D1130125

Footprints

One night a man had a dream. He dreamed he was walking along the beach with the Lord. Across the sky flashed scenes from his life. For each scene, he noticed two sets of footprints in the sand: one belonging to him, and the other to the Lord.

When the last scene of his life flashed before him, he looked back at the footprints in the sand. He noticed that many times along the path of his life there was only one set of footprints. He also noticed that it happened at the very lowest and saddest times in his life.

This really bothered him and he questioned the Lord about it.

"Lord, you said that once I decided to follow you, you'd walk with me all the way. But I have noticed that during the most troublesome times in my life, there is only one set of footprints. I don't understand why when I needed you the most you would leave me."

The Lord replied, "My son, My precious child, I love you and would never leave you. During your times of trial and suffering, when you see only one set of footprints, it was then that I carried you."

Author unknown

THE HOLY LAND TO-DAY

The Holy Land To-day

BY

M. BASILEA SCHLINK

TRANSLATED BY THE REVD. N. B. CRYER
AND MISS V. RUFFER

Evangelical Sisterhood of Mary
Darmstadt — Eberstadt — Jerusalem

FIRST PUBLISHED IN ENGLISH IN 1963

Translated from the German
HEILIGES LAND HEUTE

Printed in Israel
by
Yanetz Ltd. — Jerusalem

INTRODUCTION

THIS book is both a guide-book and a travel-book, but not after the usual pattern. It is based on the experience of a number of visits to the Holy Places, where Jesus lived and suffered, in the Holy Land. These experiences gave the desire to depict for others Jesus Christ in His words and works, in His love and His suffering, as He appears to-day against the historical background of the places mentioned in the Gospels. This is what this book wants to provide for those who take it as their companion on a journey to the Holy Land. But it should also be of use to those who seek to follow the footsteps of Jesus in spirit if they have no opportunity for such a journey. Passages from the Gospels remind us of the scriptural facts of each site. In each case the mention of the spiritual significance of the place seeks to build a bridge from past to present, to be a call to-day. Prayers and hymns, many of them composed on the spot, and meditations provide various ways of responding to this call, and to allow us to take part in the Gospel happenings.

The historical and factual descriptions, compiled by various Marienschwestern who have themselves visited the places, are only meant as further means to this, and so purely historical and artistic considerations find no place. Various archaeological publications have been consulted, and the descriptions seek to emphasize the essential facts of historical development and to underline the certainty or otherwise of particular traditions. Different points of view have been respected.

The factual descriptions are designed to enable pilgrims to find their way about without official guides, though without too much detail. Sites from pre-Christian Bible times are only noticed when they have a direct connection with Gospel events. The general plan of the book and the order in which the Holy Places are presented are meant as suggestions for a pilgrimage, and take note of the present political situation. We will gladly provide further details on request, especially about the possibilities of joining a group of pilgrims.

> And the Word was made flesh, and dwelt among us, and we beheld his glory, the glory as of the only begotten of the Father, full of grace and truth.
>
> St. John 1: 14.

Hymn

Holy Land, where God had dwelling,
He Who reigns in highest Heaven,
Hail to thee, thou land most dear
Where I find God's footsteps near,
Hail to thee, hail to thee.

Holy Land, in thee I find
Those His places who will tell
God became Man, from His throne bending,
God my Brother, Son of Man. Hail to thee . . .

Holy Land, here would I praise thee
Honour Jesus in these places,
He Who came to take our nature—hail to thee . . .

Holy Land, here I will sing thee,
Joyful adoration bring
When of miracles I hear
That He wrought in thee, O Land. Hail to thee . . .

Holy Land, here deeply mourning
I would tell all in these places
That for my sin He did bleed
That I might be saved indeed. Hail to thee . . .

Holy Land, here I love Jesus
And would shrink from all offending
Him Who suffer'd in love to me—
Now I thank Him lastingly. Hail to thee . . .

Holy Land, here may I see them,
Jesu's ways, and may walk on them,
Here where He at every footstep
Calls to follow evermore. Hail to thee . . .

Holy Land, to Him I live now,
Him, Who gave His life for me.
I would follow at His side
To prepare the way, that all men
May be ready when He cometh
Hail to thee, hail to thee.

CONTENTS

CHAPTER I

WHY WE VISIT THE HOLY PLACES

'PUT off thy shoes from off thy feet, for the place whereon thou standest is holy ground.' Such is God's word to us when we come to the Holy Land. It was His word to Moses when God appeared in the burning bush (Exod. 3: 5), and it was also the word spoken by the angel to Joshua when he was about to enter the land of Canaan (Joshua 5: 15). How much more do not these words mean when we come to the Holy Places, where God did more than give a sign and send an angel, where the Second Person of the Most Holy Trinity, God as Son of Man, walked and talked with men. This Land with its Holy Places is most truly a Holy Land.

God was made flesh. This is what we adore, in contrast to those who see Jesus only as a prophet, the hero of His people. Jesus, God Almighty, became so completely Son of Man that His feet actually trod this earth, and He went over the same paths as His children, here in the Holy Land. He actually journeyed through Galilee, sought shelter with others in the inns, drank from the same wells as other travellers. Here He mingled with the crowd, and preached, and healed the sick. He trod the streets of Jerusalem and bore His Cross through them. He feared, as Man, in Gethsemane, and wept on the Mount of Olives as He beheld His city.

This Jesus, Son of God Who became Man, as one of a particular nation in a particular country and thus entered history, Him we Christians acknowledge as our Lord. No other religion has this fact as part of its creed. Yet, in these places where He lived, it often happens that those of other religions show utter reverence, such as is wholly lacking in us. How unnatural this is! For surely our reverence and adoration at the Holy Places of Jesus should be a witness to all the world, and especially to the non-Christian world, that the

Word was made flesh, that God took upon Himself our body and became Man. Our adoration here should be a potent witness that Jesus really became man, lived and suffered and died here, and rose again from the dead, all love, all glory being due to Him.

Only those who approach the Holy Places with the deepest reverence can really know that Jesus reveals Himself here to-day. Nor can we otherwise expect a blessing. God, the high and lofty one that inhabiteth eternity, Whose name is holy, He dwells with them that are of a contrite and humble spirit —so the prophet Isaiah tells us (57: 15). And contrition and humility are never so needful as when we tread this Land which God's feet also trod, and where He condescended to us and walked amongst us sinners.

Holy Places in the Holy Land which were trodden by the feet of Jesus, which heard His mighty words, which beheld His miracles, His sufferings and His dying and His rising again! Who can know all their meaning when we walk here to-day? And who does not long to come? We are ready to take long journeys in order to see great men in their own countries, and we do not begrudge the time and money for studying their surroundings and to learn more about them. How much more readily therefore should we not give time and spend money and despise difficulties to journey to the earthly country of our Lord Jesus Christ, the land where He was born as Man and in which He grew to manhood, where He not only lived but also suffered and died for us!

Wherever we cast our eyes in this land, wherever our feet lead us—everything speaks of Him, as nothing in our own land can. Who dare boast that he is everywhere in spirit with Jesus and knows and understands His life and sufferings and all His words so vividly that he has no need to see the country and consider the circumstances? We often take the word of God as a matter of course, or we give it too abstract a meaning. The actual sight of the Holy Places will help us to come closer to the deeds and the sufferings of Jesus. We all need to follow the paths of Jesus to understand more truly what took place here for us.

Every lover of Jesus who desires to understand more of His work and His sufferings is drawn to this land. He will wish to thank the Lord in his heart for His life and dying, and to bow the knee where the Cross was lifted up. And he will long to visit the spot where the Lord Jesus offered up strong crying and sweat of blood and tears for us: Gethsemane. It is there, almost more than anywhere else, that we come close to the sufferings and struggles of our Lord.

Or the lover of Jesus will want to stand upon the Mount of Olives, where Jesus ascended to Heaven, there to adore and to rejoice that we have a Lord Who triumphed gloriously and went up on high, returning home to His Father as victor, to sit at God's Right Hand. And will he not here, on the Mount of Olives, be more vividly conscious of the Lord's Return, recalling the prophecy that His feet shall stand on this same Mount from which He ascended up on high (Zech. 14: 4)? All that the Bible tells us comes alive, as also the events at the end of time to which we are approaching.

Yet, when love to the Holy Places draws us to them, we may sometimes be disappointed to find that they have been built over and that they do not come up to our expectations. Here and there we may be painfully aware of the careless way in which the Holy Places are treated. And we may question the historical reality of some of the sites. We cannot escape such questionings and experiences. It is well to be prepared for them and to encounter them in the right way.

Many of the places, such as the lake of Gennesareth, the Mount of Olives, the valley of Kidron, the Temple, Jacob's well, and others, are obviously recognizable as the ancient biblical sites. Historically they are more or less correct, though others may be more uncertain. Excavations on many of the sites are not yet completed and new finds are constantly to be expected; final certainty is as yet impossible. But even if the place should not be quite certain historically, the churches which have been erected over them give us the opportunity of thinking prayerfully about some particular biblical event—even if that event took place some miles away.

As to the painful impression when the outward aspect is disturbing, let us remember that God Almighty did not disdain to come down to our so unsatisfactory world as Man, to be laid in a manger, and to disguise Himself. The Holy Places show Him in the disguise men have put upon Him. But the loving seeker after Jesus will find Him even under human disguises. They are part of our human nature—our poor sinful nature—part of our flesh and blood.

And as we draw near the places where Jesus showed Himself to us sinners in love and mercy, let us look with eyes of love on the deeds of those who desired to keep the knowledge of these places for us, often with great sacrifice, even if their way of acting seems inappropriate to us. We seldom realize how much we owe to the guardians of the Holy Places, mostly Franciscans. Through the centuries they devoted their lives to protecting the places; and amongst them have been many martyrs.

Jesus is waiting for us to approach the places and their guardians with thoughts of blessing, not of reproach. Thus it will be easier for us to overcome our disappointment. If here and there Holy Places are not kept holy, if we hear of strife and disunity or even see them for ourselves, Jesus will expect us to accept this willingly, because all we Christians, without exception, are continually hiding Jesus by our unholy ways. We should pray the more earnestly for such places. In all the places of Jesus we are called to offer up our prayers and our love that they may be truly Holy Places. For they cannot proclaim God if their message is not lived out there. It is an inescapable fact that the Holy Land, where God once revealed Himself, is not necessarily holy for ever. Those who ask 'Are there still Holy Places to-day?' are not wildly mistaken. The Bible proclaims that there are Holy Places, and that God has called one city 'the holy city' (Isa. 52: 1) and the Temple 'his sanctuary' (Ezek. 23: 38). But we know what has happened, for example, to Jerusalem, and to the Temple. Men dishonoured the Temple and gave not glory to God; they did not live according to His commandments, but pursued their own affairs. They made the House of God into a den of thieves. Therefore this place came under judgment and destruction. And thus it was with many Holy Places. This is grievous to God. And He grieves anew when we dishonour Him by quarrels and envy and indifference in the Holy Places where He has revealed Himself.

The Holy Places summon us to make them live anew by our contrition and our love to Jesus and our adoration, so that the image of Him comes alive and is witnessed to by many. This we cannot do if we regard them as museums and 'places of interest,' wanting to see as many as possible in the shortest time and gaining but a fleeting impression of them. The Holy Places expect us to linger in prayer, encountering Jesus. So our inward preparation should be begun a long time beforehand.

How great an opportunity has God not given us if we are able to visit the Holy Places! Not only an inwardly enriching gift—provided it is not just an interesting study or a means of passing the time—but a commission, a duty. May our hearts be enkindled with desire, not only to receive spiritual blessings, but to be full of thanksgiving. Because Jesus lived here as God in human form and suffered for us sinners, the Holy Places wait for us to give Him the gifts of love.

May there be many prayers of loving gratitude! Everywhere may there be a response to Him, a surrender to the message He proclaimed, our contrition and our willingness to follow in the way of the Cross. May multitudes sing together, and the Holy Places be full of praise. And may a multitude of those who bewail their sin here adore Him Who bore our sins.

Jesus waits for those who will come lovingly to the Holy Places; for love makes the loved one loveable and attractive to others. Love will renew the impressions of His life in the places where He trod. Love will make manifest to all the world in the Holy Places Him Who lived and suffered, and was crucified, and rose again, and ascended to Heaven: the Lord yesterday, to-day, and for ever. Praise and honour and glory be to Him Who dwells amongst us, world without end.

How great a privilege it is to be able to visit His land, to follow in His footsteps, to render Him loving thanks! And more: here we may rejoice before Him in the thought of that great day when He will come again to His holy city, to be greeted with the cry of rejoicing: 'Blessed is he that cometh in the Name of the Lord!' (Matt. 23: 39). And still more: the thought of that day when the Heavenly Jerusalem shall come down and dwell amongst men (Rev. 21).

A Prayer at the Start of a Journey in The Holy Land

Lord Jesus,

We thank You from the bottom of our hearts for the opportunity which we have, as a privilege above many others, of travelling in that Land in which You lived and suffered. So we pray You to so inflame our hearts that we should enter this Holy Land with feet unshod. We realize with great shame and grief how our forefathers came here—under the sign of the Cross—and caused a blood bath amongst Jews and Muslims. We bear deep penitence for that in our hearts, since we as Christians have thus damaged Your Name over and over again and also have harmed Your Holy Sites. Mindful of this guilt of ours permit us now to visit Your Land and dwell in it with humbled hearts. Give us the grace to make amends somewhat during our journey for past faults.

Permit us to enter Your Land with God-fearing hearts and not to bear any uncleansed guilt. Help us in these weeks of pilgrimage not to tolerate the slightest sin or anything else which might imperil our fellowship as a group. Prepare us to visit the places of Your suffering with hearts full of penitence that our devotion may be seen before men. Awaken in us a new love for You so that You may rejoice in our love for these sacred places. Give us a spirit of prayer to lament at Your suffering, a spirit of worship and rejoicing with which we may fill these places of Your earthly pilgrimage. Do let us find You, O Jesus, for we long to thank You in these Holy Places of Your Land, we long to sing and be full of joy. Grant that we might make known none other but You. Grant that we, as those who have met You in spirit and in truth here in this land, may be led back to our homes richly blessed and bringing with us many blessings.

May Your angels be our shield and buckler on our journey, and may Your Fatherly hand ever be over us; so that we, in all our dangers and difficulties along the way in this Holy Land, may know relief and finally return home safe and sound. AMEN.

HYMN

Holy Places murmur ever
  That our King soon will be here.
They prepare for us and all men,
  Longing that the day appear.

And the holy ones who love Him
  Darkling know the King is nigh,
And their hearts go out towards Him
  Joying that the day is nigh.

God the Father's Arms are opened
  To receive His people dear,
That the hopes of many ages
  May be certain, true, and clear.

Tears of Jesus that He, weeping,
  Shed on Olivet in pain.
Jesu's grief unites us to Him,
  For His Love melts our heart's pain.

City of our Lord and Master,
  Salem, be thou well-prepared.
All the honours thou canst give Him
  Are to few, in triumph shared.

People of God, make yourselves ready
  For the King is nigh indeed
That ye may rejoice beside Him
  When His day from night is freed.

CHAPTER II

MOUNT ZION: THE UPPER ROOM

THE LAST SUPPER AND PENTECOST

HOW often do we not hear the name of Mount Zion in prayers and hymns. And now we are standing at the foot of Mount Zion. We know that this is not the real 'Zion,' the city of David, for this lay to the south of the old city wall on Mount Ophel, and it is no longer extant. But 'new Mount Zion,' in the eastern part of the New City, close to the boundary of the old, contains some of the most significant Gospel sites. Here are commemorated, in one room, both the Last Supper and the descent of the Holy Ghost on Whitsunday.

We reach it from the centre of the New City by either King David Street or King George Street, both of which lead off from the Jaffa Road, the east-west link, to the south-east, and they come together near the Montefiore windmill. A little farther on, to the south, just before the railway station and by the Scottish church of St. Andrew, we follow a short road leading to Mount Zion. The rocky Hinnom valley, lying along the west side of the Old City and coming from the north, is now in front of us. It turns sharply eastwards to join, in the distance, the valley of Kidron. High above the houses on the floor of the valley rise the tower and the circular building of the church of the Dormitio, the outstanding feature of Mount Zion.

Now comes the steep climb up the western slope of Mount Zion. As it is also the way to the Tomb of David, the Jewish national sanctuary, the Jewish guardian hands us a leaflet printed with Psalms, and we pass tablets inscribed with verses from the Psalms about Jerusalem which are let into the limestone walls bordering the road. At the top we reach an uneven space with pine-trees, which serves for the celebration of Jewish feasts. The fenced-in hollows below reveal excavations of the Old City.

The buildings of the so-called Citadel of David are on the left. Passing through lofty vaulted rooms we come to an inner court where sign-posts indicate the entrance to David's Tomb. In order to reach the Upper Room of the Last Supper we must go past the guardian and through a wooden lattice, on the north side of the Benedictine abbey-grounds and the church of the Dormitio. The entrance to this, for us, so important room is obscure. Through a pointed archway in a building we find an outside stairway leading to a vestibule. The plain Gothic room, which bears no sign of its significance, lies directly above the Tomb of David. We can hear prayers and singing coming from the Tomb, but we must remain silent however much we long to sing of the love of the Lord Jesus Who gave Himself to us in the Last Supper, and of the Holy Ghost.

Lastly we mount up to the observation platform, whose approach is opposite the entrance to David's Tomb. Crooked stairs lead to the roof and we stand beneath a steel-blue sky, from which once came the sound of rushing wind. Opposite lies the Mount of Olives, and far below us the city of Jerusalem lies spread out. But our eyes seek the way which our Lord may have taken from the Upper Room to the garden of Gethsemane and back again after His arrest, for the house of Caiaphas probably lay here on the new Mount Zion.

THE HISTORICAL ASPECT

The Gospels tell us nothing of the situation of the house where Jesus celebrated the Last Supper with His disciples; they only say that a man bearing a pitcher of water would show the way. Mark and Luke use the word 'katalyma' (Mark 14: 14; Luke 22: 11), which usually means a reception room for guests. The disciples were to be shown a particular room—an 'anagaion,' Upper Room (Mark 14: 15; Luke 22: 12). This was probably in an added story, and thus indicates that Jesus chose a well-to-do house for the Paschal Feast. But as there is no hint of its whereabouts in the Gospels there is no Early Christian tradition either.

But the place of the Pentecostal gathering has an ancient tradition, guaranteed by references. It is this tradition which has given Mount Zion its name. The first Christians assembled here and called it Zion, and the name was taken over from the city of David on Mount Othel. Over this meeting-place a church was built, the 'Mother of Churches.' It escaped destruction in A.D. 70 because the Jewish defence collapsed in front of the upper city, so this hill, later called Mount Zion, was unharmed. Epiphanius, a bishop born in Judaea in 315, reports that the Emperor Hadrian, during his inspection of Jerusalem in 130, found complete destruction 'except for a few houses and the little church of God which stood where the disciples went up to the "hyperoon" on Zion after the Ascension.' This witnesses to the tradition that Zion was regarded as the dwelling-place of the Apostles after the Ascension, and the place where the Holy Ghost descended at Pentecost. But according to the nun Aetheria, who took part in and described the Easter liturgy in Zion in 385, this site was also venerated as that of the Appearance of the Risen Christ to the Twelve, recounted in Luke 24: 36–49 and John 20: 19–29, and the meeting-place of the disciples from the death of Jesus onwards.

Yet this 'little church of God' above the Upper Room did not yet commemorate the Last Supper. In the Gospel accounts of the Last Supper and of Pentecost the Greek text has two different words. The 'hyperoon' of Bishop Epiphanius' account is used by Luke in Acts 1: 13, but not 'anagaion,' which he uses in his gospel for the room of the Last Supper

(22: 12). In 400 the tradition arose in Syria that both Upper Rooms were one and the same; the Syrian translation uses only one word to render both 'hyperoon' and 'anagaion.' In Jerusalem we find, between 450 and 500, that the Last Supper and Pentecost were held to have occurred in the same room, as we can see from the liturgies of that date.

Yet the commemoration of the Last Supper was only slowly accepted by the church of Mount Zion. Several pilgrim reports of the sixth century give other traditions for the place of the Last Supper, such as the Cave of Betrayal or the Holy Sepulchre. It is not impossible to think that the disciples would gather together at the place of the last Pasch. So this room, in spite of incomplete tradition, is the right spot for commemorating the Last Supper.

In about 340, a large basilica, the Upper Church or Hagia Sion, was erected over the 'little church of God,' but it was destroyed by the Persians in 614, as were almost all the churches. After this the church on Mount Zion commemorated as well the death-bed of Mary, which had probably had a special chapel in the church. To-day it is called the Church of the Dormitio. But the reports do not make clear whether the Upper Room was part of the church or alongside.

The badly damaged church of the Crusaders was acquired in 1335 from the King of Naples and given to the Franciscans, who restored the room of the Last Supper and gave it its present aspect. The Franciscans were driven out by the Turks in 1524 and it is still in Moslem ownership.

From the ninth or tenth centuries onwards, the populace venerated the Tomb of David on Mount Zion, and this is to-day the Jewish sanctuary, below the Christian Upper Room. Since 1948 the whole building is administered by Israel.

MOUNT ZION: THE UPPER ROOM

THE LAST SUPPER

From the Holy Bible

Jesus sent Peter and John with these instructions: 'Go and prepare for our Passover supper.' 'Where would you like us to make the preparations?' they asked. He replied, 'As soon as you set foot in the city a man will meet you carrying a jar of water. Follow him into the house that he enters and give this message to the householder: "The Master says, 'Where is the room in which I may eat the Passover with my disciples?' " He will show you a large room upstairs all set out: make the preparations there.' They went and found everything as he had said. So they prepared for Passover.

When the time came he took his place at table, and the apostles with him; and he said to them, 'How have I longed to eat this Passover with you before my death! For I tell you, never again shall I eat it until the time when it finds its fulfilment in the kingdom of God.' And during supper he said, 'I tell you this: one of you will betray me.' In great distress they exclaimed one after the other, 'Can you mean me, Lord?' He answered, 'One who has dipped his hand into this bowl with me will betray me.' Then, after dipping a piece of bread in the dish, he took it out and gave it to Judas son of Simon Iscariot. As soon as Judas had received it Satan entered him and he went out. It was night.

During supper Jesus took bread, and having said the blessing he broke it and gave it to the disciples with the words: 'Take this and eat; this is my body.' Then he took a cup, and having offered thanks to God he gave it to them with the words: 'Drink from it, all of you. For this is my blood, the blood of the covenant, shed for many for the forgiveness of sins.' From Matthew 26; Luke 22; John 13.

A CALL TO US

In the Upper Room we remember how Jesus gathered His disciples to celebrate the Passover for the last time before His crucifixion. Here He spoke those last discourses, with their special lustre such as only the last words of such a master could have, and which are His last legacy. They reveal Who this is Who is saying farewell, and the best and greatest of what He wished to leave to those He loved.

In the hour when Jesus was preparing to undergo a sacrificial death, He spoke not of Himself but with loving concern for His disciples. Although He sees that the night has come, with the power of darkness, when one disciple will betray Him, the others forsake Him, and even Peter will deny Him, He speaks words of gratitude and love. He thanks those who in the very next hour will grieve Him repeatedly, for continuing with Him in His temptations, and He gives them the promise that He will prepare a place for them in Heaven with His Father (Luke 22: 28, 29). And more, He promises that He will return and dwell with them, that He will send the Holy Ghost, the Comforter, and that as they now share His sufferings they may share His glory to all eternity.

Such words can only be spoken by Him Whose heart is filled with love to those who will grieve and forsake and betray Him. Here is revealed the Divine love with which Jesus looks upon mankind in darkness and sin. Although He realizes to the full the grief of what His disciples will do to Him, He looks beyond their sins and suffering as One Who is yet greater, One Who is Love triumphant in faith. This Divine Love believes and hopes for all His sinful creatures, and sees beyond their sins to that which He will make of them. Jesus' look of Love reaches to Eternity, to the Kingdom of God, where His own, those redeemed by His love, will take their place for ever.

These discourses are embedded in the Feast of Love that our Lord celebrated with His disciples. It was in this Feast, although His heart may have been heavy-laden, that He inaugurated the New Covenant, the covenant of Love, which was to be sealed by His death. In this very moment, when He is offering His life in sacrifice, one of the Twelve nearest His heart went out to betray His Master. Thus it is the Feast of true Love, the Love of Jesus which never faileth.

The human mind can hardly grasp that the Lord, Who knows all things and to Whom the hearts of all are open, could say in this hour of betrayal: 'With desire have I desired to eat this Passover with you.' But love that comes from the heart of God desires His beloved, even though they will sin against Him. We, with our earthly minds, would avoid such people. But Jesus longs to be with them and to eat with them. So the Upper Room witnesses to a love such as cannot be found elsewhere in this world. It is the love of Him Who came down from Heaven to bring us true life, the life Divine, which is true love. He showed in Himself what manner of love it is that knows no bitterness, that forgives freely, that goes to death for His enemies, and which in the very presence of sin believes in the triumph of redemption.

Whoever partakes of this Feast must believe that Jesus, Love Eternal, gives Himself and makes us partakers of His nature. Did He not say: 'Whoso eateth my flesh and drinketh my blood, hath eternal life' (John 6: 54)? This gift from Heaven to us can never be sufficiently praised. It says to us: Come and receive, in body, soul, and spirit, all those good things of His which you need for strength and for renewal. In this Feast we are made one with Jesus Himself and are taken into the fellowship of His love and His sufferings.

So we cannot but adore the incomprehensible love of Jesus here in this room where the Last Supper took place. Here we must answer that love which gave us the new covenant, by following Him in love to our brethren and in giving up our lives to them. In this Holy Feast He desires to give us the love which will enable us.

PRAYER

We thank Thee, Lord Jesus, that Thou dost say to us, as once to Thy disciples: 'With desire have I desired to eat this Passover with you,' because Thy love doth constrain Thee to us to unite Thyself to us Thy sinful creatures. We thank Thee that in this Thy Feast, in which Thou Thyself dost come to us, Thou dost give us this union with Thee, making us partakers of Eternal Life. We adore Thy love which has given us not only all good gifts but Thyself as well, Thy precious flesh and blood, that we may receive the forgiveness of sins and have part in Thy Divine Being.

Dear Lord Jesus, I will heed the call of Thy Love and answer it with my love. Joyfully will I hasten to Thee, that I may be made one with Thee. Hear my prayer and make me partaker of Thy love as I am partaker of this Feast. AMEN.

It is the Feast of forgiven sinners, the feast of Love, in which God is united to men, the feast of brotherly love, which opens to us the door of Heaven, the Presence of God.

HYMN

Supper of the Lord: He gives,
As He once did give His own,
Himself the Sacrifice of Love.
Bread and wine, His life indeed,
Is for sinners given here.
Miracle, all thought above.

Supper of the Lord: the Covenant new
Jesus hereby doth make known;
We are one with Him indeed.
Covenant with Eternal Love,
Him Who makes our spirit, soul,
One with Him, in Him indeed.

MOUNT ZION: THE UPPER ROOM

Supper of the Lord: to us this given.
Life Divine comes to us down
When we drink, O Lord, Thy Blood.
Yea, in Bread, Thy Body true
Thou dost nourish us with life
That doth make us ever new.

Supper of the Lord: O be thou praised
For the grace thou dost us give:
We receive our Lord Himself.
This His Feast will make us meet
All His suffering to share:
Praise eternal be to God.

PENTECOSTAL HALL

From the Holy Bible

Late that Sunday evening, when the disciples were together behind locked doors, for fear of the Jews, Jesus came and stood among them. 'Peace be with you!' he said.

A week later his disciples were again in the room, and Thomas was with them. Although the doors were locked, Jesus came and stood among them, saying, 'Peace be with you!'
John 20: 19 and 26.

While he was in their company he told them not to leave Jerusalem. 'You must wait,' he said, 'for the promise made by my Father, about which you have heard me speak: you will be baptized with the Holy Spirit, and within the next few days.' When he had said this, as they watched, he was lifted up, and a cloud removed him from their sight. Then they returned to Jerusalem.

Entering the city they went to the room upstairs where they were lodging. They were constantly at prayer together, and with them a group of women, including Mary the mother of Jesus, and his brothers. From Acts 1: 4–9 and 12–14.

While the Day of Pentecost was running its course they were all together in one place, when suddenly there came from the sky a noise like that of a strong driving wind, which filled the whole house where they were sitting. And there appeared to them tongues like flames of fire, dispersed among them and resting on each one. And they were all filled with the Holy Spirit.
Acts 2: 1–4a.

Pentecostal Hall

Pentecostal hall, within
Which all did rejoice and praise
As the fire came down.
Here, O Holy Ghost, may'st Thou
Now be praised, and evermore.
Here God's chosen people are
Made the Bride of Him Who comes.

New creation here came down,
Here the Bride He caused to be,
        Miracle of Heaven.
New creation here was made
to astound, yea, even fools.
        Church of God indeed!
Holy Ghost, Thou did'st descend: love from above.

A CALL TO US

The Upper Room recalls to us another great saving event: the descent of the Holy Ghost. Here took place a miracle which we still wonder at and adore, a miracle greater than any before.

The Holy Ghost, the Third Person of the Godhead, came down on earth as a mighty rushing wind. He came down in one particular place, in this Upper Room on Mount Zion. And He came upon particular people: the disciples, that unhappy handful of failures, who had not kept faith with their Lord, but had forsaken Him as He went to His Passion. Yet it is specially to these, the poor and needy, to whom the Holy Ghost comes. In them He can reveal that He is indeed Creator Spirit, Who awakens dead hearts to new life, and fills fearful hearts with courage and the power to witness.

We read in Acts 4: 31 that as the disciples were praying together 'the place where they were assembled was shaken.' For the Holy Ghost Himself in the fullness of grace came down on those gathered in the Upper Room. He came as tongues of fire on their heads, bringing them the fire of love and the courage to suffer, inflaming them wholly for God and His purposes.

The Spirit of God put something of God Himself into those hearts, enkindled the love of God in them as a consuming fire, beyond ordinary speech. They were compelled to witness to Jesus, cost them what it would.

Blessed Pentecost, when the fire of love burned so brightly that it was not only the love of God but also love of the brethren, which sought to have all things in common! The company were of one heart and one mind, moved by the Holy Ghost. Must we not adore the Third Person of the Godhead, Who doeth such wondrous things!

The Creator Spirit created a company which has persisted to this day. Must we not love Him and thank Him and glorify Him therefore? For He is the same to-day as then, and still longs to create the Kingdom of God amongst us. He still comes down upon the poor and needy children of men, when they pray to Him continually and are of one heart and one mind, claiming in faith the promises of God. Still to-day He makes men to be born anew by His life-giving power. He transforms souls, filling their hearts with the fire of Divine Love. And still to-day He is the spirit of Joy which gladdens men to laugh and sing. He still unites the separate members of the Body of Christ in the love of God. He gives His gifts of grace, as the Bible tells us: the spirit of knowledge, of faith, of wisdom, of prophecy, of preaching, of miracles. Still to-day He can soften our hard hearts that so hinder and grieve Him, till they are changed into the image of Christ. He waits for us to say: 'I believe in the Holy Ghost,' opening our hearts to Him in faith and supplication. For Jesus told us: 'If I depart, I will send the Comforter to you' (John 16: 7).

And may Jesus not specially to-day, with His Second Coming so near, desire a new Pentecost for His Body, to make ready, by His Creator Spirit, the Bride who was born in the Upper Room?

†

Disciples gather behind closed doors.
Within the Upper Room they are at one
In prayer and watching and again praying
That Jesus' promise may fulfilled be.

Their hearts are big with expectation and with longing
For things unspeakable that yet shall come.
Their souls reach up to Heaven, they seek the Light Eternal
They pray and watch and wait and pray again
That Jesus' promise be fulfilled to-day.

Once more on this new day they are together
Alone within the sacred Upper Room.
The sound of rushing wings, the Holy Spirit coming
Fills all the room as if it were the sea,
And tongs of fire descend, and their whole hearts are glowing.

O blessed Pentecost, that brought fulfilment
And washed with fire and gave the strength divine!
With high rejoicing now all the Apostles
Are filled with faith and warmth and power.
Jesus their Lord has left them not as orphans,
The Holy Ghost has come on them with power.

They praise, they sing, they witness with rejoicing
That Jesus their high Lord hath made them glad.
The whole place shakes, and thousands hear them singing.
The Spirit seizes them, repentance springs.
Their hearts are grieving, yet they are rejoicing
As fearlessly they own the Christ, the Lord.

O blessed Pentecost, O happiest dawning,
When praise and glory sounds from countless throats!
Our sins' forgiveness now is freely given,
For we are born again in th'Holy Ghost.
O blessed joy! The Spirit hath descended
With rushing sound and flick'ring tongues of fire.

PRAYER

O Holy Spirit, we give thanks to Thee that Thou didst here come down as a mighty rushing wind and didst bring to birth the Church of Jesus Christ. We thank Thee that love divine was here kindled in the hearts of the disciples and that Thou didst bestow on them the wealth of Thy gifts. We praise Thy power which transformed cowards into confessors, eager witnesses, and martyrs. We thank Thee for this miracle of Pentecost: that Thou didst reveal Thyself as the Creator Spirit calling into being what was not—the New Testament company, the mystical Body of Christ, filled with the power of love, of prayer, of sacrifice, endowed with all grace and with all the gifts of the Spirit.

Here in this Upper Room, faced with all the lack in me of gifts and graces, I will yet pray: I believe in Thee, O Holy Ghost, and in Thy creative power. Thou wilt awaken in me, even in me, the courage to witness, the warmth of love, the spirit of sacrifice.

I thank Thee that Thou dost so unweariedly work on my hard heart that I may at length attain to the image of His love. I pray Thee, inflame me with love to the brethren, even to those of other confessions, that the world may see by the love we have for each other that the Head of the Body is Love Eternal. AMEN.

Litany of Adoration of the Holy Ghost

Blessed be Thou, O Holy Ghost
flame of God's fire, Who dost come down upon us, the sinful children of men, to kindle in us the fire of divine love.

Spirit of life,
Who dost make the dry bones live and dost breathe the breath of God into our dead hearts that we may come to life and ever praise our Saviour and Redeemer.

Spirit of power and might,
Who dost put down the proud and mighty so that the one and only God may be exalted.

Spirit divine,
Who comest from God and searchest the deep things of God and revealest them to them that love God.

Spirit of joy,
Who comfortest them that mourn and makest sorrowful hearts to rejoice and fillest them with the splendour of God.

Spirit of truth,
Who dost cleave asunder joints and marrow and judgest the thoughts of all hearts and bringest to light things hidden.
Thou Who dost illumine the darkness with the shining light of the Godhead, so that we may know the way to God and may not stray from it.

Creator Spirit,
Who dost make all things new and transformest sinners into children of God.

Spirit of fulfilment,
Who formest the image of God in sinful men.
Thou Who fillest Heaven and earth as a mighty rushing wind and fillest Thy people with the spirit of adoration and thanksgiving
Thou eternal Spirit,
Who art and wert from before beginning, Who art co-equal with the Son, one with them in the Eternal God-head.

We adore Thee and we bless Thee.

†

HYMN

Great and mighty, full of grace,
Holy Dove, Thou camest down
Here within this hall.
Here Thy wings Thou didst outspread
Coming down from Zion's mount
To renew the world.

Hark! a mighty rushing wind,
Spirit sounding like the sea
On the Apostles' heads came down.
Let us praise and sing the fame
Of the Spirit's tongues of fire
Flaming in the Apostles' hearts.

Heads and hearts are both inspired
And in the love of God are drowned.
May proclaim what God has done.
Kindled now, their tongues are loosened.
Jesus now must e'er be praised,
For the flame their hearts consumes.

Sacred Hour, and Hall of Blessing
Where God came in mighty power
Down amongst His people here.
Here Thy Spirit shall have glory
Who has given grace so fully
To His people gathered here.

✝

At Pentecost the Holy Ghost gave His gifts almost wastefully. And still to-day He is the same Spirit, Who longs to bestow on us the fullness of His gifts. But only those who come empty-handed and desiring, who realize their poverty, can receive His gifts.

✝

We must be ever ready to hearken to the admonishing of the Holy Ghost. He is sensitive, and He will draw back if we grieve Him.

✝

When thou dost perceive the poverty and disorder of thy soul, say fervently: I believe in the Holy Ghost and in His divine power. Thy faith will make His power real to thee.

CHAPTER III

THE TEMPLE AREA

LET us go to the place where the Temple used to stand, the Haram-esch-Scherif, as the natives call it. From the very first sight of Jerusalem it has drawn our eyes, on account of the huge Dome of the Rock, the present-day mosque, which glitters with gold. The wide extent of the Temple area occupies about one-sixth of Old Jerusalem. Nine gates lead into it, six on the western side, three on the northern. All are open throughout the day, but only at the Bab am Naziv, the Gate of the Inspectors, can tickets and plans be bought. The Bab am Naziv is the second of the six gates on the western side (counting from the north), and it is reached by narrow lanes leading from the valley road (King Solomon Street) which comes from the Damascus Gate in the north of the city.

Passing through the arch with its gate-house above it and the sentries posted there, we see the great octagonal Dome of the Rock in the centre of the square. It is built on a raised, terrace-like platform, and surrounded with pillars, and it is reached by stairways on every side. Round about this platform are a number of small buildings all over the square: little temples, prayer-alcoves, fountains, and basins, all Muslim, remind us that this square, once the spiritual centre of the Old Testament congregation, is now soaked in centuries of Muslim history. With the exception of a Byzantine church where now the El-Aksa mosque stands, and the short period of the Crusaders, the entire Temple area is untouched by Christian history.

The Temple is familiar to us from many Bible events, and we are drawn to seek the site of the former Solomon's Porch, on the east side. Here, against the city wall beyond which we can see the Mount of Olives, is the Golden Gate, whose bricked-up exterior can be seen from the Mount of Olives. On the inside there is a gate-house dating from Byzantine times. A long flight of steps leads us down from here—about 10 yards—to the only place where we can stand on the actual ground where Jesus trod; all the rest of the area is buried beneath the deposit of centuries. A few blocks of stone invite us to be seated, to meditate the events of Jesus' earthly life which took place in this Temple area, beginning with the first time that the twelve-year-old Jesus walked here, and ending with the last entry when He was seated upon an ass—perhaps passing through this very gate.

The next attraction is the Dome of the Rock, standing on almost the same site as the Temple. Beneath the dome of this magnificent building lies the living rock on which the ancient altar of burnt-offering probably stood. The rock—called Moriah—is of unexpected dimensions: about 15 yards long and 12 yards wide, and rising to a height of about 2 yards above ground. Visitors are not commanded to keep silence, but before this rock and its history—from the sacrifice of Isaac to the symbolic offering of Jesus at His Presentation—the Christian pilgrim cannot but be silent.

Below the rock there is still a cave, probably that of Araunah the Jebusite, whose threshing-floor David bought in order to build an altar upon it. When the altar of burnt-offerings stood here, the hole in the surface of the rock served to drain away the sacrificial blood.

The so-called 'Solomon's Stables' will interest us as being buildings of the time of Jesus. They lie below the cobbled open space on the south-east, hemmed in on two sides by the wall and on the third side by the basilica-like El-Aksa mosque. The entrance is at the south-east corner of the wall, close to the 'pinnacle of the Temple' which here rises above the valley of Kidron. Many steps lead down to a large room formed by the large-scale underpinning of Herod's time.

We will end by visiting the so-called 'Wailing Wall,' for which we leave the Temple area by the southernmost gate on the west side, the Moorish Gate, and after two turns to the right, we reach a cul-de-sac. We face a high wall, about 28 yards long and

18 yards high, built of huge blocks of stone, the lower stages of which date from the time of Herod and are the last sign of the Temple Jesus knew.

Chief hours of opening: 9 a.m. to 11.30 a.m., every day except Friday.

THE HISTORICAL ASPECT

The history of the Temple is closely connected with that of the city, for since the time of Solomon, the Temple was the most important place in both its inward and outward developments. The oldest settlement of Jerusalem was on the southern spur of the hill whose northern continuation was later to contain the Temple area; it was bordered on the west by the Tyropæon valley and to the east by the valley of Kidron. The exit from this ancient settlement was probably at the well of Gihon, at the eastern foot of the hill, in the Kidron valley. Excavations have shown that this settlement was inhabited from 3000 B.C. onwards. To-day on this hill—called Ophel—is a village of the same name on the slope towards Kidron; both lie beyond the south wall of the Old City.

In the Bible Jerusalem is first mentioned when Abraham encountered Melchisedek, 'King of Salem' (Gen. 14: 18), about 2000 B.C. The beginning of the Temple history can also be assumed to go back to Abraham, for, according to Jewish tradition, Mount Moriah, which Abraham ascended for the sacrifice of Isaac, was the same elevation on which the Temple was built later (Gen. 22: 1–19).

At the time of its conquest by the Israelites under Joshua Jerusalem was still not occupied by the Israelites, but persisted as a Canaanite city-state under the Jebusites, who reigned here throughout the period of the Judges (1300–1050 B.C.), and after whom the city was named at that time. It was David who conquered the city, about 1000 B.C., and made it the centre of his kingdom. The 'city of David' occupied the site of the oldest settlement, Ophel, on the southern spur of the Temple Hill. But more important than the building of his capital was the fact that David also made it the centre of worship, by bringing in the Ark of the Covenant and planning to build a Temple for it (2 Sam. 6 and 7). But he received only the Divine command to erect an altar on 'the threshing-floor of Araunah the Jebusite,' which lay to the north of his royal palace (2 Sam. 24: 18). David obeyed this command in reparation for the sin of the census-taking, which God had visited by smiting His people with the plague. On this 'threshing-floor of Araunah' there was in the centre the rock of Moriah, on which was erected the altar to the Lord. David's plan was to build the Temple here. But the Lord forbade him to undertake this himself (1 Chron. 22: 1, 8–10).

Solomon, David's son, was however able to build the Temple to the glory of the Holy Name (2 Chron. 3: 1), about 960 B.C., and he enclosed the area with his palaces. The first Temple of Solomon conformed to the pattern given on the mount to Moses for the Tabernacle. The later buildings followed the pattern in general. The square building—orientated east to west—consisted of the outer court, the sanctuary, and the Holy of Holies with the Ark. In the innermost 'outer court' stood the altar of sacrifice, upon the rock on which David had probably erected his altar.

The conquest by the Babylonians under Nebuchadnezzar in 587 B.C. brought about the destruction of the Temple. When the captive Jews were allowed to return, in 538, under Cyrus, they erected the second Temple on the foundations of the first, which was finished in 515, under Zerubbabel. But the Holy of Holies no longer housed the Ark, for that was lost during the Captivity. The second Temple was not as magnificent as Solomon's, but it became more and more the 'heart' of Jerusalem.

In 168 B.C. the Temple was sacked and desecrated by the Greek king Antiochus Epiphanes, and Jewish worship was forbidden. In 165 B.C. Judas Maccabaeus, after his victory, cleansed the Temple. When the Emperor Pompeius assumed control of the country in 63 B.C. he left the Temple and its services unmolested. In 20 B.C. Herod the Great, whom the Romans made king, began the rebuilding, and the third and most magnificent Temple was erected.

Meanwhile Jerusalem had spread from the eastern hill, Ophel, towards the west and north-west. Beyond the Tyropæan valley, with the valley of Hinnom as the southern boundary, the so-called 'Upper City' came into being on the second hill, with a 'suburb' to the north. Thus the Temple area was completely bounded on the west by the city. Herod expanded the area southwards to double its size, and the downward slope of the Temple hill had to be evened out by under-building. This under-building produced the subterranean 'Stables of Solomon' on the south side of the Temple area, on the site of Solomon's royal palace. North-west of the Temple Herod erected the fortress of Antonia, on a rocky eminence, from which steps led down to the Temple area and gave an outlook over the whole area.

The Temple area was enclosed with walls which were pierced by eight gates. In the northern part of the eastern wall lay the Shushan Gate, which can still be seen though it is now bricked up. Since Byzantine times it has been called the Golden Gate. Tradition says that here Jesus entered the city on Palm Sunday, and from the time of the Crusades onwards the procession went through this gate every year till it was bricked up in the sixteenth century.

On all the four inner sides of the walls were pillared porches. The best known is that of Solomon, on the eastern side, towards the valley of Kidron. The conversations which Jesus held with the Scribes probably took place here. And here the twelve-year-old Jesus may have sat (Luke 2: 46). Here, according to John 10: 23, He walked at the Feast of the Dedication and spoke of the Good Shepherd. Acts 3: 11ff. tells of St. Peter's preaching here to the people. In these same porches the first Christians met together. The southern porch, the Royal porch, probably held the tables of the money-changers and the booths of those selling animals for sacrifice, whom Jesus drove out (Matt. 21: 12–13).

In the space enclosed by the porches lay the wide Court of the Gentiles. The Temple itself was in the centre of the area, raised by terraces and firmly shut off. It was surrounded by the men's fore-court, while the Court of the Women lay in front of that, to the east. The Court of the Women was reached from the Court of the Gentiles through the gate 'called Beautiful' where, according to Acts 3: 2, the lame man was healed. Mary must have brought her child here to the Court of the Women for the Presentation. And it was here that the event of the widow's mite took place (Mark 12: 41–4). The woman taken in adultery was brought here to Jesus, for the Jewish law-court was situated in the Temple area (John 8: 2–11). During the Feast of Tabernacles huge 'candlesticks' were lighted in the Court of the Women, and these most probably occasioned Jesus' proclamation of Himself as the Light of the world (John 18: 12 and 20).

From the Court of the Women more steps led westwards to the men's court where it adjoined the forecourt of the priests just at the entrance to the Temple. Here stood the altar of Burnt Offering and the laver of brass. During the Feast of Tabernacles water from the Pool of Siloam was poured out daily at the foot of this altar before the morning sacrifice as a drink offering. This procession was the only time when men who were not priests could enter this portion of the area. Here Jesus cried out on the last day of the Feast, 'Let him that thirsteth come to me and drink' (John 7: 37). Within the priests' court, raised by several steps, stood the actual Temple, a comparatively small building. The front part was the Sanctuary, where the angel appeared to Zacharias and announced the birth of John the Baptist. Behind it was the Holy of Holies, shut off by the veil, which was rent in two at the death of Jesus.

Early Christian tradition regarded also the south-east corner of the Temple wall as a significant Scriptural site, for here was the so-called pinnacle of the Temple, mentioned at the Third Temptation. From this pinnacle James, the Lord's brother and the first Bishop of Jerusalem, was said to have been cast down after he had been stoned.

The Herodian Temple was wholly destroyed only a few years after its final completion. On August 10th, in the year A.D. 70, Jerusalem was captured by the Roman general Titus. The Emperor Hadrian, who changed the name of Jerusalem to Aelia Capitolina, erected a temple to

Jupiter in A.D. 135 in the midst of the ruins, and also a statue of himself. At the time of Constantine (A.D. 335) this Roman temple vanished. Later, Julian the Apostate wished to revive the Jewish sacrifices and he encouraged the Jews to attempt a restoration of their Temple, but this was prevented by an earthquake. The Temple area remained desolate. Only at the south side, where the El-Aksa mosque now stands, a sixth century church stood till it was destroyed, as were all the other churches of Jerusalem, in 614.

When the Arabs conquered Jerusalem in 637, the Caliph Omar caused a mosque to be built on the ruins of the Temple; but the magnificent dome which now covers the rock Moriah, only dates from fifty years later, under the Caliph Abd el Malik. The octagonal building was copied from the church of the Ascension, now the mosque of the Ascension, on the Mount of Olives. The Dome of the Rock is the most important sanctuary of Islam after Mecca and Medina. At the time of the Crusades (1099–1187), when the Christian Kingdom of Jerusalem was proclaimed, this mosque became for a short time, under Godfrey of Bouillon, the church of the Order of the Templars, but afterwards reverted again to being a place of prayer for Moslems. In 1517 the Turks re-conquered Jerusalem and reigned there till the British Mandate of 1917, which lasted till 1948. An extensive restoration of the Dome was begun in 1959.

From the Holy Bible

And God said to Abraham, Take now thy son, thine only son Isaac, whom thou lovest, and get thee into the land of Moriah; and offer him there for a burnt offering upon one of the mountains which I will tell thee of. Gen. 22: 2.

Then Solomon began to build the house of the Lord at Jerusalem in mount Moriah, where the Lord appeared unto David his father, in the place that David had prepared in the threshing-floor of Aravnah the Jebusite. 2 Chron. 3: 1.

It was the practice of Jesus' parents to go to Jerusalem every year for the Passover festival; and when he was twelve, they made the pilgrimage as usual, and the boy Jesus stayed behind in Jerusalem. His parents did not know of this. After three days they found him, sitting in the Temple, surrounded by the teachers, listening to them and putting questions . . . 'What made you search?' he said. 'Did you not know that I was bound to be in my Father's house?' From Luke 2 : 41–9.

Jesus was walking in the temple precincts, in Solomon's Cloister. The Jews gathered round him and asked, 'How long must you keep us in suspense? If you are the Messiah say so plainly.' Jesus answered, 'My own sheep listen to my voice; I know them and they follow me. I give them eternal life. My Father who has given them to me is greater than all, and no one can snatch them out of the Father's care. My Father and I are one.' Once again the Jews picked up stones to stone him and this provoked them to one more attempt to seize him. But he escaped from their clutches. From John 10 : 23–39.

Then Jesus went into the temple and began driving out the traders, with these words, 'Scripture says, "My house shall be a house of prayer"; but you have made it a robbers' cave.'

His disciples recalled the words of Scripture, 'Zeal for thy house shall destroy me.'

Day by day he taught in the temple. And the chief priests and lawyers were bent on making an end of him, with the support of the leading citizens, but found they were helpless, because the people all hung upon his words.

From Luke 19 : 45–8 and John 2 : 16 and 17.

'O Jerusalem, Jerusalem, the city that murders the prophets and stones the messengers sent to her! How often have I longed to gather your children, as a hen gathers her brood under her wings; but you would not let me. Look, look! there is your temple, forsaken by God. And I tell you, you shall never see me until the time when you say, "Blessings on him who comes in the name of the Lord!"' Matt. 23 : 37–9.

The Temple Area—a Call to Us

What memories are called up when we make our way across the Temple area in Jerusalem, where the Dome of the Rock now stands! The Temple was the Holy Place of God under the Old Covenant, the Place He had chosen for Himself as a symbol of His dwelling in the midst of Israel—and therefore it was also the place which was of the greatest importance to Jesus, the Son of God, during His earthly life. We are told how Jesus at the age of twelve was drawn to the Temple. His moving words there, 'Wist ye not that I must be about my Father's business?,' give us a glimpse of what Jesus must have had to endure in being separated from His Father, far from Heaven, down here on earth. And they tell us of His longing to touch but the hem of His Father's garment in the Temple where, according to His own word, He had His dwelling (Exod. 25 : 8).

But it was just here, in the Temple area, that Jesus was made most conscious of His way of humiliation and renunciation. For, according to the revelation under the Old Covenant, the actual place of God's Presence was the Holy of Holies of the Temple, where formerly the Ark of the Covenant had stood. Should not the Son of God have had more right than any of the priests to enter here? But as a layman He could not even enter the Sanctuary, let alone the Holy of Holies. Only the priests, or rather the High Priest, had this right. Jesus was obliged to remain in the outer court. This must have been to Him not only a deep grief but also a great humiliation.

So for Jesus there was no room in 'His Father's House' for Him to work except the porches round the edge of the area. In Solomon's Porch Jesus and His disciples walked up and down. Here He would sit at the great festivals, surrounded by crowds of Jews, and would utter His great words. So powerful were His words that the servants, sent by the Pharisees at the Feast of Tabernacles to seize Him, returned saying they could not take Him because 'Never man spake like this man' (John 7 : 46). Yes, it was the Temple area which witnessed over and over again the attempts to seize Jesus. When He spoke here of the Good Shepherd telling of His great love for His people, His flock, their response was to take up stones to stone Him (John 10 : 31).

Thus the Temple area, the sanctuary of Jerusalem, as well as the city itself, became for Jesus the place of greatest suffering. Here Jesus experienced not only the rejection and hatred of the Pharisees, whose headquarters it was, but also the repeated attempts to kill Him here in this most holy place. Here Jesus, the Son of God, had to realize that the sanctuary of His Father, which He 'had desired for his habitation' (Psalm 132 : 13), had become a den of thieves. Therefore, in holy and painful zeal, He was obliged to drive out the money-changers and them that sold doves. Here He uttered the great woes to the Pharisees out of His deeply-grieved heart because their pride and hypocrisy desecrated the sanctuary of God even more than the money-changers did (Matt. 23). When He beheld daily how the sacrifices were offered so officiously, He must have felt the deepest grief because He knew how unreal the sacrifices were and how their most profound significance was lacking. The rock of Moriah, on which the animals for sacrifice were slain, must have constantly reminded Him that He must become the True Sacrifice, the 'Lamb of God,' for all these sins (John 1 : 29).

The Temple area brings before our eyes the shattering fact that God found least room in just those places which should have most indicated His Presence because He had chosen them as the sites of His revelation. Why? Because here dwelt the so-called devout, who are so devout that they worship their own devoutness instead of honouring God. The ultimate result of such an attitude, the answer of the Holy One in judgment, is shown to us by the subsequent history of the Temple, which, according to the words of Jesus, Matt. 23 : 38, is destroyed till His people shall say, 'Blessed is he that cometh in the Name of the Lord.' Therefore the Temple area calls out to us : Ye devout who frequent the holy places, who are employed in serving dedicated places, churches, and other places of God, give heed how ye handle holy things! Give heed that, without realizing it, ye do not grieve the loving Lord and drive Him away from the holy places and slay Him anew, because ye make idols of your devotion, your church-going, your prayers and your worship, and have become self-satisfied and satiated! The Temple area calls out to Christendom: Awake and see to it that your sanctuaries are not turned into markets, and ultimately into a den of thieves because ye forget that God seeks from us the broken and contrite heart that is filled with love to God and with mercy to men.

Jesus lives to-day. And to-day still we can grieve Him and His Holy Spirit, just as the Pharisees and the people grieved Him in the Temple area, when we seek our own glory in devout service and in our pride live for ourselves and not for the true serving of God and men by the surrender of ourselves. Should not Jesus, after the unspeakable sufferings of His earthly life, have a cause for rejoicing in us to-day if He finds those who give Him true glory because they no longer strive for their own honour and recognition? Should not His sacrifice be met with the true sacrifice of ourselves when we slay our own self? Only so can we bring true love and adoration to Jesus in His Holy Places, and prevent them from becoming a den of thieves, to grieve the heart of Jesus. He waits for our humbleness and love to make the Holy Places holy indeed.

Prayer at the Temple Area

Lord, here in this place where Thou didst endure so much, let me remember my sins. I humbly acknowledge all that I have done to make holy things not holy, be it in prayer, in worship, or in Communion. How often have I loved not Thee but myself, when I felt satisfaction in my devotion, my prayers, or my taking part in church life.

Lord, Thou showest me, here at the place of the destroyed Temple, how Thou dost judge such false devotion. Let me stand in the light of Thy Truth, that I may behold with Thine eyes all that is not true in my apparently Christian life, and that I may repent and not grieve and anger Thee any more. Grant that I may have not the mere appearance of a devout life but that its real power may dwell in me: the power of love and the authority that come from humility. Give me an ever humble heart because only such is the root from which my prayer and my actions can bring forth fruit for Thee. AMEN.

O Jesus, Thy heart with grief is afire, for none will own Thee as God to-day.
Few honour Thee here in Thy holiest chair, forsaken Thou art, yea, driven away.

In churches how often Thou still art alone! Thou weepest but none hear Thy call.
Thou stretchest forth arms of encircling love, but who will respond and come home to Thy hall?

Then cry out, ye stones, when all else is still, till the creature at length will bow down the knee
To Him, its true Lord, and in lowliness love, that His heart no more broken with grieving may be.

CHAPTER IV

THE POOL OF BETHESDA

PASSING through St. Stephen's Gate, in the eastern part of the city wall, and along the street of St. Anne, and seeking the site of the Pool of Bethesda, that miraculous pool of God's mercy, we shall be directed to the third door on the right, which leads to a large courtyard belonging to the 'White Fathers.' The path leads past a lovingly-tended garden of sub-tropical plants to the church of St. Anne, on our right, one of the most beautiful Crusader-churches in the Holy Land. The crypt of the church is traditionally the birthplace of Mary, the Mother of Jesus.

Behind the church, to the left, we come to the excavations of the Pool of Bethesda. A pile of debris, about 60 feet high, the result of the destructions, is a wordless history-lesson about the sorely-tried city of our God. The main outlines of the former double pool can be seen. The ruins by the sides of the pool have been partly laid bare, as well as the ruins of the churches which later on were erected on the dividing wall. The remains of these ancient walls, brought to light nearly 1900 years later, can guide our thoughts to the Pool of Bethesda spoken of in St. John's Gospel.

Times of opening: 8 a.m. till noon; 2 to 6 p.m.

The Historical Aspect

The Pool of Bethesda is mentioned only in chapter 5 of St. John's Gospel. Later sources refer to it as the Pool of Bethzatha, calling it after the suburb to the north of the Temple. But the name Bethesda did persist; the meaning is held to be 'House of Mercy.' The site of the Sheep Gate, by which, according to St. John, the pool lay, cannot be definitely ascertained; it is uncertain whether it was on the north side of the Temple area or near the present St. Stephen's Gate. The five porches described by St. John were probably built by Herod the Great; four surrounded the pool, the fifth was upon the wall which divided the pool into two. It was in these porches that the sick waited for the troubling of the waters.

The memory of the pool and of the miracle wrought there by Jesus persisted in this place. The historian Eusebius describes the five porches in the year A.D. 300, as well as the double pool; so does the Bordeaux pilgrim in 333—his is the first pilgrim's description still extant. But no healings took place here through the troubling of the waters, according to these two reports, as they had done in Jesus' day. The porches crumbled away increasingly, and gradually the pool was filled in. About A.D. 450 there occurs the mention of a 'Church of the Lame Man' on this site. But before the end of the fifth century a church to the memory of Mary—quite near the Pool of Bethesda—comes to the fore in the descriptions; this was erected over the cave regarded as Mary's birthplace. After destruction by the Persians in 614 the church at the pool remained a ruin, whilst the church of St. Mary was rebuilt.

In 1100 the Crusaders built a chapel by the Pool of Bethesda and enlarged the church of St. Mary 'in honour of St. Anne.' After the defeat of the Crusaders in 1187 the chapel by the pool was probably destroyed and the pool disappeared beneath the ruins, so that it fell into oblivion.

After the Crimean War, in 1856, Napoleon III was given possession of the area by the Turkish Sultan, in recognition of the help given to him by France. In 1873 traces of the ancient pool were rediscovered, and after the 'White Fathers'—a Greek Catholic missionary order, which now runs a seminary for Melchitic priests—had acquired the area in 1878 they started and continued excavations. These are not yet complete, but they do witness to the strong probability that this is the site of the miracle described in John 5.

From the Holy Bible

Later on Jesus went up to Jerusalem for one of the Jewish festivals. Now at the Sheep Pool in Jerusalem there is a place with five colonnades. Its name in the language of the Jews is Bethesda. In these colonnades there lay a crowd of sick people, blind, lame, and paralysed waiting for the disturbance of the water; for from time to time an angel came down into the pool and stirred up the water. The first to plunge in after this disturbance recovered from whatever disease had afflicted him. Among them was a man who had been crippled for thirty-eight years. When Jesus saw him lying there and was aware that he had been ill a long time he asked him, 'Do you want to recover?' 'Sir,' he replied, 'I have no one to put me in the pool when the water is disturbed, but while I am moving, someone else is in the pool before me.' Jesus answered, 'Rise to your feet, take up your bed and walk.' The man recovered instantly, took up his stretcher, and began to walk.

That day was a Sabbath. So the Jews said to the man who had been cured, 'It is the Sabbath. You are not allowed to carry your bed on the Sabbath.' He answered, 'The man who cured me said, "Take up your bed and walk." ' They asked him, 'Who is the man who told you to take up your bed and walk?' But the cripple who had been cured did not know. A little later Jesus found him in the temple and said to him, 'Now that you are well again, leave your sinful ways, or you may suffer something worse.'

From John 5 : 1–14.

The Pool of Bethesda—A Call to Us

Once again Jesus was sojourning in Jerusalem, probably for the Feast of Purim. The place where there lay so many sick—blind, crippled, lame—drew Him; His heart of love went out to those living in shadow, in suffering, for is He not the Saviour of His children? He approached the sick man whose burden was the heaviest, for he had lain there 'thirty and eight years,' still waiting for help. We wonder why this sick man had no one to carry him to the water when others found those to help them. The words of Jesus seem to indicate that the sickness was connected with sin, 'Sin no more, lest a worse thing come unto thee.' Perhaps the further burden, of having none to help, was due to this; perhaps also to his unattractive personality. He was left to his misery because 'he well deserved it.' But Jesus singles out this most unhappy creature. The deepest depth in which a man lies in sin and misery call out His power; He will reject no one, though He is God, Who has the right to cast off sinners. Our human charity soon reaches its bounds; it ceases when others behave badly or seem unworthy of our care. But there are no bounds to the love of Jesus; it cannot fail because He is Love Divine. His saving love draws Him specially to this poorest man, to help not only his bodily need but also his still greater spiritual need, his sin. Approaching the sick man Jesus uttered the mighty, well-nigh incomprehensible words, 'Take up thy bed and walk.' To every one's surprise this incurably sick man was able to do so.

The Pharisees scolded the sick man, 'It is not lawful for thee to carry thy bed on the sabbath day.' We see the narrow bounds of human charity when ordinances are placed above mercy. The sick man is corrected as a wrong-doer because, after thirty-eight years of infirmity, he is able at last to help himself and to carry his bed home. Yet these people cannot give him the really needed correction; they cannot tell him the truth about his sins as Jesus does. They lack the full authority of true love which can help sinners to repent through the Word of Truth. How differently from the Pharisees does Jesus speak of sinful men, to the poor and sick! And how differently He treats them! As far as Heaven is from earth, so far are His judgments, His words, His help from those we give to others. He speaks to the healed man that mighty word which still to-day goes home to our hearts, 'Sin no more, lest a worse thing befall thee.' The saving love of Jesus made whole the man who had been suffering for thirty-eight years; His Saviour's heart shared his great need, but being true love He saw even deeper, saw that the true evil of the sick man's life was not the pain and infirmity of his bodily sickness, but his sinful heart which would bring him to everlasting torment. Jesus intervenes to make the sick man truly whole, so that, released from his sin, he may live for ever in the kingdom of God. The goodness of God leads him on from healing to repentance. The loving acts of Jesus are joined to words of truth. That is what lies behind those words, 'Sin no more.'

Jesus helps the unfortunate man but having done so He warns him, for His love longs to keep him from even worse penalties which would come upon him if, after being healed, he spurned the goodness of God and sinned yet more. Jesus' love wants the man to begin a new life, in which he can be truly whole and happy. The saving love of Jesus is active still to-day. When we visit the ruined Pool of Bethesda it is as if Jesus stood waiting for us, to be our loving Saviour, to do our body and soul good. To us in our misery and distress in which no one can give us help, He speaks His word of salvation, 'I have the power to help you.' If we put ourselves in His hand then we shall stand in His great love which will not only save our bodies but also sanctify our souls. Jesus thus speaks to us, 'Take care that you respond to the goodness and help which I have shown you in your distress, by departing from your sins and living a life of thanksgiving and devotion towards Me. Begin that life to-day so that I shall not have to chastise you any more since My love will help you to know that you are healed for ever.'

Prayer

Dearest Lord Jesus,
I thank Thee that Thy name means Saviour and that Thou didst come to heal all our sickness. I thank Thee that Thou, Who didst create me, body, soul, and spirit, seest them all as a whole and desirest in Thy love to help me wholly. I beseech Thee, as Saviour, to show us Thy children Thy whole love. So I bring to Thee the sicknesses of my body and also those of my soul, that Thou mayst help me as Thou didst help the sick man at the Pool of Bethesda. I trust Thee, my Saviour, to heal all in me that is sick and sinful.

In this place I would give thanks to Thee for helping me in every bodily sickness and for giving me new life. But I would hearken also to Thy warning, and ask myself whether I have not sinned yet more in spite of Thy goodness to me, so that Thou must chastise me anew. Lord Jesus, I will to-day renounce every sin by faith in the power of Thy Redemption—every sin which Thou dost show me or cause others to show me. I would thank Thee, my Saviour, for all that Thy love has bestowed upon me in help and righteousness. AMEN.

Where else is there a saving Love like the love of Jesus

drawing Him to the most wretched so as to bring them out of the depths?

A Love that so mercifully embraces those that dwell in the shadows;

A Love so all-embracing that it wills to cure both body and soul;

A Love which will overlook no sins but will call them by their true names and call upon us to forsake them so that we may be made new, fit for the Kingdom of Heaven and for life everlasting;

A Love which has wrought redemption for us from every sin. Where can we find such love but in our Saviour Jesus Christ, Who heals all men and Who endured suffering and death for our sakes.

Hymn

Name of Jesus, Name of Saviour,
Making all wrong right,
Jesus Who didst come as Saviour
To destroy all sickness' might,
Name of Jesus, Thou hast power,
Thou dost heal us every hour.

Name of Jesus, shining, burning
Full of fire and love Thou art!
Whoso calls Thee, whoso names Thee,
Safe and sound will be in heart,
For Thy Name is God's own power,
Overcoming sin each hour.

Name of Jesus, Thou art Saviour,
Who hast broken every chain;
Rending rocks, Thou e'en dost rescue
In the power of Thy name;
Jesus' name in every hour
Can outwit all Satan's power.

Praise and thanks and love and blessing
Be to this dear Name we own.
All ye heavens help us praise Him
Through Whom victory comes alone.
Thy dear Name is God's own power—
Saviour, Victor, every hour.

CHAPTER V

THE MOUNT OF OLIVES

LEAVING the Old City by St. Stephen's Gate, we can go by the shortest way to the Mount of Olives, which the Arabs call 'Jebel el tur,' as they also call Sinai, Gerizim, and Tabor: The Mount, the Holy Mount.

But first, a short digression. Immediately on the right, once we are through the gate, we see an inconspicuous door in the wall, which leads into the Mohammedan cemetery. Behind this a path through the graves leads past the Golden Gate, giving us a matchless view on the left. In front of us lies the whole Mount with its three summits and its gentle slopes, lying like a rampart between the City and the hill-country of Judæa. The view is at its best in February, with tender green amongst the rocks. At our feet lies the deep and steep valley of Kidron. The opposite slope is thickly sown with graves to the south-west, right up to the village of Silwan, which lies by the southern summit of the Mount of Olives, also called the 'Mount of Offence,' after 1 Kings 11: 7 and 2 Kings 23: 13. On the northern summit lies the Greek Orthodox convent called 'Viri Galilei.' But it is the middle summit which concerns us most. Let us rest here awhile, for the sun is getting hotter. There are no sign-posts in this country, and this path is mostly known only to the inhabitants and seldom used. It invites us to stay awhile, to look upon the 'valley of Jesus' and 'His mountain': a never-to-be-forgotten sight.

At the foot of the middle summit lies the Basilica of the Agony, surrounded by olive-trees. It is divided from the descending terraces of the olive-garden by the wide motor-road to Jericho, whose traffic disturbs the lonely stillness of Gethsemane. Higher up the hill the onion-shaped towers of the church of St. Mary Magdalene, the Russian Orthodox monastery of Gethsemane, stand out between the huge cypresses and pine-trees. To the right is the chapel of 'Dominus flevit,' built in the shape of a tear, in memory of Jesus weeping over Jerusalem. Almost at the top we can see the tower of the Paternoster Church, whilst to the left rises the loftiest tower in the Holy Land, the tower of the Ascension, belonging to the convent of the Russian Orthodox nuns; quite near the tower is the minaret beside the mosque of the Ascension.

Whereas most of the places connected with the earthly life of Jesus in Jerusalem are difficult to ascertain on account of destruction, accumulations, or new buildings, the shape of the Mount of Olives is practically as it was 2,000 years ago. Probably there were more olive-trees on the western slope in Jesus' day, but we may well assume that the three paths are practically the same as they were when Jesus and His disciples trod them countless times. All three paths, which spread fan-wise from Gethsemane, lead to the summit. Having gazed at the Mount in its entirety from our quiet resting-place, we will continue on our way and examine the sites more closely. First we shall go back to St. Stephen's Gate and follow the road down to the bridge, which crosses the brook at the same spot where there was a bridge in Jesus' day. Our Lord must have crossed this bridge scores of times when He 'drew nigh to the city' from Jericho, or when He 'went out' to go to Bethany via the Mount of Olives. To the left, beyond the bridge, lies the entrance to the Cave of the Betrayal, which is entered from the low-lying outer court of Mary's grave.

Diagonally opposite lies the gate of the Garden of Gethsemane, with the church of the Agony where we shall want to linger some time.

Later we shall want to climb to the top. For that we must take the right-hand path, behind the church, which leads upwards in a southerly direction between high walls which allow no view of the city at first. But soon we get more and more views. Soon—near 'Dominus flevit,' on the left of the path—we can look over the Old City. Still ascending we leave on the right a space enclosed by walls containing the so-called 'graves of the Prophets.' We encounter an old man whose appearance puts us in mind of the Prophets. Nearly at the top we have a wide view over the valley of Kidron and the Temple area, in fact over the whole of the Old City as far as the Mount of Zion, and far out into the country. The path then makes a large detour to the north and is soon again enclosed by walls. On the left we pass a convent of Benedictine nuns. Here our path joins the middle path, which is the shortest and steepest way up the Mount. At this meeting-point lies a convent of Carmelite nuns, within whose area lie the church of the Paternoster and the ruins of the ancient Eleona church.

The gate-keeper will show us the way down to the crypt and the cave beside it, where we shall want to linger, for it is one of the most significant places in which our Lord still calls to us.

Beyond the Paternoster church the path becomes a road, which we follow northwards to the Arab settlement of El Tur and the octagonal mosque of the Ascension about 70 yards beyond. Having passed through the village we come to a smaller road, about 50 yards to the right of the hotel, leading to the convent of the Russian Orthodox nuns, with its high tower of the Ascension. It is well worth a climb, for from the top we can get some idea of what Jesus saw when He looked upon His land for the last time.

Times of opening:

Cave of the Betrayal (R.C.)	8.30 a.m.—11.45	2 p.m.—6
Basilica of Gethsemane (R.C.)	8.30 a.m.—11.45	2 p.m.—6
Church of St. Mary Magdalene (Russian Orth.)	9 a.m.—noon	2 p.m.—7

Dominus flevit (R.C.): only occasionally. Key may be obtained from the Franciscans of Gethsemane.

Church of the Paternoster and the Eleona ruins (R.C.)	8 a.m.—noon	2 p.m.—7

Tower of the Ascension, in the Russian Orthodox convent, can only be ascended by special permission from the Reverend Mother.

There is a constant bus service to the Mount of Olives from the bus station outside the Damascus Gate.

THE SITE OF THE ASCENSION AND OF OUR LORD'S WORDS CONCERNING HIS SECOND ADVENT

The Historical Aspect

From very ancient times the cave over which the Eleona church was built has been revered as the site of the Ascension. The historian Eusebius reports in A.D. 330 that the Emperor Constantine chose two 'Mystic caves,' besides the cave of the Holy Sepulchre, to be honoured with magnificent buildings; these were the cave of the Nativity at Bethlehem and this one on the Mount of Olives. To commemorate the Ascension he caused his mother Helena to build a 'holy church' over it. 'For,' says Eusebius, 'the feet of our Lord and Redeemer stood upon the Mount, by this cave here shown, where, having prayed and revealed to His disciples the mysteries concerning the end of the world, He ascended into Heaven.'

The site also recalls another event which took place before the Ascension. According to Eusebius, Jesus often visited this cave and 'initiated His disciples into hidden mysteries.' It was here that Jesus would have uttered the words about the end of the world and His Second Coming (Matt. 24: 3), when He sat down on the Mount of Olives and looked out over the Temple (Mark 13: 3). The first Christians revered this cave equally with that of the Nativity and the Holy Sepulchre. Constantine found it to be a generally accepted memorial, and so caused a church to be built over it. But whereas the other two churches retained their spiritual significance through the centuries, the tradition concerning the Eleona church was lost. A few decades already after its erection the memory of Jesus' Ascension here had vanished and only His teaching and the eschatological sayings were remembered.

About the year 614 the Persians destroyed the Eleona church, as they destroyed that of the Agony in Gethsemane which had also been built in the fourth century. Because the Eleona church no longer recalled the Ascension it was not rebuilt, as was the Gethsemane Basilica. The Crusaders erected only a modest chapel in the ruins, for by that time even the memory of the eschatological sayings had died out. The only tradition remaining was that Jesus had here taught the 'Our Father' to His disciples.

The exact position of Constantine's church was eventually forgotten. In 1876 the French Carmelites built their convent and its church beside the ruins of Eleona without realizing their significance. They named the church after the Paternoster, and in their cloisters the Lord's Prayer is recorded on marble slabs in fifty different languages. The remains of the Eleona church were only discovered at the beginning of this century by excavations, and then research revived the ancient tradition that this was the site of the Ascension.

The loss of the tradition of the Ascension at the Eleona, mentioned above, was probably caused by the building over the cave, which made it difficult to represent the going up. So by the end of the fourth century the memorial of the Ascension had been moved to the central summit of the Mount, about 70 yards away from the basilica. About 378 a 'church of the Holy Ascension' was built there, also called 'Inbomon' (the Greek word for 'on the summit'). Later a monastery was founded here. In the octagonal church, whose dome was open to the sky, was revered the stone said to bear the footprints of the ascending Lord. The church must have been a model of architecture, for in the seventh century, the Arabs copied it for their great Dome of the Rock. In contrast to Eleona, it was rebuilt after the Persian destruction, and again after the entry of the Crusaders. In the twelfth century it became a mosque, for Moslems believe in the Ascension of the 'Prophet' Jesus (Isa.). In essentials the building has retained its shape through the centuries. But the arcaded porches of the external octagon have vanished, and the small octagonal mosque in the centre of the courtyard was closed in at the top by the Mohammedans. Only on Ascension Day itself are groups of the different Christian churches allowed to hold services here. The actual site of the Ascension can still be found in the Eleona ruins, and the re-erection of a basilica has started here.

The Greek Orthodox church regards the northern summit as the site of the Ascension, and they have called it 'Viri Galilei,' after Acts 1: 11.

From the Holy Bible

Jesus' days were given to teaching in the temple; then he would leave the city and spend the night on the hill called Olivet.

Luke 21: 37.

When he was sitting on the Mount of Olives the disciples came to speak to him privately. 'Tell us,' they said, 'when will this happen? And what will be the signal for your coming and the end of the age?' Matt. 24: 3.

Jesus answered and said to them, 'When that day comes, the kingdom of Heaven will be like this. There were ten virgins, who took their lamps and went out to meet the bridegroom.'

Matt. 25: 1.

Once, in a certain place, Jesus was at prayer. When he ceased, one of his disciples said, 'Lord, teach us to pray, as John taught his disciples.' He answered, 'When you pray, say, Father, thy name be hallowed.' Luke 11 : 1–2.

Then Jesus led them out as far as Bethany, and blessed them with uplifted hands; and, in the act of blessing, he parted from them. Luke 24 : 50–1.

The Mount of Olives—A Call to Us

Why did Jesus choose the Mount of Olives for His final discourse on the Last Things, and why did He choose it after His Resurrection for His triumphant Ascension to His Father? The Mount of Olives was specially Jesus' own, for when He had no safety in 'his city,' from the persecution by His adversaries, He went out at evening to the Mount of Olives (Luke 21 : 37). After He had been rejected in the Temple, 'his Father's House,' which had become a 'den of thieves,' He went to the Mount of Olives to speak with His Father in His usual place of prayer.

Here, on the slope of the Mount, Jesus wept over His city which had rejected Him, just before He entered it in triumph on Palm Sunday. And at the foot of the Mount He finally lived through His dark hour of spiritual agony. Here He fought His great fight unto death with the powers of darkness. What more fitting than that this hour of grief should be followed by the triumph of the Ascension? The Mount which beheld the lowest depth of the humiliation of Jesus, when He trembled as a Man, beheld Him again when He ascended victoriously above earthly laws and powers, to sit at the Right Hand of God as King of kings, choirs of angels doing Him homage and preparing for His triumphal entry. How different from His coming down to earth! The legions of angels who worship Him as their Creator must have gazed in wonder at the marks of His wounds which revealed how bitter a struggle it had been for Jesus on earth to redeem His children. From thenceforth the wounds of the Ascended Lord, the Lamb of God, upon the Throne would be the signs of His victory, glowing like rubies. They, His highest honour, show Him forth as the Lord who has entered Heaven as the Victor in the bitter war with Satan.

But Jesus our Lord will not stay in Heaven for ever; His love 'constraineth' Him at the end of time to return to us, as it is written, 'This same Jesus, which is taken up from you into heaven, shall so come in like manner as ye have seen him go into heaven' (Acts 1 : 11). And He shall come not only in the clouds of Heaven to fetch His own (1 Thess. 4 : 16, 17), He shall come also to the Mount of Olives to His people. For the prophet Zechariah had foretold that 'His feet shall stand in that day upon the Mount of Olives . . . and that shall cleave in the midst thereof . . . and there shall be a very great valley' for a place of refuge for His people (Zech. 14 : 4). So it is not surprising that Jesus should speak about His Second Coming to His disciples and His future Church here on the Mount of Olives.

Now that we have entered the atomic age, the words of Jesus concerning His Second Coming and the Last Things have taken on a new reality. Now 'the end of all things' of which Jesus spoke has begun. Physicists clearly tell us that we have arrived at a 'time like no other,' of which it has been prophesied that catastrophes brought about by the hands of men will come upon the whole earth. The time is near when Jesus' words about the Last Things, 'Men's hearts failing them for fear, and for looking after those things which are coming on the earth' (Luke 21 : 26), are coming true.

The other signs of His Second Coming, of which Jesus spoke on the Mount of Olives, are now being fulfilled, especially the concentration of the anti-Christian powers (Matt. 24 : 9–12), and the preaching of the gospel in all the world (Matt. 24 : 14).

Never have these words which He spoke to His disciples for the last time here on the Mount of Olives been so decisive as they are to-day. The end of time is for us a time of division and hence a time of decision.

The words of Jesus will then be fulfilled, 'Two shall be grinding at the mill; the one shall be taken, and the other left'

(Matt. 24: 41). Or as Jesus remarked in the parable of the wise and foolish virgins—all will go forth to meet the Bridegroom, but though all believe on Him, only five are accepted by Him. To the others Jesus says, 'I know ye not.'

There can be no 'middle way' any more for us, in which we can live by 'cheap grace' with a self-satisfied Christianity, for as Jesus has said, this time will be 'as the days of Noah, before the Flood' (Matt. 24: 37–9). In such a time when destruction threatens the whole world we cannot live as if the times were normal.

As was the case at the time of the first Flood so in our day and before the coming of atomic war we shall see such sin as there has not been hitherto. All that is needed is that men should act as if the time of destruction were *not* just round the corner. According to Jesus' own words, to men that is just the very thing that will bring to pass the judgment of God.

And Jesus says also that when we are in an age such as ours to-day, an age before great destruction, the same will happen to us unless we free ourselves of every earthly tie and not only link ourselves with Jesus but give our lives over to Him—unless we are fully obedient to God's commandments, to His Word and to His Will. Truly, unless we do as Jesus bids us still to-day, that is, show ourselves willing to 'lose' our 'Life' for Him—and this means everything that makes Life worth living for us—then we shall, and these are Jesus' words, be as Lot's wife (Luke 17: 32f.) and we shall be destroyed. For he who does not whole-heartedly follow Jesus or who disregards the reality which God makes plain for us to read in this atomic age, will be suddenly overtaken by the disaster with which God's judgment shall break through in a flash.

Yet before the outbreak of the atomic war which threatens us there is the opportunity for us to decide how we shall then live through that time of disaster. We have to decide whether we shall belong to those who will be called by the Lord who comes again out of the destruction of this age at the sounding of the Last Trump, as it is written in 1 Corinthians 15: 51f.

The Mount of Olives, as the setting of our Lord's words concerning His Second Advent, calls to us as with a trumpet-blast, 'Behold the Bridegroom cometh, make yourselves ready!' For only those who accept discipline, who prepare themselves by daily repentance and prayer and love 'may be accounted worthy to escape all these things that shall come to pass, and to stand before the Son of man' (Luke 21 : 36). Only those, however, who lovingly attend the coming of Jesus as their bridegroom, can in the fear which prevents and attends the present anxiety do what Jesus commands His own at this time, 'When all these things come to pass, lift up your heads, for your redemption draweth nigh' (Luke 21 : 28).

Prayer on the Mount of Olives

Dearest Lord Jesus,
I will give thanks when the darkness deepens here on this earth, for I know that the nearer the darkest hour approaches, the nearer too approaches the hour of Thy coming. Incline my mind steadfastly to look forward to Thy Return as a day of rejoicing in the fulfilment of Thy promise for the end of time.

Let me not be absorbed either by fears of approaching destruction or by the routine of my daily life, but rather let me grasp the one important fact that you are coming soon and then I must be ready to let go earthly cares so as to be ready for Thee. Help me to live for that hour of Thy coming, to be steady even in the knowledge that horrors, wars and anxiety such as have never hitherto been known in the world may be coming upon us. I would surrender myself to Thee, to live wholly to Thee and for Thee, so that Thou wilt be to me in the coming darkness of the threatening atomic war, light, comfort, and joy, the strong rock of my salvation.

Thou hast further told us that we should watch and pray, that we may be worthy to be spared destruction and to stand before the Son of Man. Help me to do according to Thy word, so that I may experience the fulfilment of Thy promises and escape from the horrors which might occur, as one whose soul is delivered from the world and united only with Thee. May my whole love belong to Thee so that at Thy coming I may be drawn to Thee as by a magnet. O make me ready to behold Thee when Thou dost appear in glory as the Bridegroom because Thou dost draw me to Thyself out of the path of destruction. AMEN.

✝

When the trumpet shall sound at the midnight hour, only those will hear it whose hearts are attuned to it. These are they who love Jesus, who wait for Him, whose hearts are ever with Him, and whose lives are surrendered to Him. They will be called in unto Him when He comes as the Bridegroom.

Hymn

Jesus, King of Glory,
  Thine be thanks and praise,
All the host of Heaven
  Joyful songs do raise.

With Thy wounds Thou comest,
  Risen from the grave,
Captivity led captive
  By Thee strong to save.

King of kings throughout the world,
  Thou the foe hast slain,
Lamb of God in deathless triumph,
  Praise to Thee again.

Prince of Glory, all shall own
  Thee, confident in pride,
Angel-legions bring Thee
  To Thy Father's side.

United as Thou art on high
  Thou canst God's glory claim;
The Son beside the Father's throne
  Dost rule o'er grief and shame.

Power and glory evermore
  Shine through all the spheres:
Thou wilt reign for evermore,
  Thou wilt wipe all tears.

Hymn

The King is come! The King is come!
Virgins be ready to welcome
Him home!
Go forth to meet Him,
Your Bridegroom to greet,
To praise Him, to love Him,
And fall at His feet.

O put on the robe that shall
Shine as the sun,
The robe of His righteousness,
Woven in one,
Lowliness also is part of that dress,
And love that is equal to righteousness.

The King is approaching,
How great is our joy!
Can there ever be more
That never shall cloy?
Come, spread out your garments
In front of His path,
His servants and subjects
That fear not His wrath.

He once came as King,
On the ass riding still,
In lowliness here
To the olive-tree hill.
He shall come as the Rider
Upon the White Horse
To gather us up,
In His followers' course.

Come, take up your palm
And sing Him alone,
For He cometh, He cometh,
The Lamb on the throne!

Go forth to meet Him,
Your Bridegroom to greet,
To praise Him, to love Him,
And fall at His feet.

DOMINUS FLEVIT

The Historical Aspect

As long ago as the sixth century, in Byzantine times, a small chapel and monastery stood here on the slope of the Mount of Olives, near the present chapel of 'Dominus flevit—the Lord wept.' This has been proved by recent excavations—in A.D. 400 there were in all twenty-four monastic buildings on the Mount. But the tradition that Jesus wept on this spot only dates back to a time later than the Crusades. The Franciscans, who have had a settlement and a small chapel here since 1891, discovered the remains of the Byzantine church in 1954, and they erected this tear-shaped chapel on the foundations of the ancient church. A large window in the sanctuary looks out over Jerusalem. The excavations also revealed ancient graves in the vicinity.

Many regard the tradition of Jesus' weeping here before He entered the city as doubtful, because the steepness of the slope would have been unfavourable to a procession. But no other site has a tradition of this incident. And it is the outlook over the city from this western slope, rather than any special spot, which recalls to us Jesus' weeping. 'Dominus flevit' is singularly well-placed for this outlook.

From the Holy Bible

When Jesus came in sight of the city, he wept over it and said, 'If only you had known, on this great day, the way that leads to peace! But no; it is hidden from your sight. For a time will come upon you, when your enemies will set up siege-works against you; they will encircle you and hem you in at every point; they will level you with the ground, and not leave one stone standing on another, because you did not recognize God's moment when it came.' Luke 19: 41–4.

O Jerusalem, Jerusalem, the city that murders the prophets and stones the messengers sent to her! How often have I longed to gather your children, as a hen gathers her brood under her wings; but you would not let me. Luke 13: 34.

Dominus Flevit—A Call to Us

'Dominus flevit' lies on the western slope of the Mount that beheld so many of the tears shed by our Lord. At the foot of the Mount, in Gethsemane, He called upon His Father, 'with strong crying and tears unto him that was able to save him from death' (Heb. 5 : 7) when the powers of darkness threatened to overwhelm Him. And only a few days earlier, before He made His triumphant entry into the city, Jesus shed tears here, not far from the Garden. He wept over Jerusalem, the city of God, of the Great King, His own city, which would not receive Him but would cast Him forth 'without the gate' a few days later to crucify Him.

The city bewailed by Jesus had been chosen to be the most glorious of all cities and nations; but it was going forward to destruction. The glory of God was to shine out in this city because a holy people dwelt therein (Isa. 62 : 12). This people was called to be a blessing, to the healing of the whole world. God had made wonderful promises to the city, 'All nations shall flow into it' (Isa. 2 : 3), and it was to 'go forth as a lamp that burneth' (Isa. 62 : 1). But Jesus wept because its inhabitants, instead of being the light of all nations, were covered in darkness. It exhibited, not love, but strife, hatred and spiritual death. Only a few days before hands had been lifted to stone Jesus in the holiest portion of the city, the Temple area (John 10 : 31). 'O Jerusalem, which killest the prophets, and stonest them that are sent unto thee!' Jesus may have found it hard to grasp, like a mother cannot grasp that her beloved child has gone to the bad, just what had happened to this city which could claim the whole love of their God. Here God had established His dwelling-place and revealed Himself in the Temple—and all that men could do was turn it into a den of thieves!

Only one who loves the dwellers of such a city could weep and lament for its downfall. It was because Jerusalem so wholly claimed His love that Jesus wept and bewailed over His city. Yes, it was for the people that dwelt therein and were the 'all righteous' (Isa. 60 : 21) amongst sinners and yet who hated and rejected the Son of God, that His love, His great love, was aroused.

Who wept with Jesus at that time? Scarcely any one! The tears and lament of Jesus over His fellow men are however an invitation to us and call for a response. For how can God's own fail to join their tears and lamentations to His? Yet it may be that we should weep and lament first of all over our own malice and wickedness, and the judgment that 'must therefore come upon us.'

'Dominus flevit' looks for the response of repentant tears from all who come here. For Jesus has wept over me, my sin and my rejection of Him. He has wept when I have not realized 'the things that belong to my peace,' when He called to me and came to me in my daily life. How often do we not reject His comings in favour of our own wills and desires, in defiance of His shepherding! We do not respond when He calls us to follow Him in humble obedience.

It is not of the tears shed by Jesus during His First Coming that 'Dominus flevit' speaks to us; it reminds us also of the tears which will be shed at His Second Coming, though not by Him. When at the end of time Jesus shall appear in glory, here on this Mount of Olives which will break in half to become a refuge for His people (Zech. 14 : 4), they will mourn with great mourning the things they have done to Him. But when He is acclaimed as their King, then shall their sorrow be turned into joy. Then will be made manifest the fruit of Jesus' tears, the fulfilment of the promises made to His city, when 'all flesh shall come in unto it.'

But there must be preparation for that day. The way must be made ready for Him, as it was for His First Coming. Who should make ready His way but we who already acknowledge Him and call upon His name? Let us repent, therefore, and weep over our defiance and our continuing in sin. The thought of that day, when all the people of God shall come to repentance, shall be His consolation.

PRAYER

Dear Lord Jesus,
we bow before Thee, because Thou didst here weep for us obstinate sinners, and because Thou dost still weep when in spite of all Thy coaxing and loving care we will not forsake our sins and follow Thee, our Good Shepherd.

May Thy tears, through the power of the Holy Spirit, soften my heart that I may weep for every occasion that I have grieved Thee by my disobedience.

How I long, Lord Jesus, that Thou Who hast loved us with so great a love, shouldst be able to grieve no longer, but to rejoice. Receive me unto Thyself, that I may become a joy and consolation unto Thee in the midst of Thy suffering which Thou dost still support for Thine own people.

Take Thou my will, and let me follow Thee in lowliness and obedience—obedience to every inspiration of the Holy Spirit, in faith in the power of Thy Redemption, so that I by repentance and prayer may prepare Thy way before Thee. AMEN.

HYMN

The Lord doth weep with bitter grief,
He cries aloud to find relief
Upon that Mount of Olives,
'I call'd you to your heavenly home
And longed that you would with Me come
But yet you would not follow.'

The Lord doth weep with bitter grief,
He cries aloud to find relief
Upon that Mount of Olives,
'I longed to bring you holiness
That you to God's high goal might press
But all you wished was Judgment.'

The Lord doth weep with bitter grief,
He cries aloud to find relief
Upon that Mount of Olives,

'I opened wide Heaven's castle gate
That you might there proceed in state
But you would not be welcomed.'

The Lord doth weep with bitter grief,
He cries aloud to find relief
Upon that Mount of Olives,
'My people, who are called God's Race,
Being blind and deaf heed not My face
And do not share My sorrow.'

The Lord doth weep with bitter grief
He cries aloud to find relief
Upon that Mount of Olives,
'O make your way to your true home;
I long that you should no more roam
But come and dwell with Me.'

Hymn

Draw ye near, draw ye near!
Hear Love's voice that calleth ever,
'Children, come ye home to Me!
I do wait for thee and thee.'

Come assemble, come assemble!
You the Shepherd's little flock.
Lie in penitence and sorrow
At the feet of Him Who loves you.

Hear His call, hear His call!
The Good Shepherd calling ever,
'Children, come ye home to Me!
Pastures green I have for ye.'

Come ye home, come ye home!
The Father's arms are open wide
To welcome you for evermore.
Come ye home, come ye home.

GETHSEMANE

The Historical Aspect

St. John, in his report of the events of the night before Good Friday, says that after the Last Supper Jesus went forth with His disciples over the brook Kidron, where was a garden. The other Evangelists say that Jesus went, as He was wont, to the Mount of Olives, to a place which was named Gethsemane. These indications lead us to the church of to-day, for the road that crosses Kidron reaches the Mount of Olives at this point. So we can almost certainly accept the tradition that this is the actual place where Jesus was 'sorrowful unto death.'

The place which was named Gethsemane, of which Matthew (26: 36) and Mark (14: 32) speak, was confidently regarded by the Christians of Jerusalem as the place of Jesus' Agony and Betrayal, according to the evidence of the historian Eusebius about the year 330. Eusebius describes it as lying by the Mount of Olives. According to various ancient sources, Gethsemane, in popular tradition up to the end of the fourth century, meant only an enclosed portion of the 'place,' containing the cave where the Apostles slept and where Jesus was betrayed. That Jesus was taken prisoner in front of this cave was a tradition dating back to the first Christians. Therefore this spot was deeply impressed on the popular mind, and the Agony came to be commemorated here as well.

About the year 400 St. Jerome accepted Eusebius' report, but made it more definite by saying that Gethsemane lay 'at the foot of the Mount of Olives.' He adds, 'A church has now been built over it.' Thus he applies the name Gethsemane to the whole territory, including the church. In this church, on the other side of the road from the cave, the Agony was specially commemorated, according to the report of the nun Etheria (385), who describes the church as 'ecclesia elegans.' This was the Station where Jesus suffered His Agony 'a stone's throw away' from the sleeping Apostles and the place of Betrayal.

The church mentioned by St. Jerome is the strongest evidence for the authenticity of the Station, for this sanctuary had already been erected in the fourth century over the place of Jesus' Agony.

This magnificent church was destroyed by the Persians in 614, as were many other holy places. A small church on the same spot, built in the eighth century, and a large one of Crusading times, were also destroyed, so that by the middle of the fourteenth century no traces could be seen. But the assertions concerning the oldest church and the authenticity of the spot were vindicated in 1909 when with the excavations the Franciscans came upon the foundations not only of the ruins of the medieval basilica but also of those of the 4th century church. During the building of the oldest church the roof and sides of the cave where Jesus prayed had obviously been removed, so that only the end wall remained, and the ground on which Jesus had knelt. The High Altar was placed against this wall, with the rock of the Agony visible in front of it.

In the present church, which was built from 1919 to 1924 on the foundations of the fourth-century one, by means of offerings given by Roman Catholics of all nations, this arrangement has been retained, so that the yellowish limestone rock, most probably drenched by Jesus' sweat and tears, is, though railed in, visible from the High Altar.

Behind the church a part of the original rocky region, as it may have been in Jesus' day, has been preserved.

In the little flower-garden in front of the church, which came into the possession of the Franciscans in 1666, are eight very ancient olive-trees. They seem to be a sign from the earthly life of Jesus. An olive-tree does not die; it continues by means of new shoots. So it is quite possible that the stump of the tree venerated as the Tree of the Agony did indeed hear and see that Agony.

From the Holy Bible

Then Jesus went out and made his way as usual to the Mount of Olives, accompanied by the disciples. When he reached the place he said to them, 'Pray that you may be spared the hour of testing.' He himself withdrew from them about a stone's throw, knelt down, and began to pray, 'Father, if it be thy will, take this cup away from me. Yet not my will but thine be done.'

And now there appeared to him an angel from heaven bringing him strength. And in anguish of spirit he prayed the more urgently; and his sweat was like clots of blood falling to the ground.

When he rose from prayer and came to the disciples he found them asleep, worn out by grief. 'Why are you sleeping?' he said. 'Rise and pray that you may be spared the test.'

Luke 22 : 39–46 and Matt. 26 : 42.

Gethsemane—A Call to Us

Jesus often went to the Garden of Gethsemane, whose name means 'oilpress.' Luke 22 : 39 says that He went 'as he was wont.' He prayed much in this garden, and spoke to His Father in the solitary nights. And surely the angels again and again descended upon the Son of Man, for did He not say to His disciples, 'Ye shall see heaven open, and the angels of God ascending and descending upon the Son of man' (John 1 : 51).

Gethsemane must have been an oasis for Jesus. After all He experienced during the day—the pressing crowds, the arguments with the Pharisees, and their persecutions—He found here at evening, beneath the olive-trees, a place of quiet. Gethsemane was His place of refuge. Here He could be alone with His Father. He probably used one of the caves, of which there are many on the Mount of Olives; these were often used as places for prayer at this time.

So, on Maundy Thursday, Jesus probably took His way to His usual cave. But this time, when He began to pray, He did not find His Father waiting for Him, nor legions of angels, nor Heaven opened. This time it was Hell that was opened, and the Prince of Hell, Death, waiting for Him, to struggle with Him, the Son of man and the Son of God, a struggle costing Him the sweating of blood. This time Gethsemane, true to its name, became for Him 'the press.' It is God Himself Who here treads the press. He chastises His only-begotten Son, and He does so for our sakes, for us who as His true but sinful children should be chastised and beaten by Him. He uses a scourge more terrible than any we could imagine: Satan himself, with legions of evil spirits. Yea, He delivers Jesus into the power of Satan in his most terrible form, as Prince of Death (Heb. 2 : 14).

In this place there now took place the most decisive as well as the most terrible battle that the world has ever seen. A like situation occurred only in the garden of Eden, when Satan provoked another battle, with the two first human beings. But in this first battle he was not obliged to exert himself. Though it was a matter of life and death for the whole human race, the incredible took place: Adam and Eve hardly defended themselves against Satan. They practically never gave battle, but surrendered almost at once. So there was no struggle, and they had no need to sweat blood. Because they were not prepared to fight, this attack from the Enemy could only end in deadly defeat.

Satan was easily and swiftly victorious. From thenceforth Death reigned over men, and none could save them from death's power.

But now was come the hour when He who is Life itself came against Satan, Prince of Death, who appeared with all the powers of his kingdom, with the army of all the evil spirits. Would Jesus in this hour, in His human weakness, also give up the struggle as Adam and Eve had done, capitulating to the fiend of Hell? Satan made three tremendous attempts to make the Son of God abandon the fight and let Himself be overcome. But Jesus defied Satan. He accepted this dreadful battle against Hell and Death and Sin. In the pains of death He fought with Satan at the rock of the Agony, that Agony whose name the Gethsemane church bears. He fought for us to the end—till He sweated blood. He fought for those who have not accepted the challenge because they will not take sin seriously.

And what was this terrible struggle between Heaven and Hell about? Satan's object was to force a word from the lips of Jesus, a word such as Adam and Eve uttered, a word of mistrust, of doubt of the love of God, and of refusal to accept His Will. But each attack of the Enemy produced but the contrary word: FATHER. 'Father, if this cup may not pass away from me, except I drink it, thy Will, not mine, be done.'

'Father!' said Jesus in that hour when He could no longer understand God's Will, when He might well have lost His trust in Him. What may Satan not have suggested to Him, as he suggested to the first man, 'Hath God said . . .' Did it not seem as if Jesus' whole work of Redemption were about to be destroyed, with Death's hand stretched out to seize Him so that Redemption could not be completed on the Cross? But Jesus replied with the one word that sent Satan packing; that word of trust in the love of God, uttered in the midst of deepest pain and temptation, 'Father!' This word was the powerful sword-thrust by which Satan was defeated.

This word, 'Father!' must have sounded through every region of Hell and have made the evil spirits tremble, for it told them that they were defeated. And it must have rung through Heaven, echoing a thousandfold, so that the angels adored, and the Father's heart rejoiced and He again said, 'Thou art my beloved Son in whom I am well pleased.' In this dreadful hour Jesus not only resisted the Enemy unto blood; He fought him with the right weapon: loving trust in the love of God.

Truly, God did not tread the press in Gethsemane in vain. He chastised the Son in so many ways till soul and spirit and body were nigh unto death. Streams of blessing flowed forth, and are still flowing throughout the world. They make the weak and sinful children of men victorious in their battles with Satan, followers of Jesus ever fighting. They are privileged to repeat the words of Jesus, 'Father, thy will be done!' 'Father, I cannot understand, but still I trust.' Jesus still waits for such fighting followers, fruits of His Agony in Gethsemane. For if we fight thus in hours of temptation, we shall have the victory, to His glory.

Prayer in the Church of the Agony

Dearest Lord Jesus,
I thank Thee that Thou didst go through that terrible night of temptation, of utmost struggle with the powers of Hell, costing Thee blood and sweat and tears, for love of us. I thank Thee that Thou didst overcome these temptations with the word 'Father!' When Thou couldst no longer understand God, Thou didst bow beneath His Will in deepest darkness. For this I adore Thee.

Here, in the place of Thine Agony, in gratitude for Thine unimaginable pain, let my answer always be, 'Father!' I would bow beneath the mighty Hand of God when He chastises me; I would trust His fatherly love when I cannot understand. Let me thus be victorious in temptation, and grant that I may be crowned victoriously, as the true follower of Thee Who didst fight against the Enemy, against sin, in Gethsemane. AMEN.

Ways of victory in temptation:

Do not be impressed by temptations.
Trust God's Love, though you do not understand.
Humble yourself beneath God's inscrutable leading.
Acknowledge that God's thoughts are higher than our thoughts.
Seek not to understand God's ways by unredeemed reasoning.
Honour God's commandments and keep His Will holy.
Absolute obedience—wanting naught but His Will.
Keep fast hold of His promises.
Believe that God is Yea and Amen.
Live by faith, faithful to the end.
Wait for God's good time.
Believe that His choice is wonderful always.
Hold fast to the fact that God is Love and that He decides what is best for His child.
Remember always that temptation is the way to glory.

Hymn

Gethsemane, hark to His grief,
His tears, His prayer for relief,
The Son of God trembles and sighs,
And none with love answer His cries.
He is alone, all alone.

Gethsemane: hark to His prayer,
See, how He looks for His friends
For help and for comfort in pain,
To show how much He must bear.
But, see, His friends are asleep.

Gethsemane: hark how He strives
With powers of death that overwhelm Him
And shake Him with their utmost might.
His soul is plunged in darkest night.
By man and God forsaken.

Gethsemane: thou place of pain!
I praise God's love again, again.
For me, for me did Jesus weep,
From might of death and hell doth keep.
How can I ever thank Him!

✝

My Jesus, I would kneel beside Thee
On the Rock of Thy deep woe,
I would stay in love beside Thee
When through death's valley I must go.
I would stay beside Thee, ready for all that betides me,
Till to glory I shall come, till I reach my blessed Home.

✝

Jesus, worthy of all praise,
To be sung in countless songs,
Thou that didst 'Yea, Father' utter.
When the cup of pain was filled,
Scorn and evil wrought their will,
'I will drink it,' Thou didst say.

Jesus, here I can but praise
And Thy glory ever raise,
Lay at Thy feet mine own will.
I, the sinner, bow before Thee,
Bend my will, whate'er befall me,
Joining it to Thine own Will.

✝

The 'Father' of utter resignation brought Jesus through the deepest night of temptation to victory.

Thus is opened unto us the way of victory through every night.

THE CAVE OF THE BETRAYAL

THE HISTORICAL ASPECT

Ancient reports tell us of this important site of one of the events of the Passion. From the historian Eusebius we learn that about A.D. 330 the place where Jesus was betrayed and where He endured the Agony in the Garden was still vividly commemorated by the people of Jerusalem, and the Bordeaux pilgrim, whose description is the earliest still extant, about 333, found the site of the Betrayal to be the cave still pointed out to-day. At that time, in the fourth century, the name Gethsemane was used only for this cave, which commemorated the Agony as well as the Betrayal. But about 385 a magnificent church was erected, somewhat to the south, to commemorate the Agony. The cave kept the commemoration of the betrayal and arrest of Jesus; when the church of the Agony was destroyed, that commemoration was again attached to the cave for a time. The description by Etheria, about 385, shows how vividly the arrest was revered here. When during the Maundy Thursday procession the appropriate portion of the Gospel narrative was read out here, the crowd would burst into a clamour or weeping, loud enough to be heard within the city.

The tradition that Jesus was arrested in front of the cave of the Betrayal continued uninterruptedly, so that the Crusaders accepted it without question. But the supposition that the cave was also the site of the Apostles' slumber has not so ancient a tradition. The Crusaders ignored it. The English pilgrim, Saewulf, wrote in 1102 that 'here in Gethsemane is the place of prayer where Jesus left Peter, James, and John'; so at that time the cave was regarded as the place where the three apostles slumbered, but later on the other eight apostles were included in the commemoration, so that no particular spot can be assigned with certainty to the place of slumber. At one time tradition transferred the Last Supper to this cave, which was then furnished with tables and benches of stone. It is by no means certain that a church was ever built over the cave, although some ancient reports refer to one. To-day the cave is a chapel. The natural roof remains, unlike that of the church of the Agony in Gethsemane, so that the bare rock is visible. The chapel is cared for by the Franciscans.

The Tomb of the Virgin, from whose courtyard the cave of the Betrayal is reached, is an ancient Sanctuary, where the burial of the Virgin Mary has been commemorated since the fifth century. The church has been destroyed several times, and to-day only the crypt remains, within which is the tomb (Greek Orthodox).

From the Holy Bible

The third time Jesus came and said to them, 'Still sleeping? Still taking your ease? Enough! The hour has come. The Son of Man is betrayed to sinful men. Up, let us go forward! My betrayer is upon us.'

The place was known to Judas, his betrayer, because Jesus had often met there with his disciples. So Judas took a detachment of soldiers, and police provided by the chief priests and the Pharisees, equipped with lanterns, torches, and weapons, and made his way to the garden. When he reached the spot, Judas stepped forward at once and said to Jesus, 'Rabbi,' and kissed him. Then they seized him and held him fast. Then the disciples all deserted him and ran away. From Mark 14 and John 18.

The Cave of the Betrayal—A Call to Us

Three happenings, closely connected with each other, give special importance to this cave—the Apostles' slumber, the betrayal by Judas, and the arrest of Jesus by the Temple guards. None of these happenings can be called to mind without the other two. It was Judas, one of the disciples, who brought about the arrest, and Jesus' suffering was greatly increased by the disappointment of finding the apostles asleep during His darkest hour. Here, where they might have been of the greatest help to Him, they forsook Him, instead of praying and watching with Him, and giving Him their support. Why did the Apostles fail Jesus, instead of sharing His grief? They had refused to acknowledge ways which meant suffering and a cross; in the time before Peter had cried out, 'Be it far from thee, Lord!' (Matt. 16: 22). So they could not see that Jesus was the Lamb of God, although John the Baptist had thus addressed Him. They would not realize that He must be put to death for our sin, the Lamb for sacrifice, whose apparent end was defeat; and thus they did not understand why Jesus showed Himself in weakness and temptation in Gethsemane. They were 'offended' at Him, as Jesus had foretold, because they wished to see only the victorious Messiah, come to establish the Kingdom of God here on earth, thus ensuring honour to them. They wanted to be eminent rather than to suffer and be humiliated; instead of being willing to lose their lives for His sake, they wanted to keep them. So strong was this desire that they ignored Jesus' words, 'Whoever would follow me, let him take up his cross.' They would not accept it because it seemed to them too difficult and hence impossible.

Only this could have made them so apathetic and uncaring as to fall asleep in this hour of grief. And so at the arrest, when the Cross beckoned to them, they fled in all directions. Thus they emphasized the indignity of the arrest of Jesus. He was left to face the guards and the Pharisees alone, as one to Whom His followers did not consider it worth while to be faithful. What sadness the avoidance of the Cross by His disciples brought Jesus!

At this cave we can realize to what our shrinking from the Cross can lead us. Our faith and our love are worthless unless we accept the words of Jesus about taking up the Cross and following Him as the determining influence in our lives. The decisive thing is whether or not we are, in our daily lives, prepared to take our Cross, whatever it may be—humiliation, degradation, unjust accusation, contempt, loss—from the hand of God, believing that it will become a blessing to us. Judas reveals to us to what lengths we shall be driven if, however great our veneer of piety, we covet honour and riches and refuse the way of lowliness and poverty that Jesus went. It was this that finally made Judas a traitor, and such an attitude will no less cause us to fall in more exacting times of trial, to leave Jesus or betray Him.

In Gethsemane the disciples did not yet know Jesus risen victorious from the grave. But we do know the Risen Christ. We know that suffering will be turned into glory and weeping become rejoicing, and that the life lost for Jesus' sake will be the life saved. Jesus looks for us to be His true followers, not forsaking Him and grieving Him, but ready to go with Him to prison and to death, ready to 'lose our lives' for Him day by day. But that means following Him when we do not feel like doing so or when to do so is repugnant. It is then that we shall be able to prove that we are His true disciples who stand with Him whatever it costs.

†

Whoso is daily prepared to 'lose his life' will be true to Jesus in the time of trial and will be able to give his life for Him.

HYMN

Betrayed stands Jesus all alone
And there is no one by His side,
A prisoner He passes on,
Reviled and bound tho' now He is
Soon to be numbered with the thieves,
Tho' Lord of all men in the world.

O weep, at what has come to pass
At what this spot so sadly saw!
Betrayed, forsaken is the Lord.
The band of Twelve who loved Him once,
Now having fled, have moved Him sore—
Who is there now to go with Him?

PRAYER

Dear Lord Jesus,
with shame we confess that it was Thy disciples who forsook Thee in the hour of arrest, adding to the sorrow of Thy way of pain. We, who would be Thy disciples, are still the same to-day, ignoring Thy loving call to follow in the way of the Cross. Forgive our grieving of Thee by our unwillingness to bear the Cross—now as then—which, in the hour of trial, has so often led to our betraying Thee.

Jesus, enable me to stay by Thee, to follow Thee whithersoever Thou goest. Make me ready to take up the little crosses of my daily life, to be faithful in the hour of trial, so that I may ever be found at Thy side, whatever may come, even unto prison and death. AMEN.

†

Judas revealed that he priced Jesus at thirty pieces of silver. The other disciples showed that they did not think it worth while even to share His arrest.

To-day Jesus is looking for disciples who will consider nothing too costly to become His followers.

†

Here Thou wast taken and bound,
My dearest, loving Lord.
Here Thou didst walk in grief,
My King and God.
The liberty that Thou didst give,
Was led to cruel death.
Here let's adore the Lord of life,
Who chose the bonds,
To make us free.

†

Jesus' disciples slept out their unwillingness to face the Cross in that most sacred hour, in which God's Son was ready to lay bare for them His heart in its deepest pain and bitterness of soul. His heart will only comprehend those who are open to His grief.

CHAPTER VI

THE VALLEY OF KIDRON

THE Mount of Olives is the beginning of the Passion-area. When seeking to follow the footsteps of our betrayed and arrested Lord, we shall come to the valley of the brook Kidron, which He must have crossed when He was being led away to the house of Caiaphas and Annas. We leave the site of the Betrayal and go along the motor-road to Jericho for about 100 yards to where the road forks, one way leading steeply downwards to the valley.

There are no springs here, and for most of the year the valley is dry; only in the rainy season does water run down the steep sides and traverse the desert down to the Dead Sea. The river-bed is several yards higher to-day than at the time of the Passion, owing to the accumulation of debris from the often-destroyed Temple-wall. Along the narrow stony paths Jesus must have been dragged as prisoner.

That part of the valley which divides the city from the Mount of Olives has, since the fourth century, also been called the valley of Jehoshaphat, from the words of the prophet Joel (3 : 2). Thus this valley of the Passion has a further significance as the traditional scene of the Second Advent and the Last Judgment. Many Jews, and also Christians and Muslims, made their graves here, so as to be ready for the Last Trump; the Jewish graves are on the western slope, with the Muslim ones opposite, by the Temple area. Jews from Eastern Europe used to come to Jerusalem in old age, so that they could be buried here, for they held fast to the promise, 'Whosoever shall call on the name of the Lord shall be delivered' (Joel 2 : 32). Passing thousands of destroyed Jewish tomb-stones and crossing the bottom of the valley, we come to the village of Siloam. All the time we are conscious of a strange atmosphere of expectation and waiting.

Opposite the steep south-east corner of the city wall, the

pinnacle of the Temple, lies the monument to Absalom, on the left, easily recognized by its steep cone. Beside it are the so-called graves of Jehoshaphat, James, and Zacharias,

dating back to the first and second centuries B.C., which Jesus must have looked upon. They must have witnessed His sorrowful passing on that night of Maundy Thursday.

The slopes on both sides are a mass of stones and rubble. We discern the village of Siloam on a slope of the Mount of Offence, and beyond a bend of the road, to the right, on an outlying spur of the Temple hill, the village of Ophel. High above its houses rises the church of St. Peter in Gallicantu (the Cockcrowing), on the eastern slope of the new Mount Zion.

The road has now reached the bottom of the valley. To the right are two school buildings, behind which we go down some steps to the well of Gihon, also called the well of the Virgin, the only well in the Jerusalem of antiquity. Here many Old Testament scenes come alive for us. It was from here that David looked out upon Jerusalem, and from here Joab, his captain, 'got up the gutter,' an underground conduit leading into the city (2 Sam. 5 : 8), and here too Solomon was anointed king (1 Kings 1 : 38, 39). The view now opens out to the south, and in front of us lies the 'Mount of Evil Counsel,' with its tree-clad summit. This name comes from the tradition that it was here, in his country-house, that Caiaphas gave the counsel to put Jesus to death (John 11 : 47–50). To-day it is the seat of the United Nations.

The left-hand side of the road is richly green because of the so-called 'Garden of the Kings,' which are irrigated from the Pool of Siloam. Fig-trees grow close together in the lush grass and vegetables, and soon we can see a bubbling spring flowing from the Pool of Siloam. If we follow along the valley a little farther southwards we come to another site well known to us from the Passion narrative, a steep-sided ravine on the west : the valley of Hinnom; above it, on the slope, lies Aceldama, the 'field of blood' (Matt. 27 : 7, 8; Acts 1 : 18, 19), an ancient cemetery for pilgrims. Close to it there is an Orthodox monastery. A little farther on the left, right amongst the houses, is the well En-Rogel, where Adonijah, David's son, appealed to the people in order to get possession of the throne (1 Kings 1 : 9).

But our chief interest must be the way taken by Jesus as prisoner. Assuming that the house of the High Priest lay on the new Mount Zion, the cohort, bringing their prisoner from Gethsemane, would have left the valley of Kidron before this point. If we follow the path by the outflow of Siloam we come to the pool itself, surrounded by trees. Still to-day the Pool of Siloam is connected, as it was in Hezekiah's day (2 Kings 20 : 20), with the well of Gihon by a subterranean conduit along which we can take our way. We know the pool from the description of Jesus telling the blind man He had healed to come and wash here (John 9 : 7). The memory of this healing made this a place of prayer from early times. The earliest mention of a basilica here dates from the middle of the fifth century; it was destroyed by the Persians in 614. To-day a minaret rises from the ruins of the Byzantine church.

To reach the church of the Cockcrowing, the place of St. Peter's repentance, on the slope of the new Mount Zion, we take the left-hand path, passing behind the minaret. The path is steep and stony and leads us through the houses of Ophel. Later on we pass the wall surrounding the property of the Assumptionist Fathers who are the guardians of St. Peter in Gallicantu; finally the path ends in the wide new asphalt road which comes from the Mist Gate and leads right on to the church.

From the Holy Bible

And all the country wept with a loud voice, and all the people passed over : the king also himself passed over the brook Kidron, and all the people passed over, toward the way of the wilderness.

2 Sam. 15 : 23.

At the same time Jesus spoke to the crowd. 'Do you take me for a bandit, that you have come out with swords and staves to arrest me? Day after day I sat teaching in the Temple, and you did not lay hands on me. But this has all happened to fulfil what the prophets wrote.'

Then the disciples all deserted him and ran away.

The troops with their commander, and the Jewish police, now arrested Jesus and secured him. From Matt. 26 and John 18.

†

My Saviour goes in pain,
Beloved Lamb of God.
O let me follow Thee
Along Thy path so plain.
Let me bewail the sins
That brought Thee to this grief
And enter now within Thy heart
In this dark night of grief.

The Valley of Kidron—A Call to Us

The valley of the brook Kidron—valley of tears—crossed by the weeping King David, prototype of the King of kings, Jesus Christ. David was accompanied by a weeping crowd and consoled by their sympathy. But Jesus our Saviour, our Lord and King, was left alone. He was forsaken by His disciples when He passed along this same road—only the Temple guards and the contemptuous Scribes and Pharisees accompanied Him. David went this way when obliged to flee from his son Absalom. The Son of God was harried by His children whom He loved. David walked here as a free man; Jesus was bound, like a criminal or a beast led to slaughter.

What a way! Jesus' feet must have been sore from the sharp stones of the narrow paths, and His weary body, which had struggled hours before in the sweat of blood, must have felt each step an unspeakable burden. Was there perhaps a fulfilment of Ps. 110 : 7, 'He shall drink of the brook in the way; therefore shall he lift up his head?'

He Who, more than all, had the power to bind and lead others, here allowed Himself to be bound by the evil wills of

His creatures and dragged along, because His children, the Scribes and Pharisees, had refused the good and almighty will of God proclaimed by Jesus. Now He wishes to impress on them and on us, who still refuse to receive His words, this image of Himself as the prisoner: He wishes to call us even more urgently and to beg us to 'Let yourselves be bound to the Will of God, to His leading. Accept His sovereignty as ye look upon Me, the prisoner delivered up to the bonds of My children, letting them work their will on Me, Who am yet their Lord and God. Will that not move you and change your hearts, so that ye give up your wills to Me and reach out your hands to Me that I may bind them and thus lead you, even if it be to where ye would not? For though the way that I lead you is hard, yet it is the good, the best way of the wisdom and love of My Father. His way will lead you to a shining goal, to eternal glory, making you ready to dwell where peace and joy, love and blessedness shall reign for evermore, in the Kingdom of My Father.' Will we not hearken to this request of our Lord in bonds in the valley of Kidron?

✝

If we surrender our wills to God we shall be strong, for we shall be united with the living Lord to Whom nothing is impossible.

✝

He who surrenders his will to God has chosen the better part. For he then is led by the will of Him Who alone is wise and good, and he will be led by the best way.

✝

Love gives to the beloved all its wishes and wants, as the best of all gifts. Shall we refuse such a gift to God when His Son allowed Himself in love to be bound by our wills and led along the way of sorrows?

Prayer

I thank Thee, dear Lord Jesus, for taking the hard way through this valley for our sakes. I thank Thee that Thou, Who hast the power over all men and their powers, didst allow Thyself to be bound by Thine enemies, so that we might be loosed from the bonds of our own will. Thou knowest how my own will and wishes and opinions over and over again prevent me from bowing beneath Thy will and the will of those whom Thou hast ordered to be above me; how always I desire to be free and to decide for myself. Redeem me from the bondage of my sinful will, which can only lead me to perdition.

Here I would give up to Thee all my own will and wishes. Henceforth I would be bound to Thee, Lord Jesus, to Thine only wise and only good Divine Will, however it may come to me through those whom Thou hast ordained to be over me. I would be wholly obedient to Thy Will, believing in the power of Thy Redemption which has gained this obedience for us in torments here. I glory in that Thou hast freed me from the bonds of my sinful self and hast bound me by the love of Thee alone to Thee and to Thy Will. AMEN.

Hymn

Bound and led thru' Kidron
Through that sad valley
Bearing grief and sorrow
And all of it for me.

All alone Thou goest
None to follow Thee
Only angels weeping
As God's pain they see.

Stretching out before Thee
Is a path of pain
Which, like all the prophets
Leads to death again.

Quietly, submissively
On that way Thou goest
Just as if it were Thy sin
Made Thee suffer so.

Who will bless Thee Jesus
For this proof of love
O, that I may evermore
Show my thanks enough.

✝

O holy steps, by which my Lord,
Though God, Creator, bore such grief,
So gentle, like the Lamb of God,
He yet was dragged a prisoner bound
That He might sin's bands loosen.
O holy steps, now be adored
On which God has for sin atoned.

CHAPTER VII

ST. PETER IN GALLICANTU

From the road going to the Valley of Kidron there forks off on the right a new road which leads to the property of the Assumptionist Fathers, which is like a park with many cypress-, pine-, olive-, and pepper-trees, and to the new hotel above the church.

Before we reach the hotel a little footpath forks off on the left through the park which, as commemorating Jesus' way of suffering, we select to get to the church. This path leads straight on to the excavated steps of the 'Scala santa,' the 'Holy Stairs,' which Jesus must have almost certainly trodden when He was led to the Palace of Caiaphas as a prisoner.

According to archæological reports the stones date back at least to Jesus' day if not to a still earlier time. Near the church further excavations are shown to us.

Even if we have no proof of Him being kept there the underground dungeon under the church will tell us and remind us in a very moving way of the night when Jesus spent hours of sufferings after the trial before Annas and Caiaphas.

The church is open from 8 till 12 a.m.
and 2 till 6 p.m.

THE HISTORICAL ASPECT

This church is the memorial of St. Peter's repentance after his denial and brings vividly before us the events of Maundy Thursday night, the time when Jesus stood before Caiaphas. According to ancient pilgrim-reports, the house of Caiaphas lay on a slope of Mount Zion. The Bordeaux pilgrim in 333 and St. Cyril of Jerusalem in 348 speak of it as being well-known. The Empress Eudoxia is said to have built a church in the ruins of the house of Caiaphas, about 460, to commemorate the Apostle's denial and repentance. Other reports, between the sixth and ninth centuries, confirm this. It was probably destroyed by the Persians in 614. But in 630 it again appears in the liturgical calendar of Jerusalem, in reference to the Palm Sunday procession to the sites of the events of the Passion. The procession went 'to St. Peter's, where formerly stood the House of Caiaphas.'

As these reports do not give the exact position nor tell of subsequent developments, various opinions are held. In the seventh century reports speak of a church dedicated only to St. Peter's tears, not to his denial. The present guardians regard it as the 'St. Peter's' mentioned above, which was re-built after the Persian destruction. This church, called the church of the Repentance, was again destroyed in the tenth century, and again re-built by the Crusaders. The English pilgrim, Saewulf, mentions it in 1102, and is the first to call it 'in Gallicantu.' So it can be assumed that the Crusaders' church stood where 'St. Peter's' had stood, but commemorating only the weeping, not the denial, till it was destroyed in 1330.

Others regard the church of the Repentance as having been a separate sanctuary, apart from the House of Caiaphas. When the commemoration of the Repentance was separated from that of the denial, and taken to be on the south-eastern slope, the tradition of the Repentance became attached to the place where the present church 'in Gallicantu' now stands. The House of Caiaphas, in whose courtyard the denial took place, and thus also the basilica are assumed to have stood on the summit of Mount Zion. It is also assumed that the ruins inside of an Armenian monastery, north of the so-called Hall of the Last Supper, are the remains of this.

The church of St. Peter in Gallicantu was re-built in 1931 by the Assumptionist Fathers, who are its guardians to-day. They began excavating in 1888, and discovered the stairway made out of natural stones, the Scala santa. Ancient tombs and other buildings, both Jewish and Christian, also came to light here.

From the Holy Bible

Then they arrested Jesus and led him away. They brought him to the High Priest's house, and Peter followed at a distance. They lit a fire in the middle of the courtyard and sat round it, and Peter sat among them. A serving-maid who saw him sitting in the firelight stared at him and said, 'This man was with him too.' But he denied it. 'Woman,' he said, 'I do not know him.'

A little later someone else noticed him and said, 'You also are one of them.' But Peter said to him, 'No, I am not.' About an hour passed and another spoke more strongly still, 'Of course this fellow was with him. He must have been; he is a Galilean.' But Peter said, 'Man, I do not know what you are talking about.' At that moment, while he was still speaking, a cock crew; and the Lord turned and looked straight at Peter. And Peter remembered the Lord's words, 'To-night, before the cock crows, you will disown me three times.' Luke 22 : 54–62.

THE PLACE WHERE ST. PETER WEPT BITTERLY— A CALL TO US

How significant it is that St. Peter shed his bitter tears of remorse here on the slope of Mount Zion! It must have been not far from here that he had, but a few hours earlier, insisted, 'And if all shall be offended at thee, yet will I not be offended' (Matt. 26 : 33). For these words were probably uttered when St. Peter went with the other disciples and with Jesus from the Upper Room down Mount Zion through the Valley of Kidron to Gethsemane. There Jesus warned them that this night He, the Shepherd, would be taken and that His sheep, instead of crowding round Him, would be scattered in all directions. But St. Peter had insisted, after the personal warning from the Lord, 'If I should die with thee, I will not deny thee in any wise.'

Now, a few hours later, after the arrest of Jesus, St. Peter may have looked down on the path to the Valley of Kidron when he went apart from the people to be alone with his grief. Then he must have remembered that talk, and he must have been cut to the quick when his Lord looked upon him with that look full of unspeakable grief, such as could only come from the loving heart of Jesus : full of grief and yet full of love.

Can he realize it? Was it really he who, about six hours before, down below in the Valley of Kidron, had stood beside his Master and had uttered those great words that he would never deny Him? And now this dreadful thing has happened : he has become a traitor, he has betrayed Him Whom he loved best of all—Him, for Whose sake he had left his family and his trade, on Whom he had staked his whole life. In the very hour when he might have given signal proof of his faithfulness, he not only failed Him Whom he should have helped, but he had also denied Him. He fled from Gethsemane instead of letting himself be bound with Jesus. Now he gazes down upon the paths along which, a few hours earlier, his Lord and Master had been driven by a scoffing crowd to face His judges. But Peter had not been at His side; he had not even been in sight. From a distance, where he was safe from pursuit, he had watched the procession.

And then he had stood in the courtyard, while his Master was set before the judges, and like a sacrificial lamb had allowed all the evil and unjust accusations to be hurled at Him. Not one of the judges had noticed Peter; only an unimportant serving-maid, who established that he had been a follower of the accused Jesus, and who thus, so to speak, also passed a judgment upon him. But Peter, who had not, like his Master, been unjustly judged, but had only been obliged to listen to a true word, though it was uttered in scornful astonishment, had refused to accept even this. He had repudiated it, and thus increased the wrong: he had denied his beloved Lord—now, just when He was in deepest grief and shame and desolation.

Peter's Master could accept the unjust judgment because He was willing to bear the Cross and, in utter humility, to accept the sentence of death upon the Cross. But he, Peter, who as a sinner merited every sentence, shrank from the Cross; it seemed too hard to him to share the shame and persecution of his Master. Therefore he had denied and repudiated the judgment that lay in the serving-maid's words. How pitiful he is—he has forsaken and denied his beloved Master. Peter, the Rock, the man of strength, was compelled to weep bitterly on this slope of Mount Zion.

This slope, along whose paths Jesus passed forsaken, because His disciples were not willing to follow Him to shame and imprisonment, beheld much of their sin. But now it also witnessed the new life born from the tears over repented sin: tears from which springs love stronger than ever before—love which has the power to remain faithful, even unto death, as Peter afterwards proved.

In that hour Jesus stood in the house of Caiaphas before His judge, and the bitterest part of the way yet lay before Him. But now He received consolation from him who had denied Him. For Peter's tears, which the all-seeing eye of Jesus must have seen from afar, were consolation and assurance to Him on His dark path. He who had sinned against Jesus, now wept over his sin, and thus became the great lover and follower. So the sufferings of Jesus and the way He trod because of our sin were not in vain, even for Peter.

Here, where we remember St. Peter's tears, Jesus, Who still suffers and strives for His children, waits for souls who will reply to His suffering by weeping over their sins with ever-renewed repentance. He waits for those who sorrow, not unto death but unto life and love, because their tears are for that which they have done to Jesus, and because their faith acknowledges His forgiving love. How precious are such remorseful tears!

Prayer

Lord Jesus,
we give Thee thanks that at the outset of Thy way to judgment Thou didst utter the words, 'I am he!' Thus Thou didst deliver Thyself into the hands of Thy pursuers and judges, as if Thou hadst been guilty, so that Thy disciples went free. Thou didst deny Thyself and Thine innocence, and thus Thou didst cover us and our guilt.

We adore Thee, Lord Jesus, and confess that we so often are like St. Peter, doing the opposite: denying the Lord and protecting ourselves, unwilling to accept judgment even from a serving-maid.

Lord, Who didst give St. Peter the grace to turn again and to weep over his sin bitterly, grant to me too the grace of repentance for every declaration, whether in thought or in word, 'I am not he,' with which I seek shelter from reproaches, yet deny Thee. Let me ever accept Thy true judgment upon me, even where it is uttered by others as Thy instruments. Give me grace like St. Peter's, that out of a broken and contrite heart, I may love Thee more and more and follow Thee along the way of the Cross unto the end. AMEN.

Hymn

I pray Thee, Holy Spirit,
  To grant me greatest grace,
Repentance for my sinning,
  To bow before Thy face.

I pray Thee, Holy Spirit,
  To soften my hard heart
That I may yet weep afresh,
  And tell of His sore smart.

I pray Thee, Holy Spirit,
  That Thou would'st in my heart
Pray ever with Thy groanings,
  Unutterable, apart.

I pray Thee, Holy Spirit,
  With love my heart to fill
That I may seek, repentant,
  Them I have used so ill.

✝

Jesus' look of sorrow when Peter sinned against Him ought to reach our sin too and to make us 'weep bitterly.' Our remorseful weeping over our sin against Jesus is the measure of our love for Him.

Alas, alas, my sin
  Hath hurt Thy loving Heart,
Hath added to Thy pain,
  And launched its grief-filled dart.
My heart can hardly feel
  All I have done to Thee.
Have mercy, sweet Lord Jesus,
  And look again on me.

Yea, Thou hast looked upon me,
  Jesu, mine own heart's choice,
Thy grace to me hast given,
  My heart can but rejoice.
For me the Cross Thou bearest,
  That I may e'er go free.
My heart, cease not rejoicing,
  From sin Thou art set free.

Jesus, all praise and glory
  My life shall henceforth give.
That Thou hast purged my sinning,
  That I may henceforth live
To give Thee love unending,
  To praise Thee without end.
O love, of grace eternal,
  I low before Thee bend.

CHAPTER VIII

THE FORTRESS OF ANTONIA

THE SITES OF THE SCOURGING, CROWNING WITH THORNS AND OF THE CONDEMNATION OF JESUS

WHEN we come from the Valley of Kidron we can again find traces of Jesus' sorrowful way within the city wall. From St. Stephen's Gate we take the street of St. Anne, which is wider than most of the alleys of the Old City. About 200 yards along it we come to a narrow, overgrown arch which is the beginning of the Via Dolorosa, the most significant road in Jerusalem. It will lead us first of all to where formerly stood the so-called fortress of Antonia which lay on the north-west angle of the Temple area in Jesus' day. At first sight the various buildings prevent any clear notion of the fortress, but here we can find the sites of the Scourging, the Crowning with thorns, and the Condemning to death.

Just beyond the archway a ramp leads up to the Moslem school from whose courtyard the various processions to follow the Way of the Cross start out (see p. 112). A chapel dedicated to the Crowning with thorns could formerly be reached by crossing this courtyard, but it is no longer accessible. Our present goal is the chapel of the Scourging and that of the Condemning to death, which lie on the other side of the road, on the right, in the precincts of the Franciscan Bible Institute. We enter just beside the arch, and crossing the inner court, filled with flowers, we reach the chapel of the Scourging, on the right, towards the east. A large crown of thorns reminds us at the same time of the Crowning with thorns. In the chapel of the Condemning to death on the left side of the courtyard, which also commemorates the laying of the Cross upon Jesus, we see a part of the ancient pavement of the fortress, Lithostrotos, which continues westwards.

The building on the right, next to the Franciscan Institute, also speaks to us of the sufferings of Jesus. It is the 'Ecce Homo' Basilica, and belongs to the Sisters of Notre-Dame de Sion. The 'Ecce Homo' archway, which spans the street and penetrates the church, is called after Pilate's words, 'Behold the man.' It was probably not the spot where Jesus was shown to the crowd, for the arch only dates from the second century A.D., and was not given this name till the sixteenth century, because stones of the pavement on which Jesus stood had been built into it.

In the crypt of the church we can see the excavated portion of the Lithostrotos, and the symbols of the 'Game of Kings' carved on the surface of the great paving-stones . The pavement continues beneath the adjoining house (Greek Orthodox), whose portal is inscribed 'Prison of Christ,' but also called Praetorium. Here we can go down into a dungeon hewn out of the rock, and we are reminded of the words 'Then the soldiers took Jesus into the common hall.' Lingering here, as we surely want to do, we hear from afar the noises of the street and the inevitable call from the minaret; but the 'crying-out' of the stones seems louder to us, calling us to give honour to our dishonoured Lord.

The chapels of the Scourging and the Condemnation (R.C.) are open all day; the Lithostrotos (R.C.) can be seen from 8 a.m. to noon, and from 2 to 6 p.m.; the Praetorium (Greek Orthodox) is open all day.

The Historical Aspect

According to the Gospels, the Mocking and Crowning with thorns and the Condemning to death took place within and without the palace of the Roman governor, called 'Praetorium.'

Through the centuries there have been many different opinions as to where Pilate had his residence and where resounded the cry of 'Crucify!' According to the Roman custom, whereby the governor took over the former Royal residence, Pilate would have had his abode in Herod's palace, which stands in the western part of the city, near the Jaffa Gate, and where we can still see one of its great towers, the Phasael tower. Many scholars think that the Judgment must have taken place in Herod's palace and that the Lithostrotos, the pavement, is buried underground in this part of the city.

But probably Pilate would occasionally 'sit in the seat of judgment' in the fortress of Antonia, the military headquarters of the Roman garrison. Being in the north-west corner of the Temple area, it was like a watchtower over the whole space. Especially if a riot could be expected, Pilate would have moved his 'praetorium' for the time being into the fortress. But there is no direct evidence that this was so during the Passion.

The fortress was wholly destroyed in A.D. 70, and for centuries the whole area was so covered with buildings that its exact site was forgotten. Oral tradition regarded this as the beginning of the Via Dolorosa, though it had lost all memory of the fortress. This tradition was verified when excavations at the end of the nineteenth century brought to light the foundations of the fortress and its surroundings. When Père Ratisbonne, the founder of the order of Notre-Dame de Sion, began, in 1857, to build a convent for the Sisters beside the 'Ecce Homo' arch, portions of the pavement were discovered. The huge paving-stones are roughly carved with geometrical patterns and a figure with a diadem of rays, with the letter B, which probably stood for 'Basileus' (the Greek word for 'King'); so the whole indicates the 'Game of Kings,' with which Roman garrisons used to amuse themselves, as excavations in other Roman military sites show, and which they probably played in connection with Mocking and Crowning with thorns. The pavement extends beneath the whole Antonia area, and was probably the outer court to which the public had access, and which was surrounded by the barrack buildings. In the adjoining inner court, to the east, the apartments of Pilate probably lay, and this would be the place where Jesus was interrogated by him. Even if many scholars do incline increasingly to regard Herod's palace as the scene of the events preceding the Crucifixion, yet we can be gratefully mindful of these traditional sites of the opening events of the Passion.

From the Holy Bible

Jesus was led into the Governor's headquarters and they opened the case against him. Pilate went out to the Jews. 'For my part,' he said, 'I find no case against him. But you have a custom that I release one prisoner for you at Passover. Would you like me to release the king of the Jews?' Again the clamour rose, 'Not him; we want Barabbas!' (Barabbas was a bandit.)

Pilate addressed them again, 'Why, what wrong has he done? I have not found him guilty of any capital offence. I will therefore let him off with a flogging.' But they insisted on their demand, shouting that Jesus should be crucified.

Pilate could see that nothing was being gained, and a riot was starting; so he took water and washed his hands in full view of the people, saying, 'My hands are clean of this man's blood, see to that yourselves.' Pilate then released Barabbas to them, but he had Jesus flogged.

Pilate's soldiers took Jesus into the Governor's headquarters where they collected the whole company round him. First they stripped him and dressed him in a scarlet mantle; and plaiting a crown of thorns they placed it on his head, with a cane in his right hand. Falling on their knees before him they jeered at him, 'Hail, King of the Jews.' They spat on him, and used a cane to beat him about the head.

Jesus came out wearing the crown of thorns and the purple cloak. 'Behold, the Man!' said Pilate. 'Take him and crucify him yourselves, for my part I find no case against him.' But the Jews kept shouting, 'If you let this man go you are no friend to Caesar!' When Pilate heard what they were saying he brought Jesus out and took his seat on the tribunal at the place known as 'The Pavement' ('Gabbatha,' in the language of the Jews). It was the eve of Passover, about noon. They shouted again, 'Away with him! Away with him! Crucify him!' Then he handed Jesus over to be crucified.

From Matt. 27; Luke 23; John 18 and 19.

Lithostrotos—A Call to Us

Here, in Lithostrotos, we recall the Crowning with thorns and the Mockery, made more vivid by the symbols of the Game of Kings.

Ignorant soldiers helped to pass the time by playing this game in hopes of some winnings. Maybe they also played it because of the desire for greatness that dwells in every human heart, the desire to be first, to be king. They were not permitted to be lords in real life so they essayed to play the rôle a little in their gambling.

Into their guardroom was brought One Who was truly a King, King over all peoples. But the soldiers could not recognize this any more than that they took their game seriously. They took Him into their game and made a mock of Him. They could only scorn Him, Who called Himself king and yet had neither land nor people to reign over, for His people had rejected Him. Who but a madman would still insist that He was a king? They mocked Him, instead of mocking themselves, whose minds were filled with idle dreams of greatness: their pretended greatness was entirely without foundation, and so their pretence was only a joke.

They, like all of us, were but miserable creatures with nothing kingly about them. Blind to their own futility, they were equally blind to His true character.

Yet, they, like Pilate, and all those who shared these grief-filled hours with Jesus, could have realized that here amongst them was One Who was truly royal. Perhaps they did dimly realize this, only to be driven on thereby to degrade that royalty. Are we not the same to-day? We are only satisfied when we have reduced Jesus to a figure of fun and folly, for then He can make no demands upon us and we need not obey Him and surrender ourselves to Him.

Jesus, the King of kings, allowed Himself to be thus mocked, and denied by his fellow men, suffering humiliation even as a lamb before its shearers is dumb. He allowed His dignity and His glory to be abased in order to redeem the sins not only of the soldiers and of those who encouraged them, but all our sins of pride and cruelty.

Even to-day He is still mocked, even by the devout amongst us men who strive so hard for greatness and honour. We despise Him in thought and in word, to-day as in the past, and doubt His claim to be a King when we demand of Him: Where is Thy power to prevent both wars and suffering? Where is Thy Kingdom, Thy people, Thy throne? Do not all the nations, even the so-called Christian ones, fail to recognize Thee? Rather, they regard the laws of Thy Kingdom—such as the Sermon on the

Mount—as the ravings of an exalted fool. Thine own people, Israel, does not yet recognize Thee, and the people of the New Covenant hardly do so. How this must grieve the heart of our Lord! To-day He still receives so little kingly honour and must see how few there are who are 'meek and lowly of heart,' ready to surrender their lives to His leading, instead of seeking their own honour and grandeur.

Here, in the place where we recall the Crowning with thorns, God reminds us how greatly His Son was humbled. Before such a scene Heaven itself is dumb, and angels bow in wonder before their humiliated Creator and Lord Who surrendered all His divine dignity and the glory which God had set upon Him. They could not understand that 'God so loved the world that he gave his only-begotten Son' to be mocked and humiliated. But we can understand, for He endured it for us, that we might be truly lowly of heart as men have not been since the Fall.

Who, contemplating this thorn-crowned Lord, could remain unmoved and unwilling to give praise that He endured so much to humble our pride, or be unwilling to confess with shame their constant striving for worldly recognition and honour?

He who bears within his heart the image of his Lord crowned with thorns, which challenges us continually to cancel our earthly strivings, will feel impelled to take his stand beside the humiliated Jesus and to say to Him, 'I will follow thee whithersoever thou goest.'

PRAYER

Jesus, dear Lord,
I bow before Thee, and render Thee thanks that Thou, our Creator, our Lord and God, Ruler over Heaven and earth, didst allow Thyself to be crowned with thorns in mockery because of our claims, our pride and our self-glorification. Forgive us for still being so eager for our own honour and glory and for not denying ourselves before God and man. I confess with shame that while beholding Thee, crowned with thorns, I still dare to seek the highest place, to demand recognition, to desire to have power over others.

Jesus, by this Thy grievous suffering beneath the crown of thorns, Thou hast redeemed us from this striving for earthly glory for greatness and the chief seats, from this sin of Lucifer, which binds us to him. I truly believe that if I humble myself Thou wilt make me like Thee, meek and lowly of heart. I hereby renounce all claims to honour or admiration.

O Lamb of God, I would follow Thy way of lowliness, and give glory to Thee by a wholly surrendered life. To Thee must be given as much homage and glory as Thou didst suffer pain and shame, until Thou comest to Thy Kingdom in which every knee shall bow before Thee. AMEN.

†

The image of Jesus mockingly crowned with thorns is still with us. Therefore He waits for disciples who will honour Him. But only out of the depth of a contrite heart can Jesus receive true homage, the homage due to Him as King of kings.

†

Because so few are ready to accept humiliation and thus to take the place meet for them, Jesus took it for us. But the true lover of Jesus will choose this place.

†

Hymn

There is a scene in Heaven's Hall
Before which angels prostrate fall
The Lamb that's crowned with thorns.
And yet though angels can it see
They cannot tell what it can be
For they need not salvation.

The sight of pain and grief they see
Must make them weep, whoe'er it be.
But they could hardly guess
That here the lord of Life would hang,
The Lord at whose glad birth they sang,
Now veiled beneath the shame and crown.

A sight which pierces very deep
And could make e'en the Father weep
As He beholds such grief :
Tormented by this crown of thorn
But even more by sinners' scorn
His Son, He sees, stands thus bereft.

The Trinity of Father, Son,
And Holy Ghost unite as one
To weep at what They see.
Yet out of all this Sorrow grew
A portrait that is traced anew
A Face that's full of grace and peace.

There pours forth from this face of Love
Which, though beneath the thorns above
So mildly bears the pain,
The power which ever stronger flows
Than all that men can do by blows
To reconcile fierce enemies.

There is a scene in Heaven's Hall
Before which angels prostrate fall
And thus give Him their praise.
This scene which shows the Father's heart
Of Love for men, to bear their part
Of sin, is what the angels see.

My heart doth greet Thee, Jesus,
My Jesus, dearest Lord,
Mocked, spat upon, and wounded,
Be Thou for e'er adored.

I hardly dare behold Thee,
Thou Who didst suffer so,
Thou Who dost ne'er reject us,
Thou Who wast brought so low.

For all my pride and hardness
Thou in the dust didst lie,
Thy shame and Thine abasement
Repair my strivings high.

Now let me be the lowest,
Nor seek a higher place
But ever in thanksgiving
Bow down before Thy Face.

The Place of Scourging—A Call to Us

The thought of the scourging paints terrible pictures in our minds as we remember the start of the Via Dolorosa in the Franciscan chapel. Jesus was bound to a pillar and given over to the will of the mercenaries, who covered His holy body with bleeding wounds. He was near collapse. The words of the Psalmist came true, 'I am a worm and no man' (Ps. 22 : 6).

Yet this cruelty was ushered in by Pilate with the words, 'I find no fault in him. Take ye him and scourge him.' So we have the paradox that the Roman governor, though trained in law, gives an innocent man up for scourging. Why did he act so unjustly? To keep the crowd quiet and to avoid arousing hostility to himself. He thought that he could keep his hands unsmirched by condemning Jesus to scourging instead of to death, though he must have known that scourging could result in death. But in that case it was the soldiers who were to blame for having carried out their duty too thoroughly. So Pilate washed his hands publicly, rejecting responsibility for the suffering of Jesus.

Thus Jesus, the spotless Lamb of God, Who stood dumb before His shearers, was bound to the pillar of scourging.

Unknowingly, by saying that he found no fault in Him, Pilate proclaimed that Jesus bears our sins.

'My sins and those of all men
In number as the sands,
Have brought Thee to this suffering
By rude and cruel hands.'

It is scarcely credible that it was men like us, mere creatures of God, who wounded Jesus, the Son of God, in such a fashion. God prepared a body for His Son, holy and without blemish. Men were unworthy even to touch it, but they not only touched it but wounded it so that 'it was more marred than any man's.' It was we who caused the blood of Jesus to flow. And now we, His murderers, can be healed by His stripes. Who can grasp such forgiving and such love? In adoring love we here ponder the mystery of how the wounds of Jesus are fountains of salvation for our sins.

There is a fountain filled with Blood
drawn from Emmanuel's veins,
And sinners plunged beneath that flood
lose all their guilty stains.
Dear dying Lamb, Thy precious Blood
shall never lose its power,
Till all the ransomed Church of God
be saved to sin no more.

(*William Cowper,* 1731–1800)

Here in this spot Jesus might well therefore speak to us in our deepest being and say to us, 'Do not retaliate when you are being wounded—whether they are the wounds to the soul by evil and malicious speech, or wounds to the spirit by abuse or wounds to the body by persecution. Consider My wounds which proclaim the eternal law of God that from pain and grief—though only of course if you admit your sinfulness and bear it humbly as I have—Life and blessing result more than from anything else which we can do.' Jesus is seeking such as can bear their wounds in that way for it is with them that He can build His kingdom. Here at the spot where we recall His Scourging we need to ask ourselves whether we are 'bearers of wounds' or 'the cause of them.'

And Jesus goes on to ask whether we fully appreciate the punishment which He bore for the sins of us men so that we should hate every sin of the flesh, beginning with every lustful glance which is already adultery. Is not the whole point of Jesus' loving and patient bearing of the countless wounds which He received in His sacred body that we should thus be released in our bodies from the instinct to sin and be re-established in purity and the beauty of holiness? Christ's prayer for us in this sacred spot is that His sufferings for us shall not have been in vain but that we shall respond to Him with our love and hate sin, though bearing it like Him.

✝

'I gave my back to the smiters, and my cheeks to them that plucked off the hair: I hid not my face from shame and spitting.' Isaiah 50: 6.

PRAYER

Dear Lord Jesus,
Who wast scourged until Thy blood poured forth for our sins, I bow before Thee, remembering Thy bleeding body and in deep thanksgiving that by Thy stripes I am healed—that Thy Blood redeems me from all my sinful desires.

Let the image of Thy so sorely wounded body dwell deep in my heart and speak to me clearer than any spoken call to repentance, of the power of my sin, which hath caused Thee to be beaten so dreadfully. Lord Jesus, give me a deep hatred for the sin which brought and still brings Thee such unspeakable suffering. In the power of Thy Redemption I would avoid all sin and would renounce all my sinful longings and my desire to 'live my own life.'

Holy Spirit, hear my prayer and so transform me that my life may show forth how the wounds of Jesus have brought me healing, how His Blood has cleansed me from every sin, and how I am more than conqueror. Grant that my life may praise the might of Jesus' wounds that praise and thanksgiving may always be His. AMEN.

HYMN

All the powers of Heaven bow low
  With veiled face at what they see;
God's own Son cries to the Father,
  'Why hast Thou forsaken Me?'
There He stands, bound to the pillar,
  Stripped and miserable, He
Has to bear their many lashings
  On the way to His dread Tree.

Like a lamb before its shearers
  Dumb He stands before them all,
Scarcely can one recognize Him
  Bowed beneath the blows that fall,
For His face is all distorted
  With the pain and grief of soul;
Yet despite each stroke that sears Him
  He still yearns to make men whole.

O Thou dearest, best-loved Saviour
  Almost breaks Thy heart with pain?
No, Thou goest on still further,
  Full of love, Thy Cross in train.
Bleeding from a thousand scars
  Like a sacrificial Lamb
Thou dost take the way to Calvary,
  There to die, the great I AM.

✝

Who can estimate the love of Jesus Who for us took on the form of a man and allowed Himself to be so tortured in order to atone for our sins of the body, to free us from our sinful ways and to gain for us a new and spotless resurrection body?

The Place of Condemnation and the Laying-on of the Cross—A Call to Us

As now the chapel of the Condemnation stands under the chapel of the Scourging it serves to declare this fact—that they didn't stop at scourging Jesus.

The Scourging of Jesus ordered by Pilate was the first step taken by the Governor to save himself; he took the second step to save his position and to avoid appearing as Caesar's enemy. Pilate condemned Jesus to death, delivering up the innocent Son of God, and thereby he laid upon himself the hardest debt of all—of having delivered up to death the guiltless and pure Son of God.

So the astounding and incredible thing came to pass: the innocent and sinless One, Who had power to condemn and to destroy His judges in this very moment, accepted their condemnation. He accepted it meekly, and allowed the Cross, the instrument for carrying out the sentence, to be laid upon His wounded shoulders.

The chapel of the Condemnation awakens in us the deepest shame. Jesus was condemned because over and over again we refuse to accept the judgments passed upon us, mostly with justice. Nothing is so hard for us as to acknowledge our faults when we are made aware of our wrong-doing or evil-speaking.

Hence the One Lord Jesus Christ stands before the judgment-seat on behalf of all. He bows beneath the condemnation, takes up the Cross and goes to death. He did this for us, for you, for me, who so lightly judge the words and deeds and intentions of others, usually without justice because we are unaware of their motives, whilst we ourselves resent judgment. And so we fail miserably when God lays a cross upon us; not ours the words of the Penitent Thief, 'We receive the due reward of our deeds.' But we all need a cross to purify us and make us fit for glory.

Jesus, Who needed no purification, took up the Cross as if He had been a criminal fit only to bow beneath such a load. Here we cannot but be deeply moved by the humility of the Lamb of God. He took up the Cross for us, for we are no 'lambs' but 'oxen' who kick against the pricks.

Now Jesus waits for us to thank Him for so incomprehensible an action. He waits for us to honour truth henceforth instead of lying, and to receive reproaches and judgments from others, because as sinners we are mostly in the wrong, even when others are not correct in their judgments. He waits for us to bow before Him in memory of His sinless acceptance of the death sentence, instead of excusing ourselves and even laying the blame on others. He waits for us not only to accept judgment, but to be willing to bear whatever cross He may lay upon us and say, 'Lay on! I will bear it willingly, for I would follow Thee in love and thanksgiving.'

†

Jesus, Who was sinless, humbly allowed Himself to be condemned to bear the Cross for us. He did this so that henceforth the Cross would not be a sign of death but a symbol of those who, though bearing a cross humbly, yet have a way of escape in the knowledge that as sinners we need chastisement.

†

PRAYER

Dear Lord Jesus,
I adore Thee and thank Thee that Thou, the sinless Son of God, wast condemned unto death, though guiltless, for our sake.

I adore Thy love and humility, that Thou tookest upon Thyself all my guilt as if it were Thine, only so that I might be set free at the Judgment. Thou hast borne the burden of the Cross as a condemned man. Beholding such love, I would humble myself and fall down at Thy feet.

My Lord Jesus, in gratitude I would bear in utter submission the Cross which is given me by the Father. I desire to learn from Thee how to bear my Cross in humility and patience, although Thou didst bear it unjustly, and I justly. Humbly I bend my will to take it upon me, knowing what hidden blessing and what glory it will bring. Lord Jesus, grant that I may be Thy true follower, through whom Thou shalt gain fruit from Thy sufferings. AMEN.

Hymn

Quiet and forebearing goes He
  Like a lambkin to the Cross,
What a picture of longsuffering
  For our sins portrayéd was;
Not a sound from Him, complaining,
  Does there issue from His lips,
Only in His face is anguish
  As He bows beneath the whips.

Yes, Eternal Love is shown us
  In the very midst of pain,
For from ages everlasting
  God did Calvary ordain.
Jesus did submit to sorrow
  That by love He might bring home
Sinners who, His suffering ended,
  Might no longer hopeless roam.

Thus for those along Life's pathway,
  Who, whilst seeing, do not see,
There is still no understanding
  That He has borne all for thee.
He has borne for men their burdens—
  Yet who realizes this?
Who is there that really thanks Him
  By avoiding sin's abyss?

CHAPTER IX

VIA DOLOROSA

(See Map on page 312)

OUR greatest desire surely, when visiting Jesus' city, is to follow along His path of pain to Golgotha. From the site of the fortress of Antonia, where we visited the place of His condemnation and His taking-up of the cross, we make our way through the Old City to the church of the Holy Sepulchre, along the winding lanes which are called the Via Dolorosa. The actual path which Jesus trod is buried beneath many layers of rubble, owing to the many destructions which have come upon the city. But yet these narrow lanes, though dark and in part built-over, still give us the impression that time has stood still.

Part of the Via Dolorosa, the Bazaar, is shut off from all motorized traffic by iron palings, and here the typically oriental kind of life holds sway, mostly in the open street. Dense crowds surge between the open shops on either side of the road, and strange smells assail our nostrils. The jabbering of the shopkeepers mingles with the cries of 'Baksheesh' from swarms of children and the jostling of overloaded donkeys. No chapel of the Stations of the Cross could make the Way of the Cross come so alive for us as does this street-scene, resembling that of the first Good Friday.

Thousands of feet—native and foreign—tread this road; do any of them realize that it is not an ordinary road? It must be a rare occurrence for any one here to kneel where Jesus fell to the ground if we judge by the demeanour of the people.

But once a week—on Friday afternoon—it is possible to realize what a singular road this is. A procession to the fourteen Stations of the Cross takes place—a custom which has grown up gradually since the time of the Crusades. Nine of the Stations are taken from the Gospels; the other five are based on traditions of varying antiquity. If on a Friday we come to the courtyard of the Moslem school just after 3 p.m. we shall find a few Franciscans surrounded by quite a crowd of people. From this 1st Station, the Condemning to Death of Jesus, the procession, preceded by a group of men who take it in turns to carry a wooden cross, emerges on to the street to reach the 2nd Station, the laying-on of the Cross, which is commemorated outside the chapel of the Condemnation.

Then the procession passes under the Ecce Homo arch. At this point the Via Dolorosa leaves the area of the former fortress and descends the valley of Tyropoeon. Following the procession we turn left along King Solomon Street, which comes from the Damascus Gate. At the corner another halt is made, for here is a chapel, commemorating the First Fall of Jesus beneath the Cross, which is served by Armenian Catholics (3rd Station). We can but rejoice that at this hour prayers and hymns resound at every Station amid the usual turmoil of the crowds. The 4th Station is only a few steps farther on: Jesus meets His Mother. There is a church in the courtyard, also belonging to the Armenians, and a chapel by the road-side, whose lintel bears a bas-relief of the scene.

About 20 yards farther on the Via Dolorosa turns to the right, away from the valley road. At the corner we see the inscription over the doorway of the chapel, 'Simon Kyrenaeo Crux imponitur'—'here the Cross was laid on Simon of Cyrene.' This 5th Station is Roman Catholic and belongs to the Franciscans. Wide steps lead up a narrow lane spanned by many arches and vaultings. Half-way up, on the left, beneath the first large vault, the procession halts at a chapel commemorating Veronica's deed of compassion when, according to a legend, she wiped Jesus' face with her veil (6th Station). This chapel is served by the Little Sisters of Jesus, founded by Charles de Foucauld, who have here adopted the Greek Catholic Rite.

At the upper end of the lane we come to the busy Bazaar, on the opposite side of which we find a small Franciscan chapel commemorating Jesus falling the Second Time (7th Station); the 8th and 9th Stations can no longer be approached directly, but we shall not miss them if we follow the procession. The procession turns aside into the Street of St. Francis, on the right, just beyond the Franciscan chapel. About 12 yards farther on we see a cross on a high wall with the inscription: 'IC XC NIKA —Jesus Christ conquers'; this is the 8th Station: Jesus meeting the Daughters of Jerusalem.

To reach the 9th Station we return to the Bazaar, also called Damascus Street, and about 50 yards farther along, forcing our way through the chattering crowd in this great shopping street, we climb a stairway leading to the courtyard of an Abyssinian monastery, where the 9th Station, the Third Fall, is commemorated. But the real site of this is in front of the Coptic Church which lies behind this courtyard and which is reached by a dark passage on the right beyond the courtyard.

Although we are now quite close to the church of the Holy Sepulchre we cannot reach it directly but must return to the Bazaar. At the end of the heavily built-up area we turn right by the Russian Hospice, and passing the Lutheran church of the Redemption, we come to the high wall which cuts off this short street. Here a small door leads into the courtyard of the church of the Holy Sepulchre, where the last four Stations are.

To-day we can follow the whole way in about a quarter of an hour. Who knows how long it took Jesus in His weakened state, bowed beneath the weight of the Cross? The upward path to Golgotha was far steeper then because of the lower level.

The Muslim School (1st station) and the chapels of the 3rd, 4th, 6th and 7th stations are open only at the time of the procession.

From the Holy Bible

Jesus carrying his own cross went out to the Place of the Skull, as it is called (or, in the Hebrew tongue, 'Golgotha'). On their way out they met a man from Cyrene, Simon by name, and pressed him into service to carry his cross.

Great numbers of people followed, many women among them, who mourned and lamented over him. Jesus turned to them and said, 'Daughters of Jerusalem, do not weep for me; no, weep for yourselves and your children. For the days are surely coming when they will say, "Happy are the barren and the wombs that never bore child." ' From Matt. 27; Luke 23; John 19.

Jesus then said to his disciples, 'If any one wishes to be a follower of mine, he must forsake himself, take up his cross and come with me.' Matt. 16: 24.

Via Dolorosa—A Call to Us

Via Dolorosa—begin the great lament,
Via Dolorosa—now show us with intent
The depth of Jesus' pain,
As for us the cruel cross He bore
And took on Him our load so sore,
Till on the Cross He died.

Via Dolorosa, the one true path of pain on this earth, because it was trodden by Him Who was not only human as we are, but Son of Man and Son of God, and Who therefore went this way, not for the chastisement of His sin, but voluntarily, without any sin, out of love for us. Via Dolorosa, a path of pain unlike any other, because Jesus here bore all the pains of mankind together with the Cross which He carried along this way. We all have crosses to bear, but who bears the cross like Jesus? He bore it as a criminal, and yet He was the Holy One. He bore it as one condemned to death, yet He was Life. He bore it, crowned with thorns and spat upon, though One to whom all glory in heaven and on earth is due. He bore it, bound and scourged, Whose body alone is wholly pure and without blemish. He bore the Cross as one forsaken by all, for His nearest friends, His disciples, had fled, and He was obliged to tread this bitter path alone. And, for His greater dishonour, a stranger was compelled to help with the load because none of His disciples had offered, and hence He was devoted in love to all men, in a special way and like no other.

Via Dolorosa, path of pain, which heard the sighs and plaints of the Heart of Jesus and which saw Him fall. Via Dolorosa, path of pain without equal, for where else has a path of pain been trodden as Jesus trod this? Without complaint to God, without questioning, without any resistance, without reproaches to His tormentors, condemned because of His good works. Who has trodden the path of pain with such humility, His heart saying: 'Lay on, I bear it willingly'? Who has trodden the path as meekly as Jesus, Who, when He was reviled, reviled not again, as, weary unto death, He bore His heavy Cross to Golgotha to suffer the terrible experience of crucifixion? Via Dolorosa—where else is there such a path of pain, a route which bore so guiltless a martyr in all His agony, and from the sides of which He who sought to do them good earned such contempt?

Via Dolorosa, that road on which a guiltless one suffered, not for the guilt of just one nor even for any particular nation, but for the guilt of millions, the guilt of a whole world, the weight of which made the Cross so heavy that He could hardly bear it to the end. Who else has borne a Cross which broke soul and spirit as did this one? The weight of the sin of the whole world, and the humiliation of God's judgment and chastisement, lay on One Who was willing to be a cross-bearer, and offered Himself for this out of love for us.

Via Dolorosa, thou holiest street in the whole world, along which God passed in penitence for His earthly children—thou art worthy to be traversed to-day by those whose hearts are humbled, worshipping Him. Here every other word needs to be silenced and every other act cease. The only thing to compare with our Lord and Saviour's most holy act in this street would be a holy act on their part. Ought we not to reverence His lowliness, prostrate ourselves in the dust and render praise for the fact that He did not tire but continued His way until He had completed it?

Yea, God and all Heaven wait for gatherings of people on

this road who will hold it sacred because of the sufferings of our Lord, and who will re-hallow it by holiness of life. Our Lord Jesus waits for true cross-bearers who have heard here His call to follow, and who bear the cross humbly and without complaint, meekly, loving as He loved.

Prayer

Jesus, dear Lord, we would bend low upon Thy path of pain, on which Thou wast bowed low by the weight of the Cross that caused Thee to fall. Thou, guiltless, wast compelled to bear it because we, the guilty, are unwilling to bear what our sin lays upon us. We pray Thee to forgive the times in our lives when we were unwilling to bear our cross, or rebelled against it, or threw it away. Yet we believe, on this Thy path of pain, that Thou, our Crossbearer, hast redeemed us from all avoidance of the cross, and made us to love it. Every time that I meet something difficult in life against which I might revolt do Thou help me to say again, 'I will bear it gladly.'

So we will take up our cross and follow Thee, saying: Thy Cross I do receive, for from Thy Hand it comes. In love and humility I will bear it after Thee, O Jesus. Grant that it may prepare me to be one day at Thy side, before Thy throne, and let me, as a real bearer of the cross, draw many others to take up their cross in love. May this be for Thee a source of joy and the fruit of Thy path of pain along the Via Dolorosa. AMEN.

'Take up thy Cross and Follow Me!'

Whoever belongs to Jesus cannot choose a path different from the one Jesus took. Love must follow the way of the Cross with Jesus.

Whoever loves Jesus loves the Cross, for it is part of Him.

The Cross which weighs heavily on thee will glorify thee and will at length bring thee to heaven. Is it not therefore worthy of all honour?

If he who once stood afar off will be my yoke-fellow, then let him take up the Cross—for the ways of all cross-bearers lead to God's Throne.

He who knows that he is a sinner accepts the burden God lays upon him, for he knows that sinners need chastisement in order to become like Him.

Do not carry thy Cross like a slave but like a lover of Jesus. Then it will begin to glow.

If thy Cross is heavy, so will also the blessing it bears be heavy.

If you possess nothing but your Cross, regard it still as a most precious treasure, for it conceals all that the human heart can long for: freedom from the power of sin, peace, and blessedness.

The lower you bow beneath the burden laid on you by God, the stronger and more wondrous can His might be revealed through your Cross—both now and in all Eternity.

✝

Via Dolorosa, Thou path of His great woe,
Via Dolorosa, He bore His Cross alone.
Via Dolorosa, Where deaf'ning tumults are,
Via Dolorosa, O path from God so far.
Via Dolorosa, Where stiff-necked pride is found,
Via Dolorosa, He comes bowed to the ground.
Via Dolorosa, Who knows all Jesus' woe?
Via Dolorosa, Who loves alone can know.
Via Dolorosa, God still will bear the load
And all for our relief.
Who is there that can to-day
Share in His great grief?

VIA DOLOROSA

✝

He is longing for a soul
  That will bow as low as He
And in love will bear the Cross.
  Whose can such an offering be?

Hymn

I kiss Thy Cross,
It comes from Thy dear Hands
Thy gift to me
And if Thou canst not spare me
I will receive
This love-token from Thee.

I kiss Thy Cross,
Thou gavest it to me
For love alone,
That it for life eternal
Should bear much fruit—
And take away my tears.

I kiss Thy Cross,
That Thou Thyself didst bear.
And there on high
Thou wilt one question put to me:
If I have walked
Behind Thee with my Cross.

I kiss Thy Cross,
I know its blessing true
For all of gold
Is every Cross we bear for Thee,
To show to us—that all Thy Love is free.

Therefore Thy Cross
In love I will take up,
My dearest Lord,
Upon the Cross Thou did'st hang
To set us free
From shrinking from the Cross.

And so I sing
The song of that dear Cross,
My Lord, my Christ.
The song which tells of how the Cross
Gives glory evermore
To Thee to Whom we sing.

Hymn

Jesus bears His heavy burden
To the place of death decreed.
O what form of martyr's suffering,
Who its meaning now will heed?
God Himself the Cross is bearing
That belongs to sinners here,
And not one of all who watch Him
Can prevent the end that's near.

Jesus, Jesus, burden-bearer
Of the sins of all the world,
In Thy pity for us sinners
Thou hast placed Thyself with us,
That Thou could'st still bear the burden
From which all yearn to be free.
Thou did'st bear for every sinner
All the pain of that dread Tree.

Jesus, Thou didst walk so weary
Through the streets beneath Thy load.
Thou would'st be the Cross's Bridegroom,

Never resting from Thy load.
Without ceasing Thou proceedest
To become the Victim true
Of the Cross which when erected
Means we may find Heav'n anew.

For our love Thou wouldest suffer,
For our gain Thou choosest death,
For our sakes Thou bearest meekly
Blasphemy and mocking breath.
For our sakes Thou still art bearing
That hard Cross to Calvary
For Thy love saw not Thy suffering
But our chains that Thou could'st free.

Jesus, Jesus, burden-bearer
For this poor and darkened world,
Jesus, King, yet Man of Sorrows,
Satan from his throne hast hurled.
Thou hast won the victor's trophy
On the tree of Calvary.
Victory's song shall sound for ever
For Redemption made so free.

CHAPTER X

THE CHURCH OF THE HOLY SEPULCHRE

WE will devote a whole day to visiting Golgotha and the Holy Sepulchre, so that we can have plenty of time for these most important Holy Places. The Church of the Holy Sepulchre can be reached either via the Via Dolorosa (see p.112) or direct from the Damascus Gate in the north wall of the city. From the Gate we descend a wide stairway and reach the iron posts which separate it from the Street of the Bazaar. We already know the last part of the street from our Friday visit to the 'Way of Sorrows,' and we have already seen the entrance to the church. To-day we go through the small doorway in the wall to the forecourt of the church, which is surrounded by various chapels and a convent. The main entrance to the church is next to the bell tower and is almost wholly hidden by the scaffolding which supports the ruinous building.

The interior is dark, and a general view is impossible. We get the impression of a conglomeration of innumerable churches and chapels in a variety of styles of architecture. But we are only concerned with the two focal points: the place of the Crucifixion and the Tomb where Jesus was laid. Immediately inside the entrance a narrow flight of steps leads up to the Calvary chapel (Greek Orthodox). The original skull-shaped rock is now entirely covered in marble and surrounded by walls and altars. The chapel itself is only partly built on the rock, the rest of the foundations are artificial. Later, in the Adam chapel, below Calvary, we can see a little of the original rock which has here been exposed, showing the cleft in it. In the Calvary chapel, on the right side, is a mosaic floor, which commemorates the 10th Station (Jesus stripped of His garments); it is Roman Catholic. The altar behind indicates the 'Nailing to the Cross,' with a large frescoe (11th Station, Roman Catholic). The altar on the left is the site of the 'Lifting-up of the Cross' (12th Station, Greek Orthodox). There is a continual flow of pilgrims coming to kneel here; they bend down under the altar to kiss the ground at the round opening in the rock which is supposed to show where the Cross was erected. A small altar between the larger ones, dedicated to the Mother of Sorrows, commemorates the 'Descent from the Cross' (13th Station, Roman Catholic).

It is hard not to be able to pause here in complete silence; but we are surrounded by the continual noisy coming and going of groups of people speaking in all languages. Yet we feel compelled to spend a long time here; for here, on Golgotha, more than at any other Holy Place, our crucified Lord should receive unending praise and worship.

As we descend the stairs again we come to the Stone of Anointing, opposite the main entrance. This commemorates the embalming of Jesus' body. Half-way to the left we come to the tomb-chapel, the 'little church within a church' (14th Station). It consists of an entrance-place, called the Chapel of the Angels, and the actual tomb. In order to look into the tomb we must wait awhile, for many pilgrims are continually pressing forward. Eventually we can, like Peter in the Gospel story, bend down to pass through the low, narrow opening which leads from the chapel of the Angels into the Tomb. Its walls are covered in white marble, as is also the raised shelf for the reception of the body, on the right. Nothing is to be seen of the rock of the Tomb, and yet here we are in the very place in which our Lord rose from the dead.

The Historical Aspect

We may be surprised to find the site of the Crucifixion and of the Tomb both under one roof and in the centre of the city. But excavations have revealed with some certainty that the district of the Church of the Holy Sepulchre lay outside the city wall at the time of Jesus, and that it was only enclosed by a new wall about A.D. 40. About the middle of the nineteenth century remains of the ancient city wall were found to the east and south of the church, and when the Russian pilgrims' hospice was built the threshold of a gateway was discovered.

Calvary must have been close beyond this gate. Not a hill, as we generally assume, but only a large rock rising out of the ground. At the foot of this rock was a space with gardens and tomb-chambers hewn out of the rock, amongst which will have been Joseph of Arimathæa's family sepulchre and his own new tomb (John 19: 41). The tomb-stones, dating from Jesus' day, which can still be seen inside the church, are called after him. These tomb-chambers are the strongest evidence for the accuracy of the site, for according to Jewish law tombs had to be away from living quarters.

The rock of Calvary was probably not a usual place of execution, or else a counsellor like Joseph of Arimathæa would not have had a garden-tomb so close. The title, 'the Place of a skull,' probably came from the appearance of the rock. Jesus was probably executed here, immediately beyond the city wall, so that the sentence could be quickly carried out before the Sabbath.

After He had been taken down from the Cross He was laid in the near-by grave belonging to Joseph. The Gospels give some details about it, which can still be partly traced in the church of the Holy Sepulchre. Being exceptional, in that it was intended for only one body, it would have consisted, according to John 20: 1–10, of an outer chamber as well as the actual tomb-chamber. The opening into the latter was so small that the disciples had to stoop down in order to look in (Luke 24: 12). The tomb must have been to the right of the doorway, for it was there that the women saw the seated angel (Mark 16: 5). It must have been a coffin-like cavity, for Peter could only see the 'napkin' when he looked right into the hollowed-out tomb (John 20: 7). A large stone secured the entrance to the whole, which was found rolled away on the Resurrection morning.

This site of the Death and Resurrection of Jesus was obliterated in A.D. 135 by the Emperor Hadrian, after he had put down the last Jewish insurrection under Bar-Kochba. A Roman temple was erected over it. Hadrian wanted to root out every remembrance of the Jewish religion and also of Christ. But it was this very eagerness, resulting from hatred, which preserved the memory of the site, since it was specially marked out by the temple built over it. So in 326 the Emperor Constantine caused it to be brought to light again. His mother, Helena, herself supervised the work. The whole Christian population and the garrison, involving thousands of Roman soldiers, assisted eagerly. During the course of a few months Hadrian's marble buildings were demolished and with great joy the rock of the Crucifixion and the unbroken Tomb were rediscovered, according to the Gospel reports. The other rock-tombs were also laid bare. This labour of love has preserved for us Golgotha and the Tomb on a site which has never been in question, even after 200 years of being covered over.

Constantine erected an immense basilica over this Holy Place. Part of this was circular, with the tomb-chamber in the centre. The rocks surrounding it were removed, so that it had the appearance of a stone hut, and a magnificent baldachino on pillars was erected over it.

The actual basilica, with its five naves, called the Martyrion (Witness) was joined to the circular building, the Anastasis (Resurrection), by a pillared courtyard, in which the rock of Golgotha, a square sculptured block 15 feet in height, rose up, crowned by a platform on which the Cross had stood. This building was finished in 336, but was destroyed by the Persians in 614. It was re-built, but finally destroyed in 1009 by Sultan Hakim. Only the crypt of Helena beneath the central nave and the adjoining cave in which the True Cross was said to have been found were spared. The Tomb itself was several times exposed to these various destructions.

Re-building was begun in 1048. The Tomb was re-built on the rocky foundations, and also the round church above it. A chapel was built to cover Calvary, and further chapels were added. The Crusaders took charge of this territory and enclosed it in a huge building with a large dome over the Tomb, and a smaller dome which to-day covers the so-called Choir of the Greeks. This building was completed in 1149.

After the final defeat of the Crusaders in 1187 the Saracen ruler allowed the Christians to continue using the church on condition that the entrance was guarded by Moslems. This office became hereditary in the same family who still retain possession of the key to this day. The Franciscans acquired the right of looking after the church from the Sultan in 1342. They have suffered many persecutions through the centuries. The Moslem rulers divided the rights to the church of the Holy Sepulchre, so that gradually the Roman Catholics, the Greek Orthodox, the Armenians, Copts, Syrians, and Abyssinians all established themselves, though the Abyssinians were not able to retain their share. The Crusaders' church was frequently damaged and restored again, but it retained its essential shape. But in 1808 the Round Church over the Tomb was destroyed by fire; it was re-built by the Greeks. Fifty years later the dome had to be renewed. After the earthquakes of 1927 and 1937 it was threatened with collapse. But the various churches could not come to agreement about restoration, and in 1938 the British Mandate was obliged to shore up the building within and without by steel scaffolding.

This cluttered-up appearance of the church still persists even though in 1962 the work of restoration has been started at long last. It is not enhanced by the hideous buildings dating from recent centuries which surround it nor by the bricked-up doorways and windows and the erection of party-walls. To-day it should really be called 'the most wretched church in the world,' 'without form or comeliness': a shattering illustration of the present sufferings of Him who here wrought His work of redemption for us.

All these changes have had their effect on Calvary and the Tomb. The rock of Golgotha, the historic site of the Crucifixion, is unrecognizable at first glance. And the Tomb only retains fragments of the original rock. But the foundations have remained, and the measurements are still the same as those found by Constantine. The stone which was rolled in front of the entrance, and which pilgrim-reports attest right up to the seventh century, was probably broken up during the Persian destruction. A portion of it is supposed to be built into the chapel of the Angels and is pointed out as such. The exterior shape of the tomb-chamber has changed many times through the centuries: sometimes it was in the shape of a pyramid, sometimes it boasted a tower. The Greeks gave it its present shape during the re-building of 1810.

In spite of all these transformations we can be thankful that the authenticity of the site of Calvary and the Holy Sepulchre is better attested than almost any other. The different churches are united in proclaiming that these sites did indeed witness the events of Good Friday and the joy of Easter Day.

The church is open from 4 a.m. till 7 p.m. (though not regularly).

From the Holy Bible

Then they led Jesus away to a place called Golgotha (which means 'Place of a skull'). They crucified him there, and the criminals with him, one on his right and the other on his left. Jesus said, 'Father, forgive them; they do not know what they are doing.' One of the criminals who hung there with him taunted him, 'Are not you the Messiah? Save yourself, and us.' But the other answered sharply, 'Have you no fear of God? You are under the same sentence as he. For us it is plain justice; we are paying the price for our misdeeds; but this man has done nothing wrong.' And he said, 'Jesus, remember me when you come to your throne.' Jesus answered, 'I tell you this: to-day you shall be with me in Paradise.' Near the cross where Jesus hung stood his mother, with her sister, Mary, wife of Clopas, and Mary of Magdala. Jesus saw his mother, with the disciple whom he loved standing beside her. He said to her, 'Woman, there is your son'; and to the disciple, 'There is your mother.'

Then there came a darkness over the whole land; the sun was in eclipse.

Then Jesus gave a loud cry and said, 'My God, my God, why hast thou forsaken me?'

After that, Jesus, aware that all had now come to its appointed end, said in fulfilment of Scripture, 'I thirst.' Having received the wine, he said, 'It is accomplished! Father, into thy hands I commend my spirit'; and with these words he bowed his head and gave up his spirit.

There was an earthquake, the rocks split and the curtain of the temple was torn in two from the top to the bottom.

The centurion saw it all, and gave praise to God. 'Beyond all doubt,' he said, 'this man was innocent.' And the crowd went home beating their breasts.

From Matt. 27; Luke 23 and John 19.

✝

Abyss of Mercy divine,
What deepest grief God bears
For us and for our sins.
We kneel before the Cross
And we adore the Lamb
In sorrow for our sin.

Calvary—A Call to Us

Calvary—close to the City of God, the City of the Great King, and yet 'without the gate,' and thus a place of shame, to which Jesus was led like a malefactor to suffer the cruel death of crucifixion. A place of pain as none other on earth, telling of indescribable suffering. Here the Son of God, Who had come down to earth as the Saviour and Redeemer of His people, was assigned the place considered suitable to Him, the place of a criminal. The earth had no other place for Him than 'the place of a skull.'

What has Calvary beheld? A wooden Cross laid upon the

ground as often before, waiting for a guilty criminal to be laid upon it. But once it was the Lamb of God, pure and holy, Who had chosen for Himself this ghastly death-bed. Jesus voluntarily gave Himself up to have His hands and feet pierced by nails, driven in with rough hammer-blows by His children. These hammer-blows resounded through the heavens, and angels bowed their heads and wept that their Lord, the Son of the Living God, had to bear such terrible pain for the sins of mankind. Then the Cross was lifted up and rammed into the ground trembling with its weight—a burden heavier than the whole world, for it was the Creator Himself, Who had taken upon Himself the sins of men. The Cross rose towards Heaven, as if it would thrust open the doors of Heaven, because here upon the accursed wood sin was being taken away and Paradise thrown open. And the wood reached deep into the earth, as if it would penetrate the depths of Hell and open up the realm of death, for it bore Him Who would lead forth, out of the shadow of death, all those who had waited so long for deliverance. And the arms of the Cross reached out on either side to encircle the world with the arms of love to call the world back to the bosom of the Father.

Truly, here on Calvary, on the Cross, hung Love everlasting, which, though dying, called mankind and all creation home with the words, 'I thirst!' Love called men home with words of forgiveness for His tormentors, 'Father, forgive them, for they know not what they do!' It was poured forth in the words, 'Behold thy mother!' and gave the beloved though forsaken disciple a mother and a home, and gave the mother a new maternal care. Love, which in the hour of utmost pain gave thought to the sufferings of others. The cry, 'My God, my God, why hast thou forsaken me?' revealed how Jesus bore the whole dereliction and rejection of mankind within His soul. Yet He said, 'My God!' and surrounded God in love with this word, 'My.' The cry, 'Father, into thy hands I commend my spirit,' showed how true His love was, which trusted His Father even in the darkest hour: and finally Jesus utters the mightiest word of love, 'It is finished!' —the hard way of Redemption for all the sons of men was followed through to the end, the work of love was finished. Love has conquered indeed; she has allowed herself to be not provoked, but has borne all, has not avoided agony, but has loved as no other has loved and is for the enemy's sake departed into a martyr's grave.

The depths of Jesus' pain correspond to these depths of love —a fullness of pain such as no other can bear because no other love is so great. The Son of God as Man suffered the greatest pain, in body, soul, and spirit, without any relief, yet He suffered in double measure, feeling Himself forsaken of God. Only the Son of God could suffer thus. Rejected as man, and experiencing as God the apparent failure of His work. The sum of His spiritual sufferings can never be told, for none can know the depths of such Love despised and rejected. As to His bodily suffering, there is hardly a more terrible death than that of crucifixion, which so dragged asunder every limb that many suffering it went mad. Cramp wracked the pierced and straining nerves. And finally suffocation overwhelmed the victim, who could never lose consciousness.

Thus on Calvary died Jesus, Son of God. And Calvary tells of the power of Jesus' love, as deep as the sea and as wide as the world. It tells out the tale that this love is unending, embracing foes and tormentors, stronger than the pains of death. It tells that the heart of Jesus was broken in love, bearing the most cruel death for love of us. Calvary cries, 'Ye sons of men are loved "to the end," each creature of God is loved, even thou art loved!'

Golgotha speaks of the Triumph of Love, of how Love is greater than all things, and has overcome both death and hell, since Love, when it goes into sorrow bears redeeming power. This accursed tree thus becomes a Sign of Redemption since He Who has died on it is Eternal Love.

Calvary proclaims a redemption embracing all creation, the whole world, till all shall be included in these words of Jesus, 'See, I make all things new!'

We can but fall down in adoration, praising such a redemption wrought for sinners. We can only give thanks for such redemption by choosing the way of His love, which shrinks not from suffering, which accepts every sacrifice, and prays for its enemies. Jesus waits for the fruits of our sacrifice, He waits for us, the members of His Body, to be filled with His Spirit, that we in sacrificial love may help to save sinners, that His Kingdom of Love may soon come.

Prayer in the Calvary Chapel

Dear Lord Jesus,
in this holy spot where Thou didst for us sinners surrender Thy life unto death, I adore in deepest humility Thine incomprehensible love for us. I adore Thee, O spotless Lamb of God, slain for us upon the Cross. It was we who by our sins brought Thee to such hideous pains of death. But Thy love gave to us, through Thine unspeakable sufferings, the forgiveness of all our sins. How may I comprehend that all for us Thou borest such pains upon the Cross and hast forgiven us. A thousandfold I thank Thee, dearest Lord, for all that was done.

I would praise Thee here before Heaven and earth for all that Thou hast done. I give praise too that Thy Love reaches to the deepest places and embraces all, suffering though it was.

I praise Thee for Thy blood shed for me, making me clean from all sin, making me a new creature, a child of God. Again I praise Thee, here on Calvary, that Thou hast redeemed me from Hell.

My only prayer then is : Help me, so that my whole life may truly witness to Thy Redemption of Thy children. AMEN.

THE TOMB OF JESUS

From the Holy Bible

Now at the place where he had been crucified there was a garden, and in the garden a new tomb, not yet used for burial. There, because the tomb was near at hand and it was the eve of the Jewish Sabbath, they laid Jesus. John 19: 41–2.

The Sabbath had passed, and it was about daybreak on Sunday when Mary of Magdala and the other Mary came to look at the grave. Suddenly there was a violent earthquake; an angel of the Lord descended from heaven; he came to the stone and rolled it away, and sat himself down on it. His face shone like lightning; his garments were white as snow. At the sight of him the guards shook with fear and lay like the dead.

The angel then addressed the women, 'You,' he said, 'have nothing to fear. I know you are looking for Jesus who was crucified. He is not here; he has been raised again, as he said he would be. Come and see the place where he was laid.'

Matt. 28: 1–6.

The Tomb of Jesus—A Call to Us

The Tomb of Jesus and the place of His crucifixion, both under one roof? Would we not expect Calvary to be far from the place of Resurrection because Calvary is the place of sharpest pain and of defeat, the place where Jesus' path seems to end in an abyss of pointlessness and His work to be in vain?

Calvary, where Jesus was mocked, apparently confounded, done to death as if He could never live again. Calvary, whose name fills the whole world with horror—and close beside it the Tomb, speaking of victory and joy. How can they be so close together? Only in the wisdom of God, so that their proximity in space may lead us to see their spiritual proximity. The Tomb beside Calvary proclaims: There is no defeat which, in self-surrender and faith, does not bear the seeds of victory. Here Jesus, slain upon the Cross, rose again, and put all enemies under His feet.

The watchmen, who were to ensure that He remained powerless in the Tomb, became as dead men when He rose again. He Whose heart had ceased to beat, Whose limbs had been powerless in death, lived and moved, and moved the stone. Neither the rock of the tomb nor the powers of death could hold Him fast. The gravestone is thus a sign that Jesus, though previously powerless and unable to do anything against His enemy, was now risen in the almighty power and glory of God. For now He has overcome the mightiest enemy of all mankind, yea, even of God Himself, the enemy—Death.

The tomb beside the Cross of Calvary proclaims to us: there is no eclipse of work that is done for God, without a Resurrection to follow. There can be no cross upon which our life or our work is broken, which cannot bring forth new life. There is no pain, however grievous, no darkness, borne in union with Jesus, but will end in the sunlight of Easter, in glory and joy, beginning here below and fulfilled hereafter 'when there shall be no more weeping, neither shall there be any more pain' (Rev. 21: 4).

To all who come to the empty Tomb now, that Tomb proclaims, 'Jesus lives, Christ triumphs! To Him is given all power on earth and in Heaven. Jesus is the conqueror of every power of death. Jesus has trodden sin beneath His feet, for, lo, He is risen! The sins of the whole world, which He took with Him to the Cross, could not hold Him. He conquered them, for He lives!' The empty Tomb shouts to us, 'Jesus has bruised the head of the serpent which bruised His heel. Jesus has broken the power of Satan. None can now be held in Satan's bonds who calls upon the Risen One, for Christ is the stronger.'

The empty Tomb waits for Resurrection songs of praise. It calls us in our struggle with Sin and against all powers which may afflict us, not to despair but to believe in the Stronger One Who will burst all fetters, so that all may lie beneath His feet—the feet of Jesus Christ, the Prince of Victory.

Can the victory of Jesus over death in this site of His Resurrection ever be sung and spoken of enough? So Jesus awaits, here where 'He rose for us,' those who will pray, rejoicing in Him and believing in His victory for their life.

Prayer at the Tomb of Jesus

Lord Jesus,
we rejoice that Thy grave could not hold Thee, the Lamb of God, Who paid the price of our redemption. Thou hast conquered death and hell, and hast opened the prison-doors of our Sin. I praise Thy victory, Thou Conqueror Who wilt make us triumphant over our sins. Praise and adoration be to Thee, our Lord, who didst undergo death for us and so gloriously rose again, giving us the blessed hope that, as members of Thy Body, we shall rise again in glory to live for ever in Thy Kingdom. Hallelujah! AMEN.

†

From the night of deepest sorrow
Joys of God spring into light.
Jesus, Victor, bursts His Tomb.
Praise the Lamb Who thus hath triumphed,
Who in Death hath slain His foe
And by Love hath dispersed gloom.

Litany of Victory

Jesus, Thou .hast broken Satan's power, for Thou art risen. Alleluja!
Jesus, Thou hast conquered as the Lion of Juda, for Thou art risen. Alleluja!
Jesus, Thou art the Conqueror, under Whose feet all enemies must be set, for Thou art risen. Alleluja!
Jesus, Thou hast overcome death, that we too may rise in glory, for Thou art risen. Alleluja!
Jesus, Thou hast conquered all the powers of hell and of sin, even in my life, for Thou art risen. Alleluja!

Jesus, Thou canst break the fetters that bind all men, and Thou hast broken my own sinful bonds, for Thou art risen. Alleluja!

Jesus, Thou art the strong Redeemer, Whose Redemption is for me, for Thou art risen. Alleluja!

Jesus, Whom the grave could not hold, grant that as a member of Thy Body the grave of sin may not hold me either, for Thou art risen. Alleluja!

Jesus, Thou art the triumphant Lamb who hast taken away the sins of the world, for Thou art risen. Alleluja!

Jesus, Thou hast the keys of hell and of death and art alive for evermore, for Thou art risen. Alleluja!

Jesus, Thou art the Lord to Whom is given all power in Heaven and on earth, for Thou art risen. Alleluja!

Jesus, Thou sittest at the Right Hand of God and settest Thy kingdom over all the kingdoms of the world, for Thou art risen. Alleluja!

Hymn

He cometh forth from death's dark night,
The Easter sun rejoiceth
Because of Judah's Lion.
The watchers are as men long dead,
The cross's doom is over now
For Christ our Lord is risen! (repeat)

The heavenly host sings victory,
Proclaims the foe is trodden down
That brought Him to the Cross.
The evil power is broken down,
For Jesus hath the victory won,
The Easter sun rejoiceth.
For Christ our Lord is risen!

The Lion of Judah's Tree, with power,
Hath bought for us the life divine,
Hath death's great might dispersèd.
Hearts that were dead have waked again
Because the Easter triumph sounds,
They love, rejoice, and pray.
For Christ our Lord is risen!

And He Whom Easter's victory thrills
Pours forth His heart and conquering sings
As if all Hell were ousted.
My heart rejoicing knows the Lord
And calls Him Victor, Jesus blessed,
For He is truly Conqueror!
And Christ our Lord is risen!

CHAPTER XI

BETHPHAGE

OFTEN have we heard the Gospel story of the entry of Jesus into Jerusalem, with its mention of the place where the ass was in readiness for Him. To-day we will go to Bethphage, which is now a Franciscan convent and church, lying in a hollow by the eastern slope of the Mount of Olives.

One way of reaching it is by the motor road from Jerusalem to Jericho, from half-way along which a road leads off leading to Bethphage and the Mount of Olives. But if we want to follow Jesus in spirit we will go on foot along the path He must have used so many times; this leads from the middle summit of the Mount of Olives, and will bring us to the church of Bethphage after about 15 minutes' walk. We go past the Carmelite convent and the church of the Paternoster, descending the narrow road eastwards. To the north lies the property of the Russian Orthodox monastery; eastwards we look over the tops of the Judæan hills to the mountains of Moab. Southwards lies the flattened summit of the Herodium. We can see the motor-road to Bethany and Jericho on the right, down in the valley, and the new road to Bethlehem passing the Mount of Evil Counsel.

A few houses of the village of Et-Tur are scattered on the slope. Soon we reach the extensive Franciscan property, surrounded by walls and cypress trees, and we enter the church, remembering the hour when Jesus started from here on the road to Calvary, entering Jerusalem uncrowned and misunderstood.

The church is open from morning until evening.

THE HISTORICAL ASPECT

Bethphage, whose name probably means 'House of Figs,' is described by the Gospels as lying on the eastern side of the Mount of Olives, in the neighbourhood of Bethany with which it is generally coupled. But the exact situation cannot now be determined. It is said to have lain 'over against' (Luke 19: 30), which probably means a little to the north of, the spot to which the disciples brought the ass and where Jesus mounted upon it. An ancient tradition connects the place now called Bethphage with Jesus' mounting on the ass. We can easily imagine the scene. The path coming up from Bethany was a bad one, hard for both a rider and his mount; but here, in the hollow of Bethphage, it became easier, so that the procession could best start from here.

There was a church here as far back as the fourth century. According to Etheria, it also commemorated the meeting of Jesus with Martha and Mary as they hastened to tell Him of Lazarus' death. This church, mentioned up to the seventh century, was probably destroyed later. But the memories of the place remained. The report of the Russian Abbot Daniel, at the beginning of the Crusades, about 1106, makes it clear that both events were commemorated on the same spot.

But the Crusaders lost the memory of the meeting with Martha and Mary, and their church commemorated only Palm Sunday. The German pilgrim, Theodoric, tells us in 1172 that the stone 'by which Jesus mounted upon the ass' was also pointed out. This mounting-block, with its frescoes and inscriptions, was found in 1877. In 1880 the Franciscans acquired the land and erected their church in 1883. During the building they discovered the remains of the medieval church. In 1950 they restored and completed the frescoes on the block: these depict the bringing of the ass, the entry into Jerusalem, and the raising of Lazarus.

FROM THE HOLY BIBLE

Rejoice greatly, O daughter of Zion; shout, O daughter of Jerusalem: behold, thy King cometh unto thee: he is just, and having salvation; lowly, and riding upon an ass, and upon a colt the foal of an ass. Zechariah 9: 9.

As Jesus approached Bethphage at the hill called Olivet, he sent two of the disciples with these instructions, 'Go to the village opposite; you will find tethered there a colt which no one has yet ridden. Untie it and bring it here. If any one asks why you are untying it, say, "Our Master needs it." ' This was in fulfilment of the prophecy.

The disciples went and did as Jesus had directed and brought the donkey and her foal; they laid their cloaks on them and Jesus mounted. Crowds of people carpeted the road with their cloaks, and some cut branches from the trees to spread in his path, then the crowd raised the shout, 'Hosanna to the Son of David! Blessings on him who comes as king in the name of the Lord!'

When Jesus came in sight of the city, he wept over it.

From Matt. 21 and Luke 19.

Then I saw heaven wide open, and there before me was a white horse; and its rider's name was Faithful and True, for he is just in judgement and just in war. And the armies of heaven followed him on white horses. Rev. 19: 11 and 14.

Bethphage—A Call to Us

Never can we forget Bethphage, for here Jesus showed Himself as King. From here He was to enter His royal city as the Son of David; but this entry ended in the crowning with thorns and the death on the Cross of Calvary.

Here once were tethered the ass and her foal needed, yea chosen, by their creator to serve Him for His royal entry. The ass was deemed worthy to bear this most precious load, such as had never before been borne: the Creator of the World, God Himself. By this act dumb creation was drawn into the service of God. Here Jesus, the servant of all, His power hidden, yet revealed Himself as Lord. For He said, 'And if any man say ought unto you, ye shall say, the Lord hath need of them; and straightway he will send them.'

Bethphage also speaks of Jesus' poverty, for He had to ask for the ass, possessing none Himself, though every other person in the Orient is the owner of an ass. He had to borrow the mount for His royal entry, He Who is the Lord and Creator of all things. And it speaks of His obedience. Why did He here mount the ass, when He well knew that His entry was in vain? He would never be acknowledged as king, but would end as a criminal on the Cross. But, obedient to the Word of God, 'that the Scripture might be fulfilled' Jesus mounted the ass in order to enter Jerusalem. So Bethphage proclaims that all prophecy and all the promises of God are 'Yea' and 'Amen.' Here was fulfilled the word, 'Tell ye the daughter of Sion, behold, thy king cometh unto thee, meek and sitting upon an ass, and upon a colt, the foal of an ass.' And here was revealed in what a literal and actual way, and not simply a figurative sense, God brings to pass His promises once uttered.

God is the Lord, and He bringeth His counsel to pass, by fulfilling it Himself. He, the Son of God, who is to be received as a King, entered His City, meek and lowly, sitting upon an ass, that He might make of Himself an Offering and be killed as the Lamb of God.

As He mounted the ass, hearing the joyous cries of His disciples and of the multitude, His heart must have been heavy. For He knew that even His disciples were not loyal subjects and that their rejoicing was in vain. They did not want to serve a lowly king but an earthly monarch. They wanted to secure power and earthly honour and were not prepared to allow Jesus to tell them what He, as their Lord, wanted.

They disputed amongst themselves. Jesus alone was meek. A wide gulf yawned between that which filled the heart of Jesus and their hearts: He was mourning, whilst they rejoiced. The heart of Jesus must have been filled with grief, for there is nothing so grievous as sham affection or hypocritical respect, rendered by one who is not ready to give this love with utter devotion or this respect with obedience.

And so, a little later, He wept over the city, where even worse was awaiting Him.

Once Bethphage was the starting point of the Palm Sunday procession. To-day it awaits another entry, when He will come as King of kings. According to the signs of the times, of which Jesus spoke, that entry may be near. So Jesus calls to us, 'Prepare ye the way.' When He comes again He will be surrounded by a multitude of those who have learnt to accept Him wholly as their Master, to accept His will and His leading. They will be like unto Him, meek and lowly and obedient. For these He waits to-day, the Captain of our salvation.

Prayer at Bethphage

Dear Lord Jesus,
we bow before Thee, Thou only most high, who didst begin Thy reign, upon a borrowed ass, in meek obedience. Thou didst desire to overcome us by Thy humble love, that we might willingly accept Thy rule. But tears and sorrow were Thine, because we are haughty and rebellious in heart and will not have Thee to rule over us.

Let Thy tears bring me to repentance, that I may in true lowliness bow before Thy feet. I would give Thee the rule over all my life, saying, Do with me as Thou wilt, lead me, send me, wherever Thou wilt—I would do according to Thy word. Help me to live in expectation of Thy return, to prepare for that day, that I may truly receive Thee as King. Rouse all Thy people to such preparation that Thy sorrow may be turned into joy and that we may truly cry, 'Hosannah.' AMEN.

Hymn

He rode upon the gentle ass,
The Father's Son come from above:
But none doth honour Him enough,
For none have humblest love.

He came, obedient as a slave,
To see that God's word comes to pass.
He enters in His city now
Though there they make for Him a Cross.

He came, disguised in lowliness,
A king in pain and shame.
But soon He will in glory come
His Kingdom thus once more to claim.

Then shall we all rejoice with Him
At this His marriage-feast,
Who, lowly once, is now most High
Yet welcomes all from great to least.

BETHPHAGE

✝

The blind obedience of Jesus to His Father's will led Him to enter Jerusalem humbly, sitting upon an ass, knowing that His Royal Entry would lead to His crucifixion. His blind obedience wrought redemption on Golgotha. Such obedience will bear much fruit to-day.

CHAPTER XII

BETHANY

THIS place that so much attracted Jesus, and which He visited so often, calls out to us to recall His words and deeds there. We must visit the tomb of Lazarus and the church of the Franciscans. To-day Bethany is a wholly Moslem village, known as El-Azariyeh (Lazarium), lying about 2 miles from Jerusalem, on the motor-road to Jericho. But we will go on foot from Bethphage, by a rough and stony path leading from the Franciscan property down to the valley, in a south-easterly direction; this path is most probably the one that connected the Mount of Olives with Bethany of old. Surrounded by the hills of the near-by Judæan desert, we see Bethany on the slope before us: a place of such poverty-stricken cottages that they look like ruins amidst the numerous trees. We can see the site of Lazarus' tomb from afar, because of the minaret beside it, and the dome and tower of the Franciscan church.

The path leads straight to the entrance of the tomb and, about 18 yards farther down, to the church. If we come by the road we reach the church first, by taking a left-hand turn where the road curves sharply within the village. We must descend some steep steps to reach the tomb, for it is no longer at ground-level in the garden, as it was in Jesus' day. To begin with, we enter the outer chamber, where Jesus' weeping is commemorated. A few steps lower down is the actual tomb, very like that of Jesus Himself. There are three shelves in the rock-walls, showing that the tomb had been intended for three dead. But there is nothing to commemorate the mighty victory over death won by Jesus in this place. We must seek out the church in order to meditate quietly on the meaning of Bethany.

The church is open all day, as is also the tomb.

BETHANY

The Historical Aspect

According to John 11: 18, Bethany, in Jesus' day, lay 'about 15 furlongs,' i.e. less than 2 miles, from Jerusalem. Lying half-way up the south-eastern slope of the Mount of Olives, it was a spot even lovelier than it is now, a last green idyll before reaching the bare hills of the Judæan desert. Excavations between 1951 and 1953 revealed that it was situated somewhat to the north-west of the present El-Azariyeh, towards Bethphage. This verifies the genuineness of the tomb now shown as that of Lazarus, for Jewish custom demanded that tombs should be well away from habitations.

The first Christians must have been well aware of its significance for the raising of Lazarus excited not only the village but also the chief priests (John 11: 46ff.). The tradition is of very early date. In the fourth century a three-aisled church, even orientated, was built over the tomb, but this was destroyed by an earthquake. The church was built up again in the fifth century. After being several times damaged and altered it was joined up, in the twelfth century, with the church that was built beside it for a convent of Benedictine nuns; the tomb was approached from the crypt of this second church. After it had been turned into a mosque, in the sixteenth century, when the Muslims bricked up the original entrance to the tomb, the Franciscans obtained permission to make a new entrance from the road. In the sixteenth, or, according to other reports, in the seventeenth century, they constructed the steep staircase which still leads down into the tomb.

The tomb of Lazarus is still in Muslim hands, and the minaret of the mosque rises behind it, in place of the former Christian church. But at the end of the nineteenth century the Franciscans were able to acquire some houses lying to the east of the tomb. They started excavating in 1949 and laid bare the remaining walls of the different periods of the Lazarus church. In 1952–4 a new round church, with three altars, was erected over the eastern half of the twelfth century church. It is dedicated to the raising of Lazarus and also to the anointing of Jesus by Mary.

From early days tradition sought to identify the house of Martha and Mary as beside the place commemorating the raising of Lazarus, and several spots were regarded as the house of Simon the leper, in which the anointing took place. But there was no clear and authenticated tradition concerning these houses. In the times of the Crusades it was assumed that the house of Simon had stood on the foundations of the Lazarus church and the house of Martha and Mary on those of the neighbouring convent church. But it is unlikely that either house stood so near to the tomb, considering that tombs had to be situated well away from dwellings.

According to the Franciscan Odoric, in 1320, 'the house of Martha lay a double stone's-throw outside Bethany.' This may refer to the so-called 'Houses of Mary and Martha,' which lie about 600 yards away from the tomb, eastwards of Bethany, to left and right of the road to Jericho. To-day there is here a Russian and a Greek property, the latter having a church, both connected with the names of Mary and Martha. Ancient pilgrim narratives speak of two separate houses belonging to the sisters, and possibly also their tombs, over which churches and convents were later erected. Excavations have shown that the oldest church dates back to Byzantine times. To-day both the Russian Sisters and the Greek church each show a stone on which Jesus is supposed to have been sitting during the conversation with Martha when she hastened to meet Him. There is also a third stone with the same commemoration in the neighbourhood in the middle of a field.

From the Holy Bible

While they were on their way Jesus came to a village where a woman named Martha made him welcome in her home. She had a sister, Mary, who seated herself at the Lord's feet and stayed there listening to his words. Now Martha was distracted by her many tasks. The Lord said to her, 'Martha, Martha, you are fretting and fussing about so many things; but one thing is necessary. The part that Mary has chosen is best; and it shall not be taken away from her!' From Luke 10.

Six days before the Passover festival Jesus came to Bethany, where Lazarus lived whom he had raised from the dead. There a supper was given in his honour, at which Martha served. Then Mary brought a pound of very costly perfume, oil of pure spikenard, and anointed the feet of Jesus and wiped them with her hair, till the house was filled with the fragrance.

Some of those present said to one another angrily, 'Why this waste?' But Jesus said, 'You have the poor among you always, and you can help them whenever you like; but you will not always have me. She has done what lay in her power; she is beforehand with anointing my body for burial. I tell you this: wherever in all the world the Gospel is proclaimed, what she has done will be told as her memorial.' From John 12 and Mark 14.

MOUNT TABOR

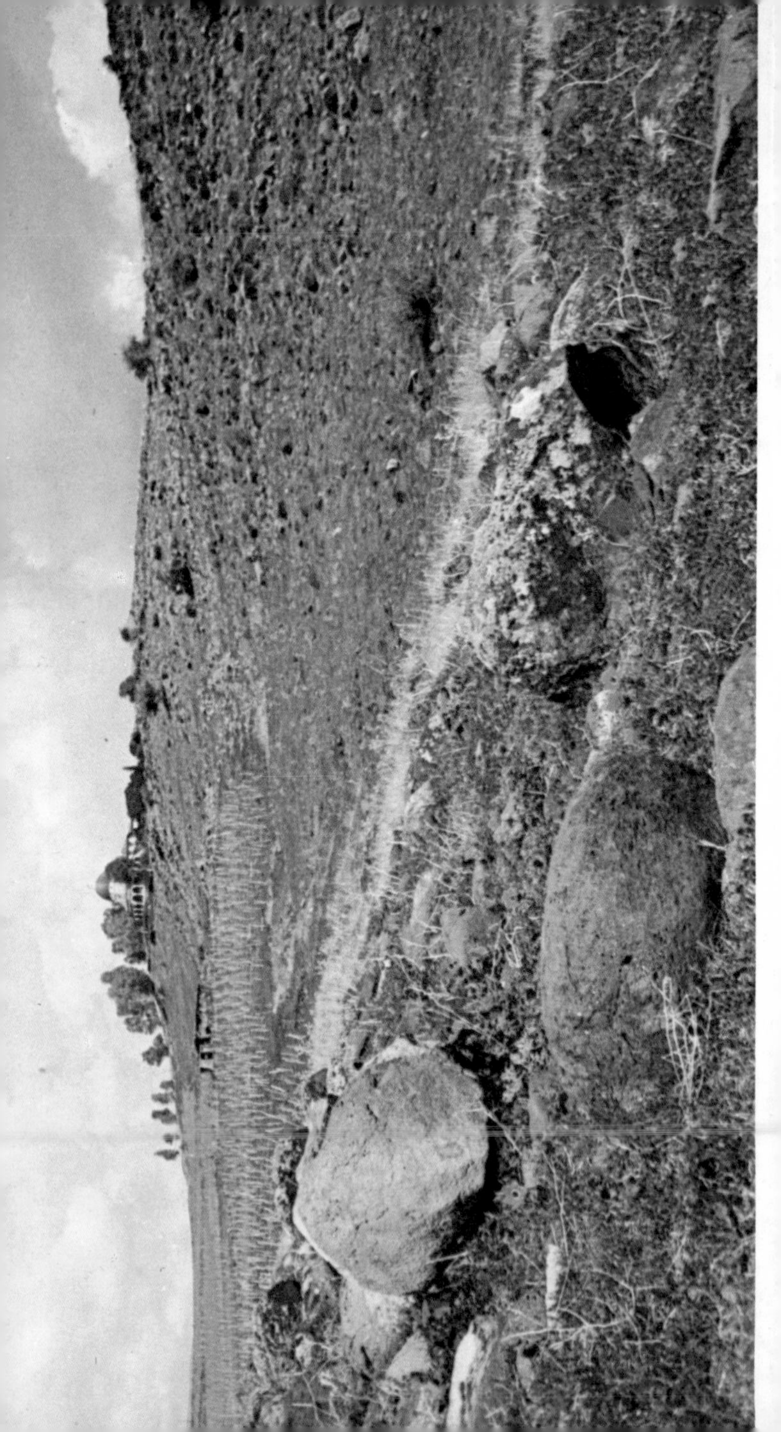

LAKE OF GALILEE

Bethany—A Call to Us

Jerusalem, the city of God, in which God, and hence also His Son, would look to expect joy and delight, had become for Jesus the city of suffering. The Temple of which Jesus had said, 'I must be about my Father's business,' had become to His grief a den of thieves. And though He felt compelled to proclaim His message in Jerusalem, under the mocking eyes of the persecuting Pharisees, yet He felt equally compelled to seek out some other place in the evenings, when His day's work had been accomplished, where He could be with those who accepted His message. This place was Bethany.

As Jesus could no longer venture spending the night in Jerusalem on account of the persecution of His enemies, even after the first year of His public activity, He probably chose Bethany as His residence when He came to Jerusalem. Here was a house in which He was made welcome. Often He was, as He said, obliged to seek like a beggar for somewhere to lay His head. In Bethany there was a house where He was received with loving words, in contrast to the angry disputes of the Pharisees in Jerusalem.

Bethany must have been the place for which Jesus had a special affection. Still to-day the name conveys to us the impression of peace and love. In Jerusalem the Pharisees wished Him elsewhere; in Bethany, Mary and Martha and Lazarus received Him with joy. And here His bodily needs were cared for; Martha saw to it that He was fed and rested. And His affairs and His griefs were sympathized with. His words were to Mary more precious than fine gold, to which she hearkened, forgetful of all else. She hearkened to His heart's desires for His people, for His disciples, for the world. Yes, she gave heed to all that caused Him delight and pain. And she realized when the hour of His great depression had come, and she tried to comfort Him by anointing Him with precious spikenard for His burial. Thus she showed her love to Jesus, whilst His disciples did nothing but criticize Him, like Judas.

Oh! How very precious for Jesus must have been the love and care which He experienced in this house at Bethany.

Of all the crowds who followed Him only a few sought Him for Himself; most followed because, as He said sorrowfully, 'they did eat of the loaves and were filled' (John 6: 26), or because they had been healed. But Jesus seeks a love which desires not His gifts but Himself. Whoever loves Jesus thus will be loved by Him in return and Jesus will reveal Himself. This becomes manifest in Bethany. Mary, Martha, and Lazarus loved Him with a pure love, so He was able to show them His heart. He loved them as His best friends. So Bethany speaks to us of the most intimate and precious things concerning Christ; of the love of Jesus to those whose hearts and homes are open to Him.

Jesus seeks a Bethany to-day amongst us, where He can enter at any time, knowing He is desired; where the dwellers are not possessed by their work and their possessions, but are ever ready for Him. A Bethany, where the inmost chamber of the heart is His, where He can dwell in the midst of work and business, where He can speak to those who ask nothing better than to listen.

And Jesus still looks for those who will be His friends as were these folk in Bethany—those who regard nothing as more important than Jesus and His company. He seeks such as desire only to love Him more and more and give Him first claim on all their time.

Jesus seeks hearts that shall be devoted to Him as were those at Bethany. He seeks the 'quiet in the land,' the Mary-like souls, those willing to be taken aside from the multitude. Bethany has become part of history because there dwelt those who truly loved Him and were at all times ready for Him. Shall we not strive to make our homes, our rooms in which we pray much, like Bethany, where He can often come to be loved and to love in return, as He did Mary, Martha and Lazarus?

Prayer in the Church of Bethany

Dearest Lord Jesus,
Thou art seeking for friends like Lazarus and Mary and Martha. Grant me that great grace that Thou shouldst be able to call me

Thy friend, sinful as I am, because I love Thee with my whole heart and keep Thy words. Let me so learn to love Thee that my heart may become Thy dwelling-place and that Thy promise may be fulfilled, that Thou wilt dwell with those that love Thee and keep Thy commandments. Cleanse Thou the house of my heart from all thoughts and feelings that would bar the entrance to Thee, from all concerns and possessions which would leave no room for Thee. Thou shalt be my first love, to whose words I will ever hearken.

I give myself wholly to Thee: the earliest and best time of the day, the week, the year shall be Thine. I will seek silence and solitude, that I may come into Thine heart and may hearken unto Thee as Mary did. May my life be lived for Thee, Lord Jesus, and not for earthly and perishing things. Grant me this grace, by Thy precious blood. AMEN.

Talk with Jesus in Bethany

'Give Me more time, more room in thy life, and I will give thee My love, in which are hidden all the treasures of wisdom and knowledge.'

I desire Thee, Jesus, only Thee; to Whom else should I go.

'Be prepared at any time to receive Me, in loving quiet.'

Thou alone givest blessing, and my heart is restless till it rests in Thee.

✝

Naught I could wish for on this earth would be lovelier than Thy coming to my heart, Lord Christ. So let me silent be, That Thou mayest come and take for Thine own my soul and all of me.

✝

To-day as in the past, the Love of Jesus seeks a refuge, where He is lovingly expected and where He can rest. He finds our hearts filled with distractions—people, work, our own interests—He longs for us to empty our hearts and lovingly to receive Him.

Hymn

Hallowed Bethany, where love comes to flower.
Hallowed Bethany, where He for an hour
Can find peace and quiet to renew His power.

Hallowed Bethany, where Christ refuge finds,
Where He can hide Himself from evil minds,
Where amongst friends He love's welcome finds.

Hallowed Bethany, thy praises we'll sound,
For thou art the spot where, though evil abound,
Before His dread Passion He there comfort found.

Hallowed Bethany, again He awaits
Until by God's Spirit He enters thy gates
And is greeted by Mary whose love ne'er abates.

THE TOMB OF LAZARUS

From the Holy Bible

There was a man named Lazarus who had fallen ill. His home was at Bethany, the village of Mary and her sister Martha.

The sisters sent a message to Jesus, 'Sir, you should know that your friend lies ill.'

When Jesus heard of his illness he waited for two days in the place where he was.

After this Jesus said to his disciples, 'Our friend Lazarus has fallen asleep, but I shall go and wake him.'

On his arrival Jesus found that Lazarus had already been four days in the tomb. Bethany was just under two miles from Jerusalem.

As soon as Martha heard that Jesus was on his way, she went to meet him, while Mary stayed at home. Martha said to Jesus, 'If you had been here, sir, my brother would not have died. Even now I know that whatever you ask of God, God will grant you.'

As soon as Mary caught sigh of Jesus she fell at his feet and said, 'Sir, if you had only been here my brother would not have died.'

When Jesus saw her weeping and the Jews, her companions, weeping, he sighed heavily and was deeply moved. Then he went over to the tomb. It was a cave, with a stone placed against it. Jesus said, 'Take away the stone.' Martha, the dead man's sister, said to him, 'Sir, by now there will be a stench; he has been there four days.' Jesus said, 'Did I not tell you that if you have faith you will see the glory of God?' So they removed the stone.

Then Jesus looked upwards and said, 'Father, I thank thee: thou hast heard me. I knew already that thou always hearest me, but I spoke for the sake of the people standing round, that they might believe that thou didst send me.'

Then he raised his voice in a great cry, 'Lazarus, come forth.' The dead man came out, his hands and feet swathed in linen bands, his face wrapped in a cloth. Jesus said, 'Loose him; let him go.' Now many of the Jews who had come to visit Mary and had seen what Jesus did, put their faith in him.

From John 11.

THE TOMB OF LAZARUS—A CALL TO US

Bethany speaks to us not only of the loving relationship between Jesus and the dwellers in the house of Lazarus. It also tells us that those whom Jesus loves must be chastened. It speaks of His leading through the dark paths of faith, trying souls like gold in the fire, that they may be able to face impossibilities, yea death itself, and come to know His glory by faith.

Jesus allowed Lazarus to die. He did not hasten to succour Mary and Martha in their sorrow. They had to endure through days of darkness, when Jesus seemed not to care, although they had begged for His aid. He lingered on the way, so that His glory and power might be more manifest. He let death intervene, so that He might show Himself to be 'the Resurrection and the Life.' In Bethany He bestowed that which His people had not known heretofore: Lazarus, whose body must have already decayed, was called out of the grave by the words of Jesus. The power of death was broken and Lazarus lived again.

So Bethany speaks to us not only through the memory of Mary and Martha and their love for Jesus, but reminds us that we must keep the flame of our love alight through the darkest hours, when He seems far from us, leaving our prayers unanswered. Bethany calls us to renew our faith in Jesus even in such hours of darkness that we may see the glory of God as He has promised.

HYMN

Thou hast the foe defeated, O dearest Lamb of God!
Thus will we ever praise Thee, O Victor thru' the Cross.
The enemy's dread power, before Thy face must flee
For Thou hast struck as lightning that has not missed the tree.

King of kings, we sing to Thee, and praise Thee as is meet,
Because Thou hast defeated the foe beneath Thy feet.
Who hath faith henceforth shall see His foes all beaten down,
For those who stand with Jesus will now receive His crown.

So from our hearts we thank Thee, O Christ, the Lamb of God,
Who bore for us such terrors upon that Cross of wood.
Yet now there is secured a victory for all;
A victory the praise of which must ring thru' Satan's Hall.

Of Jacob's tribe the hero, praise ever be to Thee.
May the whole world accept Thee its Lamb of God to be.
Around Thy throne for ever songs of joy we'll raise
For all sorrow, sighing, there shall end in praise.

Prayer at the Tomb of Lazarus

Lord Jesus,
I adore Thee in that Thou art Love and that Thou didst only lead Mary and Martha through darkness in order that Thy glory might shine out more fully.

I thank Thee that Thou dost lead me by dark paths, that I may be faithful unto death and at length be given the crown of life. Make me to understand that all faith will have its reward, if not in this life here, then above. Teach me to believe that sorrow is always turned into joy, because Thy ways are ever ways of love, whose end is not weeping but rejoicing evermore. Teach me such faith that in sure hope of Thy help and the revelation of Thy power I may persevere to the end. Jesus, I will pin my faith to Thy word, 'Be it unto thee according to thy faith,' and I will wait for the time when my faith shall end in sight. AMEN.

✝

The glory of God shall be seen by those who put their faith in Jesus in times of greatest distress and hopelessness since they are sure that He is greater than any distress. Jesus assures us that even to-day His power and might can succour our helplessness and powerlessness in the darkest hour of all.

CHAPTER XIII

THE MOUNT OF TEMPTATION
(JEBEL QARANTAL)

JERICHO and the Mount of Temptation lie about 23 miles from Jerusalem. The road goes through the Old City, over the Kidron valley bridge, past Gethsemane, and as far as Bethany, now El-Azariyeh. Then it proceeds in sharp curves through the Judæan wilderness down to the plain of Jordan. We descend nearly 3,000 feet, for the Jordan valley is the most low-lying in the whole world. After the so-called Well of the Apostles, a little way beyond Bethany, we come to a district of bare, rolling hills, mostly rock-strewn, but covered with green grass during a few weeks of spring. Flocks of sheep graze on the slopes, and Bedouin tents can be seen here and there, but there has never been a human settlement here. During the first few miles we still find pine-wood plantations but soon we come to the white sandhills and distinctly wilderness country.

In the distance the outlines of a building are seen. Half-way to Jericho we pass by the Khan el-Hathrur, the Inn of the Good Samaritan, to-day a police-post. In the ruins behind this we can still see the foundations of a former building which can be dated back to the time of Jesus. Jesus set His parable in this unwelcoming stretch of country, close to this inn. On a neighbouring hill are the remains of a Crusader's castle.

A few miles farther on, the old Roman road leaves the present asphalt one to lead along the length of the Wadi el-Qelt. Jesus must have walked on this Roman road whenever He went to Jericho; to-day it is mostly used only by the natives and their flocks. It goes in a westerly direction to Er-Riha, the modern Jericho; whilst the motor-road we are following curves away to the south-east and approaches the town from the south. Soon after the fork made by the Roman road a notice tells us that we have reached sea-level; in serpentine curves the road continues down into the valley till we come to the plain of Jordan. The descent from the hill-country to the plain is very sudden, and the flat, wilderness landscape seems devoid of all life. The last part of the road gives us a view of a neighbouring mountain-chain, from which the steep Jebel Qarantal, with its flattened summit, stands out

Before entering the city our road again joins the Roman road and the Wadi el-Qelt, which here ends in the plain. It is here, to the west of modern Jericho, that the Jericho of Jesus' day was situated. Er-Riha, the modern town, is a fruitful oasis. We are aware of this as we pass plantations of banana-palms, pomegranates, and orange-trees with their overpowering scent, interspersed with many-coloured shrubs and palm-trees. We leave Er-Riha in a north-westerly direction and head straight for the Mount of Temptation. Just before the road ends we see, 30 yards to the right, the Tell el-Sultan, with Elisha's spring at its base (2 Kings 2 : 19–22). Excavations on this hill are still in progress and are laying bare the layered ruins of Joshua's Jericho and the earlier cities still.

Now we are at the foot of the Mount of Temptation. It is still to-day a place of dreary defiles, in which a deathly silence reigns, and a loneliness such as we can imagine at the time of the Temptation in the wilderness. A stony path leads by easy curves to the top; overhanging rocks of bizarre shape alternate with stony slopes. Half-way up, about 25 minutes' walk, we come to a Greek Orthodox monastery clinging to the rock-side, and containing within its chapel the 'Cave of the Temptation.' By permission of the Greek-Orthodox Patriarch we can go through to the summit of the Mount. Reaching the platform, we find many round, flattened stones of light colour at our feet; these are just the shape of oriental bread-loaves. From the summit we can look far down the Jordan valley. We are surrounded by mountains, and on the western horizon is outlined the ridge of the Mount of Olives. To the east we see the mountains of Moab, beyond the Jordan, and Nebo. Immediately below us lies Jericho with its tropically luxuriant and many-coloured gardens. It is a view which must truly have shown to Jesus 'the kingdoms of the world, and the glory of them.' We can behold with our own eyes the settings of the different temptations with which the Tempter came to Jesus.

The Historical Aspect

Neither the Gospels nor any other sources will enable us to determine exactly the spot where Jesus underwent the Temptations: all we are told is that 'Jesus was led by the spirit into the wilderness' (Matt. 4: 1; Luke 4: 1) 'to be tempted of the devil.' It must have been a time of solitary wandering through deep river-courses, called Wadis, and over stony heights. Only later tradition gives further details, indicating Jebel Qarantal as the place where Jesus was tempted after forty days of fasting. The English pilgrim, Saewulf (1106), remarks that this tradition was vivid amongst all the Christian dwellers of the land.

The eastern side of Jebel Qarantal is honeycombed with between thirty and forty caves, some natural, some artificial, and these were lived in by hermits as far back as the fourth century. The southern side is also rich in caves. The cave that tradition designates as the shelter occupied by Jesus during the forty days was probably turned into a chapel in Byzantine times (sixth century). At the time of the Crusades, in the twelfth century, it belonged to the Canons of the Holy Sepulchre, who decorated the walls with frescoes depicting the temptations and which were still visible at the beginning of the twentieth century. The chapel was deserted from the thirteenth century onwards. Greek Orthodox monks took it over in 1874 when they established themselves here, and where their monastery is still extant.

Tradition situated the last temptation of Jesus upon the summit of the mountain, when Satan offered Him all the kingdoms of the world. A fortress of the Maccabees stood here about 130 B.C. In Christian times hermits dwelt here, and remains of a Byzantine chapel have been found. The Crusaders probably had a chapel here also. Orthodox monks began re-building it before the First World War, but it is still unfinished.

From the Holy Bible

Full of the Holy Spirit, Jesus returned from the Jordan, and for forty days was led by the Spirit up and down the wilderness and tempted by the devil.

All that time he had nothing to eat, and at the end of it he was famished. The devil said to him, 'If you are the Son of God, tell this stone to become bread.' Jesus answered, 'Scripture says, "Man cannot live by bread alone; he lives on every word that God utters." '

The devil then took him to the Holy City and set him on the parapet of the temple. 'If you are the Son of God,' he said, 'throw yourself down; for Scripture says, "He will put his angels in charge of you, and they will support you in their arms, for fear you should strike your foot against a stone." ' Jesus answered him, 'Scripture says again, "You are not to put the Lord your God to the test." '

Once again, the devil took him to a very high mountain, and showed him all the kingdoms of the world in their glory. 'All these,' he said, 'I will give you, if you will only fall down and do me homage.' But Jesus said, 'Be gone, Satan; Scripture says, "You shall do homage to the Lord your God and worship him alone." ' So, having come to the end of all his temptations, the devil departed, biding his time. And angels appeared and waited on Jesus. From Luke 4 and Matt. 4.

For since he himself has passed through the test of suffering, he is able to help those who are meeting their test now.

Heb. 2 : 18.

For ours is not a high priest unable to sympathize with our weaknesses, but one who, because of his likeness to us, has been tested every way, only without sin. Heb. 4 : 15.

✝

Jesus shows us the way, by which we can be victorious over temptation: it is always to choose that way, by which we lose our life in His.

The Mount of Temptation—A Call to Us

The tempter never finds a better field for his activities than when a soul is in trouble. Every human want, be it of body, soul, or spirit, is a point of attack by the enemy. And the wilderness, where every kind of want is felt, is a particularly favourable place of temptation. The wilderness is a place of bitterest poverty, and extreme loneliness, filled with threats and fears and wants. So when Jesus retired to the wilderness, traditionally that of Jebel Qarantal, for His 40-day fast, the tempter's hour had come. He made full use of it and staked everything on causing Jesus to fall. Care and want drive us to seize any hand that offers help. Satan knew that Jesus was 'a man like as we are,' and therefore 'in all points tempted like as we are.' So Jesus, too, must have felt the longing to escape from trouble. He was very hungry and hunger is painful; having a human body, how could He not long for food? Did He not need new strength for the work lying before Him? Surely the loaf-shaped stones at His feet could be used? Jesus, Son of the Living God, would surely have the power to turn them into bread. And His soul will repeatedly have uttered the anxious question, 'What proof is there that I am the Son of God? Am I not merely a man among men, the carpenter's son, one of many?' Now a hand is stretched out to help Jesus in His need. Satan suggests that He should cast Himself down from the pinnacle of the Temple—to which the tempter had led Him in spirit—so that He could prove Himself to be the Son of God to Whom all powers were subject. 'Thou shalt see that no harm will befall Thee; Thou wilt know Thyself to be the Son of God and wilt thus appear before men.' Thus Satan probably argued.

The purpose of Jesus' coming down to earth was to bring the Kingdom of God to men. Thirty years had already passed. He had done His work as a carpenter—but where was the kingdom? Satan had an answer for this too. The kingdoms of this world, so temptingly spread out at His feet, could in one moment of time come under His reign. The weary, painful time of waiting in vain for His purpose to be fulfilled would end in a flash. He would reign over all the world in His spirit and bring about the kingdom of peace and love.

But Jesus did not grasp the hand held out. He said, 'Yea' to the need in which He found Himself; He had the courage to remain in it, 'having done all, to stand.' He was content to wait, however long it might be, till God's hour had come. Jesus had confidence that this way of powerlessness, of humiliation, of hiddenness would bring in the kingdom of God. By such self-surrender He conquered temptation. Jesus calls to us in our times of temptation, 'Follow Me.' Do not grasp the hand of the tempter, however much ye may desire to escape from the needs of body, soul or spirit. Do not accept Satan's offer, however much he may promise to give you what you long for—money, possessions, privileges, rights, honour, friendship, by swift but doubtful ways. Be not deceived: it is Satan's hand which is stretched out to help more swiftly than God seems to do. Beware of Satan's hand, then, which seems so harmless and entices you to quick but dangerous rewards.

Give yourselves rather to God in firm faith, saying: God, the Father of His child, knows how to help and will do so when the hour has come; but He will only do so when He has tried us in the furnace, as gold is tried and so much fruit has been gained from the time of temptation.

So every temptation should be an occasion of placing ourselves in the Father's hands. Then the enemy will be powerless, and we shall come out of temptation as victors. Satan must flee and the angels of God will minister to us. God will help us in His own good time, for the Father rejoices to do good to His children.

Hymn

I would follow on Thy way, I would Thy sorrows share,
With faith to walk through darkest night.
My faith shall glorify, Thee God, for none can take away
My right to praise my Lord.

I will every pain endure, whate'er the foe may do
E'en though my heart he slay

I would Thy sorrows share, I would by faith endure
Though heart and mind dissuade me.

I would myself surrender that I might cling to Thee,
To follow through the night of faith
I here would stand beside Thee, at length Thy Face beholding
And tasting what I longed for here.

†

PRAYER ON THE MOUNT OF TEMPTATION

Lord Jesus,
I give Thee thanks that tempted in all points like as we are, yet without sin, Thou hast conquered our enemy. Teach me in the hour of temptation to oppose the tempter as Thou didst, so that I too may conquer. Give me strength to refuse Satan's help in getting my heart's desire, and to be willing to wait till Thou preparest a way out of my troubles. I will trust Thee, O my Father, for Thou knowest Thy child's needs. That shall be my answer to the Tempter, and Thou wilt cause him to depart from me. AMEN.

OUR ARMOUR IN THE FIGHT AGAINST TEMPTATIONS

Nothing is so helpful in refusing Satan's help in the hour of temptation as to hurl at the enemy that royal word: I am ready to suffer, by sorrow comes glory.

†

The tempter offers immediate assistance. You will overcome him by saying: I can await God's hour, for His help never comes too late.

†

When we are consumed by a longing, the enemy finds it easy

to entrap us. But he will flee if he sees that we are prepared to commit our ways unto God, knowing that He will bring it to pass at the right time. For He is our loving Father.

†

Temptations there must be. Without temptations there would be no crown of victory. So be prepared to fight, in spite of wounds and weeping. Only he who fights will overcome Satan by the power of Jesus.

CHAPTER XIV

THE PLACE OF BAPTISM BY JORDAN

Under the control of the Israeli Army.

WHEN we return from Jebel Qarantal we pass through the lively market-place of Er-Riha to the eastern border of the town. At a cross-roads, the old road to Amman goes off to the north-east, whilst the road going south-east leads to the Jordan. The edges of the town still have trees, but soon we again reach the flat, sandy wilderness, seldom broken by a spot of green. We can follow the course of the river in the distance by the dense vegetation of its banks.

The Jordan valley at Jericho is about 13 miles wide, and lies more than 400 yards below sea-level. It is a depression such as is hardly found elsewhere, resulting from volcanic eruption in earliest times. The sun is scorching, the hot air is entrapped, and even the wind is red-hot in this Jordan valley. The tropical heat means a sparse population, and as we follow the road to the river, under the scorching sun, we suddenly realize what is meant by that sentence in the life of Jesus, 'Then cometh he to Jordan' (Matt. 3 : 13): we recall all the bodily endurance involved, and yet unmentioned—except that Jesus went everywhere on foot.

About 5 miles from Er-Riha we come to a square, closed building of fortress-like character. It is the Greek Orthodox monastery of St. John (Deir Mar Hanna-Prodromos). There is then a short stretch of bone-dry rolling wilderness, leading to the mile-wide green banks of Jordan, with their reeds and tamarisk-trees. The road leads past a little Franciscan convent to the so-called ford of Bethabara, opposite which, on the eastern bank, is the traditional place of Baptism. On the western bank the Franciscans have erected a small chapel and a little farther on have roofed sheds where we can rest.

The river is only about 10 yards wide here, and flows round many bends with strong currents to the Dead Sea.

THE PLACE OF BAPTISM BY JORDAN

The Historical Aspect

The place where John preached and baptized was by the wilderness along the lower reaches of the Jordan. The words of the prophet about the voice crying in the wilderness (Is. 40: 3) and his exemplary life of penance drove him into the wilderness. His office of Baptist led him to seek out the river. But where exactly was the spot where he officiated and where Jesus let Himself be immersed in the waters of Jordan? St. John's Gospel describes it as 'Bethabara beyond Jordan, where John was baptizing' (1: 28). Some manuscripts add 'Bethany,' but this has no connection with the Bethany of Lazarus. Perhaps Bethany was a place near the Jordan from which John worked, with Bethabara as the actual place of baptizing, by the Jordan itself.

According to Origen in 230 and Eusebius in 300, Bethabara by Jordan was well known. But where exactly was it? The word means: house of the crossing. It is certain that John must have used a ford, to which paths led the crowds who hearkened to his preaching. Only at a ford would he have been able to immerse the candidates, for elsewhere the shores would have been too steep and the current too swift. But there were several fords opposite Jericho. Which of them was Bethabara?

The Bordeaux pilgrim says, in 333, describing the way from the Dead Sea to this place, 'From there to Jordan, where the Lord was baptized by John, it is 5 miles. This is also the place above the river, a hill by the shore, from whence Elijah ascended to heaven.' But a distance of 5 Roman miles from the Dead Sea leads us to the west bank of Jordan, to the Greek Orthodox monastery of St. John, near which the place of baptism is pointed out to-day. So the Bordeaux pilgrim indicates that the place of baptism was in this district on the east bank. And he further mentions, on the east bank, the hill of Elijah's ascension, farther inland, which we can also find to-day.

If Bethabara, and the place of baptism, lay here, it would have been a significant place in the history of the people of God. Etheria (385) and St. Jerome (400) indicate the traditions connected with this ford. It was here that the Israelites under Joshua went dry-shod over Jordan (Joshua 3: 16). Here the waters were 'divided hither and thither' when Elijah, before his ascension, crossed over with Elisha. And Elisha saw the same when he returned alone (2 Kings 2: 8–14). So this ford was exceptional for Jews, on account of their history. Both the dry-shod crossing and the neighbouring place of Elijah's ascension gave it importance. The Baptist would have chosen this ford since it was already known because of Elijah, in whose power and in whose spirit he worked. So crowds from throughout Judæa came together here.

When the Christians sought the place where John baptized they did so on historic ground. That the event was also commemorated by buildings is not referred to until 530 by Theodosius. At that time a marble pillar designated the exact spot of Jesus' baptism on the east bank. And a church was built in honour of the Baptist, probably there where the monastery of St. John now stands, on the west bank.

In later centuries tradition sometimes attached itself to the west bank, probably because the east bank was more difficult of access. But the actual spot was always taken as being 'beyond Jordan.' Still later there was a tendency to regard the more southerly ford of Hadschla as the place where Jesus was baptized because it is easier of access. But if to-day the banks by the monastery of St. John are rather steep and so less reminiscent of a place of baptism, it must be remembered that the river-bed has often changed course. So we cannot determine exactly where Bethabara was in the time of the Baptist, nor what it looked like. But is is almost wholly certain that the baptism of Jesus took place in this district.

South of the Franciscan place of the baptism are other places along the bank also commemorating this belonging to the Greek Orthodox, the Syrians, Copts, and Abyssinians. All these celebrate solemn services here on January 19th, the day of their Epiphany-feast, when they row out into the river. The Catholic service takes place on January 6th.

From the Holy Bible

About that time John the Baptist appeared as a preacher in the Judæan wilderness; his theme was, 'Repent; for the kingdom of heaven is upon you!'

They flocked to him from Jerusalem, from all Judæa, and the whole Jordan valley, and were baptized by him in the river Jordan, confessing their sins. The people asked him, 'Then what are we to do?'

Then Jesus arrived at the Jordan from Galilee, and came to John to be baptized by him. After baptism Jesus came up out of the water at once, and at that moment heaven opened; he saw the Spirit of God descending like a dove to alight upon him; and a voice from heaven was heard saying, 'This is my Son, my Beloved, on whom my favour rests.'

The next day John saw Jesus coming towards him. 'Look,' he said, 'there is the Lamb of God; it is he who takes away the sin of the world.'

This took place at Bethabara beyond Jordan, where John was baptizing. From Matt. 3; Luke 3 and John 1.

The Place of Baptism—A Call to Us

How strong a passion for repentance must have seized people at the time of Jesus that they came in crowds from all Judæa to be baptized. They came in the scorching heat of the tropical Jordan valley. Their willingness to come all this way indicated the desire for repentance. It was a whole day's travel, with a very sudden drop in height, from Jerusalem to Jericho, as well as the journey on the road from Jericho through the steamy Jordan valley to the ford, where John was baptizing.

The hearts of the people who gathered here cried out for the forgiveness of sins. Therefore they came in such crowds to Jordan in order to be baptized. It was entirely appropriate that Jesus too should come to Jordan before beginning His mission. For He had come to make sinners whole. So His place was with these people—the Saviour was with the sinners. He must have rejoiced to find that John had prepared the way, so that crowds were assembled who not only confessed their sins but asked, 'What shall we do to be saved?' These were people who wanted to change their lives, to start on a new way in obedience to God and His commands, as John the Baptist taught them.

And Jesus joined Himself to them. For the hour had come for Him to declare Himself as Saviour, as one who had come down from the throne of God in order graciously to forgive all their sins. But He did not reveal Himself as their Lord and God in kingly power; He came secretly, so that no one recognized Him. He not only sat with sinners, as He was to do later, but He was baptized in Jordan, as sinners had to be in order to receive the forgiveness of their sins. Here truly by Jordan could be seen the Lamb of God, who a few years later was to hang on the Cross, because He had taken our sins upon Him and was made sin for us. Only thus could the waters of Jordan wash away sins because the Lamb of God let Himself be baptized for the sins of His children, thus foreshadowing the Redemption.

The homeward journey of the crowds must have been a happy one with their sins forgiven. The heat and difficulty of the way would be even less felt than when they came, for they were intent only on performing that which they had been told to do in order to seal their forgiveness. Yet they who already shared something of Jesus' redemption could not have realized what had really happened to them in Jordan nor what was still to come. To-day, when the Lamb of God, the Saviour of sinners, has been revealed on the Cross to the whole world, Jordan speaks still more loudly of the blessedness of repentance. God waits for those who come here to bring their sins to Him, in memory of Jesus entering the water. Jesus waits for those who will thank Him that He has taken away the sins of the world, and who will ask, 'What shall we do? How shall we praise Thee with our new life?'

To-day the place of the Baptism in Jordan still reveals to men how those words so often used by John in Jordan, 'Repent for the Kingdom of Heaven is at hand,' will be fulfilled, as men go forth from there full of Joy and Assurance—fuller indeed than those of former days.

Jesus has made repentance the gateway to Heaven. Where souls repent they will already taste Heaven here on earth, the kingdom of joy and peace and love. And then they can cause this kingdom to shine forth in this dark world. How joyous a message sounded, and still sounds, here beside Jordan, The Kingdom of Heaven is at hand.

†

Deeper, deeper let me bow
For my sins weigh on me now
As the Lord descendeth;
Taking Baptism He ranks
Himself with sinners on those banks,
Awaiting our repentance.

PRAYER AT THE PLACE OF BAPTISM

Dear Lord Jesus,
thanks be to Thee that Thy Holy Spirit has the power to make

us listen to that which is naturally unpleasant to us: the truth about our sins. In the days of John the Baptist crowds came to the banks of Jordan for this very reason, not flinching from the hardships of the way; and Thou canst make me do the same, to long for that which I would by nature shun. I pray Thee to grant me the readiness to be told of my sins and to confess them, careless of humiliation, because Thy words of forgiveness are so precious to me. Incline my heart ever to hearken to the Baptist's cry, 'Repent ye'; and help me to turn again, there where Thou revealest that my life must be changed. I firmly believe that then new life will come to me, that I can receive a glimpse of Heaven, and something of the peace and love of Thy kingdom may thus shine out from me. AMEN.

HYMN

O Holy Ghost, come Thou to me
Grant me to have repentance free
Here by the Jordan bank,
Here where my Jesus once did bow,
As Lamb of God declared to be
And took away my sin.

Give me a heart to weep and grieve
O'er all my sin so great
And to confess before men,
A heart that ever Jesus seeks,
His grace a hundredfold receives
In sweet forgiveness then.

Give me a heart that sings Thy praise
Because I am forgiven
And Thou hast made me holy;
Daily let me share
Thy new-found grace,
O Holy Ghost, by penitence
And give me life anew.

✝

Just here where Jesus was baptized,
Do any now in penance bow?
So many come to see the place
But feel no joy, no glory now.
But God's own Son doth wait and wait
And gazes down from His high Throne,
To see if souls in Jordan bow
And weeping, all their sins will own.

What Penitence Achieves For Us

Repent and be converted—and a little bit of Heaven will enter your life.

You long for a new life full of victorious power and the fire of love—and the door to this new life is repentance.

Nothing is so blessed as repentance, for to repent means to turn from one's old life and ways, which would only bring disaster and the judgment of God, and to enter upon a new life with God and for God—a life which makes one happy and free.

Repentance could be called 'the altering of sin.' Such altering of our sin to what is good and holy is done by the Holy Spirit, to Whom we should pray.

A life in which there is not a daily act of repentance and penitence will leave us inwardly dead. It is only daily and constant repentance which makes us inwardly alive, full of the love of Jesus for mankind and full of joy.

Love for Jesus comes from repentance and penitence. Whoever desires to love Jesus more will ask Him for more and more penitence.

CHAPTER XV

BETHLEHEM

THE CHURCH OF THE NATIVITY

WE have known and loved the name of 'Bethlehem' from childhood, for it suggests all the mystery and miracle of Christmas, and so we joyfully take the road to the Bethlehem of to-day. But it is not the road that the Magi took when they sought the Babe, after their visit to Jerusalem; Bethlehem lies only about 5 miles from Jerusalem.

We come to the highest ground about half-way along, and now we can see Bethlehem in the distance, with its light-coloured houses and many towers, lying in terraces upon two hills. The landscape now changes; the earth between the stones is of darker colour, the green shoots of the spring sowing are more advanced, and there are many olive-trees in the valleys and on the slopes. This obvious fertility makes plain why the popular name of this town, on the edge of the wilderness of Judæa, is 'House of Bread.' It was here that Ruth once gleaned the corn and found favour with Boaz; and here David kept his father's flocks of sheep before he became king.

The most conspicuous of the hills surrounding Bethlehem is the Hill of the Franks, half built up artificially by Herod to be the site of his castle and also his tomb.

In the neighbourhood of the Elisha monastery our road joins the old, classic road which the frontier, drawn in 1948, has now made impassable. On the outskirts of Bethlehem lies Rachel's tomb, and tradition also makes it the spot where Rachel wept for her children. And in the weeping of the Bethlehem mothers over Herod's massacre of the Innocents, St. Matthew saw the fulfilling of the prophecy, 'Rachel weeping for her children' (Jer. 31 : 15; Matt. 2 : 18). For centuries the Bedouins of the eastern desert have buried their children round this tomb.

Behind Rachel's tomb the road to the church of the Nativity leaves the one leading on to Hebron. Our road goes round the town-centre and comes out to the east on the wide square in front of the church, which we recognize immediately by its ancient, fortress-like walls . Here, in a cave, is the historic site of the greatest miracle of all : God becoming man.

Justin Martyr, a native of Palestine, proclaimed in the middle of the second century that the Saviour was born in a cave near Bethlehem. The Emperor Hadrian (117–138), who erected a heathen temple on Calvary, also tried to obliterate the Christian significance of this cave by planting a grove of Adonis, the beloved of Venus. But it was just this which ensured the knowledge of the place of the Nativity. Origen, who lived in Palestine about the middle of the third century, wrote that the cave of the Nativity was known to every one.

Constantine erected a magnificent basilica over the cave in 325. It was even more magnificent than the one he erected on the Mount of Olives and over the Holy Sepulchre. Whilst these two were repeatedly destroyed, the church of the Nativity has remained till now, as the oldest church in the world. True, the Samaritans did damage it in 529 during their insurrection against all Christian sites, but it was restored in the same century, under the Emperor Justinian. When the Persians invaded the Holy Land in 614 and destroyed most of the churches, they spared the church of the Nativity because they recognized their own national dress in the robes of the Wise Men depicted on the mosaic of the pediment.

Later still the church escaped destruction. At Christmas in the year 1100, Baldwin of Flanders, the leader of the crusading army, was anointed king of Jerusalem. After the Crusaders had been driven out the Church of the Nativity was cared for by the Franciscans, though most of their rights were taken from them under Turkish rule. Since 1757 the church has belonged to the Greek Orthodox.

In the course of time the three great portals were bricked up and only a small doorway was left, to prevent the church being entered on horseback. If we wish to enter the church we must bend double, a truly appropriate reminder of the humility of God, born here as Son of Man. An outer court leads us to the wide interior with its four rows of pillars. The actual cave of the Nativity is beneath the altar; flights of steps on both sides of the chancel lead down to the cave. A niche in the wall indicates the traditional spot where Jesus was born as Saviour of the world. A silver star in the marble pavement beneath an altar bears the inscription, 'Hic de Virgine Maria Jesus Christus natus est'—'here Jesus Christ was born of the Virgin Mary.' This spot, too, is under Greek Orthodox care. Of the fifteen lamps burning day and night round the star, six belong to the Greeks, five to the Armenians, four to the Roman Catholics.

In another niche, three steps lower, is shown the Crib, originally a manger hewn out of the rock; it is very small, giving room for only a few cattle, whom the shepherds could keep their eye on from the actual cave higher up when, as often, they sheltered here. When Mary and Joseph came here as poor folk, the upper cave would have been the dwelling and the place of the birth, whilst the lower one would shelter the Child in the manger. Pilgrim reports have described how loving devotion covered the manger with silver and gold. To-day it is covered with marble. This spot belongs to the Franciscans, as does also the altar opposite, dedicated to the Adoration of the Magi.

The entire cave is covered with asbestos, partly disguised by white marble, and the natural ceiling has been replaced by a stone vault, so that little of its original appearance remains. But we can forget this when we realize that we are standing by the place where our Lord was born, and we can only adore and sing a few carols.

The other caves cannot ordinarily be entered from that of the Nativity, but have to be approached from the Franciscan church dedicated to St. Katharine, which adjoins it on the north. We reach this from the left aisle of the church of the Nativity via a pergola and the cloisters of the neighbouring convent. From the right aisle of the Franciscan church we descend a stairway to St. Joseph's cave, in which he probably heard the message, 'Arise and take the young child and his mother and flee into Egypt.' From this we can go into a still lower crypt, dedicated to the Holy Innocents. An artificial tunnel connects with a number of other caves in which, during the third and fourth centuries, well-known people lived and were buried: St. Jerome, 385–420 and his pupil Eusebius of Cremona, St. Paula and her daughter, Eustochium. St. Jerome founded a monastery next door to the Basilica, and in this cave he produced the Vulgate, the first Latin version of the Bible.

Our visit to the church of the Nativity should make us very grateful that this church has kept alive through all the intervening wars the historically verified spot where our Lord Jesus Christ was born.

The church is open all day.
A Protestant 'shrine' to commemorate the birth of our Lord in Bethlehem is called the 'Christmas church.' It was built some decades ago, and lies about 10 minutes' walk from the entrance of the church of the Nativity.

From the Holy Bible

But thou, Beth-lehem Ephratah, though thou be little among the thousands of Judah, yet out of thee shall he come forth unto me that is to be ruler in Israel; whose goings forth have been from of old, from everlasting. Micah 5: 2.

In those days a decree was issued by the Emperor Augustus

for a general registration throughout the Roman world. This was the first registration of its kind; it took place when Quirinius was governor of Syria. For this purpose every one made his way to his own town; and so Joseph went up to Judæa from the town of Nazareth in Galilee, to be registered at the city of David, called Bethlehem, because he was of the house of David by descent; and with him went Mary who was betrothed to him. She was pregnant, and while they were there the time came for her child to be born, and she gave birth to a son, her first-born. She wrapped him round, and laid him in a manger, because there was no room for them to lodge in the house. Luke 2 : 1–7.

Hymn

Bethlehem, I now behold thee,
Town of towns without compare,
And I bow me to the ground.
Thou dost hold the world's best treasure,
God in thee to us came down,
Here, for us, a Man to be.

Bethlehem, thou then didst harbour
God's own Son Who left His Throne
Hence to bring us to the Father.
Only he who leaves his sinning,
Small and lowly as a child
Gets the blessing from the Babe.

Bethlehem—A Call to Us

The name of Bethlehem is one of the sweetest sounds of earth, although it tells us of a dark cave and a rock-hewn manger. But here the loveliest Child ever born on earth had His first bed. He was not a child of sin like others, but a heavenly child, well-beloved of His Father, but now in human form. Cherubim and Seraphim adored Him, their Lord and Creator, Whom they praise eternally throughout all heaven, for the Father had decreed, 'All the angels of God shall worship him' (Heb. 1 : 6).

And this Lord and Creator, in unimaginable lowliness, lay in the manger, in the form of a weak, new-born infant. Full-grown as those beside Him were, they must have towered above Him. How surprised the heavenly host must have been to see Almighty God thus stripped of all might and majesty! Archangels could hardly have understood such humiliation. And what must the Father's heart have felt as He beheld His only-begotten Son, the express image of His Person, a helpless infant! He lay in the utmost poverty, in the manger of a cave. How could this be? the hosts of heaven must have asked. And they must have guessed the answer of the Father's heart, 'So God loved the world that he gave his only-begotten Son, that whosoever believeth in him should not perish, but have everlasting life.' The angel-host, cherubim and seraphim, must have adored this incomprehensible love of God to His children, a love which upholds the world in spite of its revolt and evil-doing. God took upon Himself our flesh and blood, as a tiny helpless child, so that He could come nigh to them.

Thus it was shown forth to the heavenly host and to all men that the Almighty prefers that which makes itself small and weak and humble. And when the Child had grown to manhood, He uttered this significant word to His disciples, 'Unless ye become as little children—dependent and humble—ye cannot enter the kingdom of heaven.' Heaven belongs to the child-like. God came to us in Bethlehem, lying helpless in the manger. But a helpless babe inspires all with love and joy. And so God must love those who, following Jesus' example, humble themselves and become as unassuming and unselfconscious as children. The hosts of Heaven wait to see those who come to the manger and believe in the miracle of Christmas becoming like Him. We, though grown to full stature, must renounce our wilful self-assertion, our pride and certainty, and become as little children.

God became man and humbled Himself so that we, loosed from our pride, should truly become children of the Father. If we thus bear within ourselves the sign of Heaven, the complete trust of children, unselfconscious and joyful, then the light that shines from the Manger in Bethlehem will shine out from us too, and we shall show forth to many the joy of the Holy Child. That is the call of Bethlehem to us.

Our glorious God on high has bent so low—
Will you, O Man, give up your claims below?

HYMN

O dearest Jesus, Babe Divine,
I come to bless Thee here
In Thy poor shelt'ring cave.
I sing to Thee my heart's poor song
That Thou may'st no more sadness feel
That Thou to earth hast come.

O dearest Jesus, Babe Divine,
Who would not come with gifts to Thee
To lay them at Thy feet?
Thou art so little, lowly, poor
That I must bring Thee all I have
To make Thy heart rejoice.

O dearest Jesus, Babe Divine,
Who would not seek to succour Thee,
Thou lowly Babe so small?
Thou cam'st to us in darkest night
That we in Thee might light behold.
For which we thank Thee ever.

O dearest Jesus, Babe Divine,
Who would not bless Thee here
Beside Thy lowly Crib?
From Thee shines forth the light of Heaven
Right over all the whole wide world
From this Thy narrow cave.

Who is so low as Thou art, Lord?
Then let me never rest

Till I am lowly as Thou art,
Ready to serve Thee as Thou wilt.
My neighbour I will ever see
As my dear brother true.

Here now we are, O look on us,
Forgive the evil we have done,
Who to save sinners came.
We will rejoice around Thy Crib,
'The Saviour of us all is come
Who doth redeem and save.'

Therefore, O dearest Babe Divine,
We hasten Thee to bless.
Yea, let the whole world come.
Thou camest down to earth for us
That Heaven for us might open'd be,
Therefore we praise and sing.

†

If ye become as little children ye shall know the secret of the Kingdom and shall enter into it, to love and be loved by love everlasting.

†

Hymn

O Child, so beautiful Thou art
That angels ever sing.
From Thee the light of Heaven shines
The Father's heart to bring.
O Child, the image all express
Of Godhead, meek and mild
Sinners and angels both adore
Thee, Thou most lovely Child.

BETHLEHEM

O Child, we cannot comprehend!
What man can understand
That God in Thee doth live,
That Thou from Heaven descendest
To seek and save the lost ones—
For love itself constraineth
The doors of Heaven to open
That we may come back home.

A light of Heaven shineth
Through Thee upon us here.
The Father's everlasting love
Doth rest upon us here.
The world its sickness now doth leave
For Heaven has healed all ill.
Now we can have the peace of God
By gazing on Thee still.

Since Thou hast come to earth
We are not far from Heaven;
For Thou, the shining Morning Star
Hast brought it closer to us.
O Child, from Thee by Love's own act
Doth Love itself display,
And Thou dost bring us happiness
By driving Sin away.

And we as God's beloved
Can see grief turned to Joy.
The Father's heart is open
To all who turn His way.
And Thou, O Child, dost make of us
Those who being loved, can love,
For Jesus only gives us
Such power from above.

PRAYER BESIDE THE MANGER

Dear Lord Jesus,
Thou who art Lord of lords, how low and meek didst Thou become to lay in the manger!

I adore Thee in gratefulness and wonder! Beside Thy manger I kneel down and feel ashamed before Thee. Thou, the Son of the Most Highest, Whose throne is in Heaven, enterest in such humility.

But I who am a sinner deserving only to be humbled seek over and over again to retain my own greatness, my honour and self-glory, although none of these is due to me.

To thee, Child Jesus, I bring all my sinful pride and my assertiveness and lay it down in Thy manger. Thou, the Son of God, made Child for our sakes, hast redeemed us from our pride and wilful disobedience. We pray to Thee that we may truly become children of the Father, humble, unselfconscious, unassuming and dependent.

Out of love and gratefulness I give my 'Yea' to all the ways by which Thou wouldst choose to make me lowly and humble. On every account make me childlike so that the promise may be for me: 'If ye become as little children ye shall enter into the Kingdom of Heaven.' AMEN.

CHAPTER XVI

THE SHEPHERDS' FIELD

CHRISTMAS means not only the stable and the manger, but the fields where the shepherds heard 'Gloria in excelsis.' So we take our way eastwards from the church of the Nativity to the field where the heavenly host appeared to the watching shepherds. About 30 yards along the road, which here goes down a steep hill, we come to it. On the left, in the valley, are olive-orchards, and north and east lie well-cultivated fields, beyond which, and over the bare hills, we can see as far as the Dead Sea.

The event of the message to the shepherds is commemorated by three fenced-in fields which we can recognize at once: on rising ground to the left we see the dome of the church belonging to the Franciscan field; straight ahead is a dark green grove of the Y.M.C.A., and in the valley on the right, a walled olive-orchard of the Greek Orthodox.

As we descend this view is lost, and soon after we have left the last houses of Bethlehem behind us, we come to the shepherd-village Beth-Sahur, stretching for about 1½ miles, which we must cross in order to reach the fields. Going right through this village we keep to the left at every point where roads cross. For the Franciscan field we take an ascending path on the left just beyond the church and the boys' seminary belonging to the Greek Catholic Patriarchate. After about 600 yards we reach our goal. The Franciscans built a chapel here in 1954, beside a large cave which had till then served as a sanctuary. On the slope of the property excavations in the nineteenth century revealed the remains of a very ancient church and convent, part dating from the fourth century and part from the sixth century. But the buildings must have been destroyed in very early times, perhaps by the Persians in 614.

From the main road going east, just beyond the left-hand path to the Franciscan fields, a newly-made road leads straight to the Greek Orthodox one. About 250 yards along we reach the door in the wall of the olive-orchard, in the middle of which are the ruins of the former convent 'of the Shepherds,' with a crypt. Reports from early times say that this is where the angels were seen.

But if we keep along the main road, after about a mile we reach the Protestant field, on the left. It was acquired a few years ago by the American Y.M.C.A. Here we can also see an ancient cave, like many in the neighbourhood, which may have sheltered the shepherds.

The view towards high-lying Bethlehem is specially good from the Franciscan field. We can easily imagine the shepherds hastening joyfully to the cave of the Nativity. And as if we too shared their experience, we feel compelled to burst into song. We will not be put off by the fact that there is no definite tradition about the exact place. All the three fields lie close together, and the heavenly host will not have been circumscribed by earthly measurements. All traditions agree that the heavenly host appeared eastwards of Bethlehem. So all three fields must have seen the angels that night and have heard the joyful message, 'To-day is born to you a Saviour!'

The Franciscan and the Y.M.C.A. field can be visited all day; the guardians will allow any one to enter on request. The Greek Orthodox one is only open occasionally.

From the Holy Bible

Now in this same district there were shepherds out in the fields, keeping watch through the night over their flock, when suddenly there stood before them an angel of the Lord, and the splendour of the Lord shone round them. They were terror-struck, but the angel said, 'Do not be afraid; I have good news for you: there is great joy coming to the whole people. To-day in the city of David a deliverer has been born to you—the Messiah, the Lord. And this is your sign: you will find a baby lying all wrapped up, in a manger.' All at once there was with the angel a great company of the heavenly host, singing the praises of God,

'Glory to God in highest heaven,
And on earth peace for men on whom his favour rests.'

After the angels had left them and gone into heaven the shepherds said to one another, 'Come, we must go straight to Bethlehem and see this thing that has happened, which the Lord has made known to us.' So they went with all speed and found their way to Mary and Joseph; and the baby was lying in the manger. When they saw him, they recounted what they had been told about this child; and all who heard were astonished at what the shepherds said. But Mary treasured up all these things and pondered over them. Meanwhile the shepherds returned glorifying and praising God for what they had heard and seen; it had all happened as they had been told. Luke 2 : 8–20.

†

HYMN

O happy field of shepherds,
What hast thou not beheld?
O happy field of shepherds,
Where angels' news was spelled.

Thou land by God selected
By little Bethlehem,
Thou heard'st the host of angels
Sing glory unto them.

To earth has come all Heaven
To give the joyful news:
Peace and good will to all mankind
Whom He in love doth choose.

Awake and put forth blossom,
Thou field of God's own grace,
That here the poor and lowly
May joy before His Face.

The Shepherds' Field—A Call to Us

During that Holy Night 'there were in the same country shepherds abiding in the field.' It was a night when the heavens were opened and 'the glory of the Lord shined round about them' in the darkness. Over the fields sounded the voice of the angels of God, and 'a multitude of the heavenly host were with them,' singing 'Glory to God in the highest,' and the joyful message rang out, 'To you is born a Saviour.' So the fields became fields of rejoicing.

In those days shepherds were regarded as being on the same level as publicans and sinners. But to them came the wondrous news. How could they realize that it was just they to whom the angel of the Lord was sent, and that they should behold the Saviour of the world. And where was He to be found? In a manger, in a cave! They must have been surprised for such was their own shelter. They led poverty-stricken lives, for they had no proper house, but sheltered in caves, as we can still see shepherds doing in the neighbourhood of Bethlehem. And still to-day newly-born infants are cradled in the mangers of the flocks.

That God should come down to these poor, despised shepherds was surely cause enough to make them burst forth in adoration of Him Who was ready to be poor and despised for all our sakes. He made Himself like unto them, who were such sinners that they were looked down upon by their own people. How God must have loved them, thus to come down to them, to their poor shelter! There must have been a joyful procession from the field to the cave—more joyful than any other during Jesus' earthly life. It is said that the shepherds 'came with haste.' They went to the stable, not at a comfortable, leisurely pace but with joyful eagerness and fervent expectation, leaping along the road.

Perhaps the sheep followed them, and the dogs barked, and all were filled with joy. All came to do homage to the Babe and surely the shepherds would race one another to see who would be first to greet and be greeted by the Child.

Will we too be filled with joy when we come to visit the

shepherds' field? Those who know themselves to be sinners, as did the shepherds, will receive into their hearts the joyful message, which still rings out to-day as it did then. For the poor, who know themselves to be poor and sinful, need a Saviour. For those who are 'tied and bound by the chain of their sin' there is no sound so blessed as the message: 'Christ, the Saviour, has come.'

This revelation of God's humility was given to poor sinners, the shepherds, that night. They were the first to whom Almighty God made Himself known and invited them to come to the very place where He came to earth! And still to-day His Word holds good: that He will look favourably on those of broken and contrite heart, and will make His dwelling amongst them. Joy and rejoicing shall be theirs, for whenever they bewail their sins, Heaven will be opened to them, and they will receive the message, 'To you is born Him who can save you from your sins. Ye shall behold Him, and, beholding, ye shall be changed into His image, as ye adore the Babe in the manger.'

✝

Oh, who is there can still be sad?
For in a manger laid
There is a child whose glory will
Be everywhere displayed.

PRAYER ON THE SHEPHERDS' FIELD

Dear Lord Jesus,
I give thanks to Thee that Thou hast bestowed upon us, who yearn for good news, the joyous coming of Thee, our Saviour and Redeemer. I thank Thee that Thou didst send Thine angel to tell the shepherds, who lay bound in darkness with their sin. Let me too receive this joy, that I may bear the marks of the redeemed in me. Here, in the shepherds' field, I pray Thee, dear Lord Jesus, to make me as needy as were the shepherds. Give me the broken and contrite heart that can receive the message: To me is born the Saviour, and so let me rejoice in my heart. Let me seek Thee as did the shepherds, and whenever I am painfully aware of my sins, let me hasten at once to Thee.

I thank Thee that I may be sure of receiving forgiveness from Thee and may know Thy joy. Thou wilt make this joy shine forth from me, so that others may receive faith, and find the true Saviour and Redeemer. AMEN.

WHAT WAS THE GIFT OF CHRISTMAS NIGHT TO US?

A Child, the Father's only Son,
  Came down from Heaven and left His Throne.
A lowly, hidden, Babe was He
  Who King of kings shall ever be.
A Child that is the Morning Star
  To lighten darkness near and far.
A Child of power and glory He,
  Before Whose Face the foe shall flee.
A Child, oh, 'Wonderful' His Name,
  And wonders shall Himself proclaim.
A Child Who sinners doth renew,
  A Child Who all things maketh new.
A Child from Whom all blessing flows—
  To mourners He is ever close.
A Child so humble, meek and mild—
  God's Kingdom cometh by this Child.

HYMN

O lovely, lovely Babe, who plays the shawm for Thee,
Tells Thee of the Father, counsellor and spirit
Or serried ranks of angels praising Thee?

Oh, lovely, lovely Babe, who now shall be with Thee?
Shepherds, little children, donkeys and the oxen
Here on earth they all are greeting Thee.

O lovely, lovely Babe, I take my place with Thee,
For my lips are longing and my heart's rejoicing
To sing out a song of love to Thee.

I bring Thee treasures, full, such as Thou wishest and wantest
I bring to Thee my will which can then accomplish
All that Thy dear Heart for me could want.

I'll serve Thee as I can though small and full of sin.
And I will not delay to serve Thee as I ought
But first by serving brethren I'll begin.

O, lovely, lovely Babe, I'll take my place with Thee
When the Cross presses down and Thou art forcèd low,
Then I as a sharer of sorrow would be.

I must love Thee, love Thee, more and always more.
For Thou Who art my sun, art also all my bliss
And I will ever, Thee, God's Son, adore.

Hymn

The Shepherds did hasten, we hasten our song
For none who seek Jesus can linger long.

We hasten at Christmas, for there we shall find
The Babe doth expect us, for He is so kind.

He seeth our longing, His Heart smiles to ours
The Holy Night bringeth us joy's unfading flowers.

The Shepherds rejoicing, I rejoice as do they
The Babe in the Manger my heart takes away.

The Shepherds adore Him in wonder and love.
I too by the Manger rejoice in His love.

The Wise Men are coming with gifts rich and rare,
But still better I bring Him—myself, without care.

The Wise Men gave gifts that enriched them anew,
We come to the Child, He has gifts for us too.

I give Thee my sins, and all that I have;
The Babe gives me love which from all ill shall save.

✝

O dearest darling Jesus small,
I thank Thee for Thy goodness all,
May I be Thine for ever.
Make me as humble as Thou art,
That I may dwell within Thy Heart,
Divided from Thee never.

2. Yet Thy radiance
shines the brighter
O'er our sinful misery,
And Thou lead'st
mankind in triumph
Out of death to victory.

CHAPTER XVII

EIN KEREM

LET us go 'into the hill-country' and visit the place, about five miles west of Jerusalem, in the Judaean hills, which is closely connected with the beginning of St. Luke's gospel, with the account of the meeting of Mary and Elizabeth and the birth of John the Baptist. The village is called Ein Kerem.

We come from the western border of Jerusalem, from the vicinity of the lofty Building of All Nations (Hebrew: Binjanej Ha-uma) turning left from the main road to Tel Aviv. Passing through modern residential quarters the road leads past the 'Herzl-hill' on the right, the tomb of the renowned Zionist leader, Theodore Herzl, in the centre of a court of honour. Shortly after this the road divides: straight on it leads to the high-lying University Hospital, Hadassa, and to the right it leads to the memorial place Yad Washem. We follow the middle road for about two miles down the valley of Ein Kerem, with wonderful views, part of the way, of the village and of the high lying grounds of the convent of the Sisters of Notre Dame de Sion and of the surrounding hills.

Ein Kerem lies in a hollow, in dreamy loveliness, in the midst of olive orchards and groups of slender dark green cypress trees, between which rise the towers of the various churches and convents. The terraced slopes indicate that here in the past were vineyards (Hebrew: Kerem), and the very ancient spring (Hebrew: Ein) of the village well gives a further meaning to the name: the well of the vineyard. Just before the main road turns right in the centre of the village, we see a narrow lane on the right, which leads to the church of St. John. This lies slightly above the Arab houses which surround it. Going into the church, we descend a flight of steps by the left side-altar, leading to the crypt, whose natural rock ceiling shows it to be a former cave-dwelling. Here is commemorated the birth of John the Baptist.

On the hill opposite, to the south, stands the Franciscan church of the Visitation, dedicated to St. Elizabeth. In the valley separating it from the village lie the trees and vegetable-plots of an agricultural college. A little beyond the entrance to the Russian-Orthodox convent of 'Gorni,' by the ancient well with its refreshing spring-water, a stony path leads us upward. After ten to fifteen minutes' walk we come to the lovely wrought-iron gate to the Franciscan grounds, with the Church of the Visitation , consisting of an upper and a lower building. A well in the crypt of the lower church indicates that in Jesus' day there must have been dwellings here. Many tablets, giving the Magnificat in various languages, in the outer court of the church invite us to sing the song of praise.

If we look to the north we are impressed by the loneliness of the way taken by Mary when she came from Nazareth to the 'hill-country.' Going down into the valley (see Plate 3), we again catch sight of the church of St. John.

Times of opening:

Church of St. John (Franciscan) 8–12 and 2–6.
Church of the Visitation („) 8–12 and 3–6.

The Historical Aspect

Neither the Bible nor tradition indicates the exact spot where Mary met Elizabeth, nor where John the Baptist was born. But the Greek word used by St. Luke to indicate the 'hill-country of Judaea' to which Mary hastened (Luke 1: 39), refers to the hilly district near Jerusalem. The same word is used again in v. 65 which says that when the tongue of Zacharias was again loosed after the naming of John the Baptist it was known 'throughout the hill-country.' Other descriptions of the same date use the same word for the district near Jerusalem. The place must have been within easy reach of Jerusalem because Zacharias was a priest in the Temple. The picturesque village of Ein Kerem, west of the city, corresponds to St. Luke's description. There is no very early tradition concerning the place, and several other places were formerly suggested for the site of the Visitation and the birth of John the Baptist. But eventually tradition became fixed to Ein Kerem.

It dates right back to pre-Christian times. That it was an inhabited place in Jesus' day is shown by the graves and by various finds. The first witness to indicate the biblical character of Ein Kerem is the pilgrim Theodosius, who wrote about 530. He says 'It is three miles from Jerusalem to the place where St. Elizabeth, the mother of St. John the Baptist, dwelt.' He does not give any name to the place, but the distance indicated and later witnesses indicate Ein Kerem. The first mention of the name comes in the Georgian calendar of festivals, which gives all the stations at which the Georgian church of Jerusalem celebrated its festivals. This list includes the church of St. Elizabeth in Ein Kerem.

At that time the only memory attached to it was the apocryphal story of the escape of Elizabeth by the sudden opening of a rock when she was fleeing from the Herodian massacre of the Innocents. Till the beginning of the ninth century it had been assumed that John the Baptist was born in Jerusalem and this was commemorated in a church there. Only later on did it begin to be held that Zacharias had his dwelling at Ein Kerem.

Not till 940 is there any mention of another church, besides that of St. Elizabeth, dedicated to Zacharias. In this second church, later called St. John's church, the birth of John the Baptist and the Benedictus sung by his father Zacharias were commemorated. The church of St. Elizabeth, which had originally been connected only with the legendary escape of Elizabeth, later had the gospel story of the Visitation and the Magnificat attached to it, because it was assumed that Zacharias had a 'garden-house' as well as his dwelling-house, according to Jewish custom. Tradition gradually assumed that it was here that Elizabeth 'hid herself' when she knew herself to be with child.

So this may well have been the place where the Visitation took place. Mary may have first sought the dwelling-house of her kinsman Zacharias, and then, hearing that Elizabeth had retired to the garden-house, she would have gone on to that. When she entered the garden Elizabeth would have come towards her to greet her as the mother of the Redeemer. Thus the Magnificat, commemorated here, was uttered.

At one time the Benedictus was also commemorated here —probably when the Muslims were in possession of the church of St. John. But now that commemoration has been restored to St. John's, because the circumcision and the naming after eight days would most likely have taken place in the same house as the birth.

The two-storied church of St. Elizabeth, whose beginnings go back to the fifth century, has belonged to the Franciscans since 1679. They have repeatedly restored it, and they built the upper church in 1938. They are also the guardians of St. John's, whose ruins they acquired in 1621 and rebuilt at the end of the seventeenth century.

FROM THE HOLY BIBLE

The angel said: 'Moreover your kinswoman Elizabeth has herself conceived a son in her old age; and she who is reputed barren is now in her sixth month, for God's promises can never fail.' Luke 1: 36 and 37.

About this time Mary set out and went straight to a town in the uplands of Judah. She went into Zechariah's house and greeted Elizabeth. And when Elizabeth heard Mary's greeting, the baby stirred in her womb. Then Elizabeth was filled with the Holy Spirit and cried aloud, 'God's blessing is on you above all women, and his blessing is on the fruit of your womb. Who am I, that the mother of my Lord should visit me? I tell you, when your greeting sounded in my ears, the baby in my womb leapt for joy. How happy is she who has had faith that the Lord's promise would be fulfilled!' And Mary said: 'Tell out, my soul, the greatness of the Lord, rejoice, rejoice, my spirit, in God my saviour; so tenderly has he looked upon his servant, humble as she is . . .'

Mary stayed with her about three months and then returned home. From St. Luke 1: 39–56.

MAGNIFICAT

'Tell out, my soul, the greatness of the Lord,
rejoice, rejoice, my spirit, in God my saviour;
so tenderly has he looked upon his servant,
humble as she is.
For, from this day forth, all generations will count me blessed,
so wonderfully has he dealt with me, the Lord, the Mighty One.
His name is Holy;
his mercy sure from generation to generation
toward those who fear him;
the deeds his own right arm has done disclose his might:
the arrogant of heart and mind he has put to rout,

he has torn imperial powers from their thrones,
but the humble have been lifted high.
The hungry he has satisfied with good things, the rich sent empty away.
He has ranged himself at the side of Israel his servant;
firm in his promise to our forefathers,
he has not forgotten to show mercy to Abraham
and his children's children, for ever.'

MAGNIFICAT

(Authorized Version)

My soul doth magnify the Lord, and my spirit hath rejoiced in God my Saviour.
For he hath regarded the low estate of his handmaiden: for, behold, from henceforth all generations shall call me blessed.
For he that is mighty hath done to me great things; and holy is his name.
And his mercy is on them that fear him from generation to generation.
He hath showed strength with his arm; he hath scattered the proud in the imagination of their hearts.
He hath put down the mighty from their seats, and exalted them of low degree.
He hath filled the hungry with good things; and the rich he hath sent empty away.
He hath holpen his servant Israel, in remembrance of his mercy;
As he spake to our fathers, to Abraham, and to his seed for ever.

St. Luke 1: 46–55.

THE VISITATION: A CALL TO US

Ein Kerem: the place of visitation, the visitation of Zacharias who, when he doubted the revelation of God Himself as the Living God, was struck dumb for nine months. And the place of visitation of Elizabeth, who in old age was given the miraculous expectation of bearing a child, the child of grace —John.

And the place, above all, where Mary was visited by such grace that the Magnificat sounded from her lips, the song of praise and thanksgiving to her God. And why did she thus rejoice? The highest songs of praise sound there where the soul perceives the light of God's help, His comforting, and His coming in the midst of deepest woe—in the dark night of temptation. For then it rises like a lark, soaring upwards to the sun and singing its song of thanks and praise.

Truly Mary had travelled through darkness and temptation to the house of Zacharias and Elizabeth, and here she experienced the gracious visitation of God.

The growing things, the flowers on which she stepped as she hurried to Elizabeth may well have bowed before her the pure virgin who bore so precious a treasure beneath her heart. And well may her heart have rejoiced that she was chosen to bear the Son of God, the Saviour of the world.

But well may she also have hesitated to tread the path of shame. She must go back to Nazareth, which would mean exposing herself to being despised. How could she bear that? Joseph was certain to 'put her away,' and she would be in danger of stoning, according to the Law. Was her faith strong enough to expect a miracle from God which would make it impossible for them to stone her? The voices of temptation must have buzzed in her ears: Was she not mistaken? Was it really the voice of God she heard through the message of an angel? Was God's way thus?

And the nearer she came to the house of Zacharias, the more insistent would have been the questions. What will

Elizabeth say when I tell her what is to come upon me? Will she really believe that the child I am expecting is the Son of God? Or will she reject me? She must have entered the house fearfully. But behold, God was gracious, God visited her in the midst of temptation. By leading her to Elizabeth He led her to His loving heart, that desired only good; and that revealed His decision to redeem mankind. When she entered the house an astonishing thing happened: Elizabeth, who can have known nothing of the message to Mary, greeted her with the same words as the angel: 'Blessed art thou among women.' Elizabeth bowed before her, the younger woman, as before the mother of God's Son and said 'Whence is this to me, that the mother of my Lord should come to me?'

Could Mary have had anything happen to her more wonderful, more releasing from temptations, cares and anxieties, than this heavenly corroboration of her way? For when Elizabeth called her the mother of her Lord she knew that this knowledge came from God, that she was to bear His Son, the Messiah; that He would lead her wondrously through all the difficulties with Joseph and with the neighbours; and that He would crown the miracle that she was with child by the Holy Ghost.

What a visitation of God in the house of Elizabeth this was! Mary was allowed to grasp fully her election, and the grace given to her. Her eyes were opened to behold the great and wonderful thing that God proposed for her—that she should bring the Son of God into the world. All doubts and fears and temptations must have fallen away from her, and she must have stepped from night into the full light of day, the sunlight; with Heaven opened to her she could see the angels descending upon Him Who was to go forth from her womb: Jesus. She could not but rejoice and sing that God had done great things for her who had been humbled before Joseph and before her neighbours and that He would continue so to do.

She must have found it hard to grasp, after the anticipations of shame and humiliation. She, the lowly maid, had been looked upon by God and lifted up: to be the mother of the Son of God. Ein Kerem, the place of Mary's visitation, speaks to us to-day. For God is still the same, and He will visit us when we are in darkness and in manifold temptations and give us times of refreshing. It tells us that God will bring light out of darkness, and it reveals to us God as a merciful father Who loves us and will make a way of escape out of our temptations, for His counsels work all things together for good.

So Ein Kerem, which once listened to Mary's song of praise, ought to draw the same reply from our hearts. It waits for our continual songs of praise in the night to God Who doeth such great things for poor sinful men who are ready to be humbled.

Ein Kerem waits for yet more. It waits to behold those in whom Jesus can be born again to-day because they can say Yea to the words and will of God, however dark the path, because they believe firmly in His love. God waits for such to bring Jesus to the world that has turned from God.

†

Only he who on Faith's path
 Through the dark night travelleth,
Can the help and wonder know,
 Which from God with great joy flows
To the glad sound of Magnificat.

No song like Mary's so clearly sounds
 As from a humbled heart redounds.
No hymn of praise for Jesus sings,
 As one which from a deep need springs.

PRAYER IN THE CHURCH OF THE VISITATION

Beloved Father, we thank Thee that Thou didst of Thy great goodness grant help to Mary in her way of temptation and confirm her faith, here in the place of her visitation. Thou dost reveal to us through Mary that the end of such dark paths, trodden in faith, is Magnificat. We thank Thee for the message that dark and difficult paths can lead us home to Thy heart, where joy and comfort await us. Let me take heart to follow the mother of our Lord along her way of faith, knowing that Thou hast prepared for me refreshment in the wilderness. Through manifold temptations Thou wilt give in Thine own good time the joyful light of Thy word. Let me evermore trust Thee, so that like Mary I may behold Thy glory in the midst of darkness and may sing many Magnificats to Thee. O mayest Thou not wait in vain for such songs in the night to the glory of Thy Name. AMEN.

HYMN

Over the hills the Virgin is hurrying
Bearing under her heart her treasure
The one true King of all the worlds,
Redeemer of all human kind,
Son of God, of God most high—
Who can truly know such grace?

The blessed secret, how closely she keeps it
In loving devotion to God her one Lord,
Rejoicing and weeping, for grace doth within her
Join pain with her pleasure and hallow her grief.

And yet that fair secret the hills and the valleys
O'er which she is hast'ning, they know it full well.
The birds they do sing it, the branches do murmur it:
The world's only Saviour, behold, He is nigh.

They praise the fair pure one, the mother of Him Who
Has made the whole world and redeems it as well.
The grass it is bending and tree-tops descending
Before thee, Christ's mother, thou blest over all.

We praise thee, fair pure one, the Mother of Him Who
Has formed us from nothing and saved us as well.
With grass and with tree-tops, we greet thee this morning,
Thou mother of Christ, elect above all.

CHURCH OF ST. JOHN THE BAPTIST

From the Holy Bible

In the days of Herod, king of Judaea, there was a priest named Zechariah, and his wife's name was Elizabeth. Both of them were upright and devout, blamelessly observing all the commandments and ordinances of the Lord. But they had no children, for Elizabeth was barren, and both were well on in years.

Once, when it was the turn of his division and he was there to take part in divine service, it fell to his lot to enter the sanctuary of the Lord and offer the incense. There appeared to him an angel of the Lord and said to him, 'Your wife Elizabeth will bear you a son, and you shall name him John. He will be great in the eyes of the Lord. From his very birth he will be filled with the Holy Spirit, and he will bring back many Israelites to the Lord their God. He will go before him as forerunner, possessed by the spirit and power of Elijah, to prepare a people that shall be fit for the Lord.'

Now the time came for Elizabeth's child to be born, and she gave birth to a son. When her neighbours and relatives heard what great favour the Lord had shown her, they were as delighted as she was. Then on the eighth day they came to circumcise the child; and they were going to name him Zechariah after his father. But his mother spoke up and said, 'No! he is to be called John.' They inquired of his father what he would like him to be called. He asked for a writing-tablet and wrote down, 'His name is John.' Immediately his lips and tongue were freed and he began to speak, praising God. All the neighbours were struck with awe, and everywhere in the uplands of Judaea the whole story became common talk. All who heard it were deeply impressed and said, 'What will this child become?' And Zechariah his father was filled with the Holy Spirit and uttered this prophecy: 'Praise to the God of Israel . . .'

As the child grew up he became strong in spirit; he lived out in the wilds until the day when he appeared publicly before Israel. From Luke 1.

BENEDICTUS

Praise to the God of Israel!
For he has turned to his people, saved them and set them free,
and has raised up a deliverer of victorious power
from the house of his servant David.
So he promised: age after age he proclaimed
by the lips of his holy prophets,
that he would deliver us from our enemies,
out of the hands of all who hate us;
that he would deal mercifully with our fathers,
calling to mind his solemn covenant.
Such was the oath he swore to our father Abraham,
to rescue us from enemy hands,
and grant us, free from fear, to worship him
with a holy worship, with uprightness of heart,
in his presence, our whole life long.
And you, my child, you shall be called Prophet of the Highest,
for you will be the Lord's forerunner, to prepare his way
and lead his people to salvation through knowledge of him,
by the forgiveness of their sins:
for in the tender compassion of our God
the morning sun from heaven will rise upon us,
to shine on those who live in darkness, under the cloud of death,
and to guide our feet into the way of peace.

Benedictus

(Authorized Version)

Blessed be the Lord God of Israel: for he hath visited and redeemed his people,
And hath raised up a horn of salvation for us in the house of his servant David;
As he spake by the mouth of his holy prophets, which have been since the world began:
That we should be saved from our enemies, and from the hand of all that hate us;
To perform the mercy promised to our fathers, and to remember his holy covenant;
The oath which he sware to our father Abraham,
That he would grant unto us, that we, being delivered out of the hand of our enemies, might serve him without fear,
In holiness and righteousness before him, all the days of our life.
And thou, child, shalt be called the prophet of the Highest: for thou shalt go before the face of the Lord to prepare his ways;
To give knowledge of salvation unto his people by the remission of their sins,
Through the tender mercy of our God; whereby the dayspring from on high hath visited us,
To give light to them that sit in darkness and in the shadow of death, to guide our feet into the way of peace.

Luke 1: 68–79.

THE BIRTHPLACE OF JOHN THE BAPTIST: A CALL TO US

'What think ye this babe will yet be?' the neighbours must have asked when he was born. And what did he become? He who grew up here in Ein Kerem, to a life whose greatness lay in that he was content to be nothing but the foreshadowing of a Greater. Here God prepared him whose work later was not for his own satisfaction nor brought his own message nor made his own name known, but was that of being but a Voice. Here God must have made him ready to live, not for himself but only for Him who filled his whole soul, for Jesus, the coming Messiah. With his bodily growth there grew the eager desire to be the forerunner of the One.

The dearest wish of John the Baptist was to 'decrease' before His Lord Who had come down from Heaven to earth. And so he, who did not seek the praise of men and counted himself unworthy to unloose the latchet of the Lord's shoes, rejoiced as the number of his disciples decreased whilst those of Jesus increased. Who can know how dearly John the Baptist must have loved Jesus? His whole life, all his words and all his deeds were devoted to making plain before his race the way of Jesus. Jesus should find a people made ready by His forerunner to lay their hearts at His feet. It was this devoted love which made John the Baptist the true forerunner.

But how did he attain to this self-forgetting love? What made him so powerful a preacher of repentance, whose words the people could not ignore? Surely this, that already before Jesus came to him on the bank of Jordan he had allowed the Holy Ghost to lead him to his own repentance. For the Holy Ghost had shown him Jesus as He 'Whose fan is in his hand, and he will throughly purge his floor, will gather the wheat into his garner, but the chaff he will burn with fire unquenchable' (Luke 3: 17). It was this which led him to take Jesus for his Lord and his Judge.

John the Baptist was the first who turned to repentance and

let his pride be brought low. He spent many years in the wilderness before he came forth to preach repentance (Luke 1: 80). He did not wear the garb of repentance for outward impression, but being in earnest he practised it daily (Matt. 3: 4). This was the root from whence sprang his power as a preacher and as one who made ready the way. John the Baptist had lived out himself the repentance to which he called others. Brought low under the judgment of Jesus he was prepared to be the herald of the coming Lord. He was no longer himself, only a Voice; but a voice full of power, heard by thousands (John 1: 6–8). Thus were fulfilled the words of the prophet: 'The voice of him that crieth in the wilderness, Prepare ye the way of the Lord, make straight in the desert a highway for our God' (Isa. 40: 3).

John the Baptist, who prepared the First Coming of Christ, still speaks to us, now when the Second Coming seems to be near. To-day, on the threshold of a new age of salvation, 'the ends of the earth,' Jesus again waits for those who will be ready to prepare the way, who, like John the Baptist, devote themselves, in love to Jesus, to removing the boulders of sin from the hearts of the old or the new Israel; those ready to be the ones in whom judgment shall begin; those with power to call to repentance because they live daily in the spirit of repentance, and who seek to be nothing. Only these will be His true messengers. Jesus seeks forerunners ready for His coming. He is standing at the door, as the One Who is coming. But He cannot come if the way is not ready. Shall not we, here in the footsteps of John the Baptist, hearken to the call of Jesus? Will we not become forerunners who allow their consuming love for Him to shine out, their love for their Bridegroom and King, that many hearts may be enkindled to a like love.

To be a Forerunner of Jesus Means

To desire eagerly to prepare many souls for His coming, to remove all stones of sin out of one's heart so that they may be removed also from the hearts of others.

To seek not one's own honour and glory, but that the mighty may be brought low for the coming of Jesus, that He may find the paths made straight.

To be ready to remain in the shade, so that the light of God may shine forth.

PRAYER

We give Thee thanks for the lowliness of heart that did suffer Thy coming to be prepared by a human forerunner who made the rough places plain amongst Thy people. Here will we give thanks to Thee that John the Baptist was such a forerunner for Thee. Here we will remember Thy words concerning Thy Second Coming in glory, when the Bride shall be made ready. Let us watch, that we may know how near the midnight hour already is, the hour of Thy return. Let us not be deaf to Thy call, now, when Thou seekest those who will prepare Thy way before Thee. Help us to take the way that John the Baptist took, the way of daily repentance, that we may have power to turn others to Thee. Kindle in us evermore the same love that John the Baptist had for Thee. AMEN.

HYMN

Let me prepare the way Thou shalt go,
Let me remove ev'ry stone from Thy path
That for Thy coming the way may be straight.

Let me prepare the way Thou shalt go,
That Thou may'st soon come to us here below
And be Thy children's rejoicing in woe.

Let me be first in repentance to bow
Then let me lead many others to Thee,
That Thou as King may'st proclaimèd be.

Let me but follow the way Thou dost go,
Let me make smooth the rough places below,
That the day of rejoicing may dawn here below.

CHAPTER XVIII

EMMAUS

NOW let us go to Emmaus. Two places in particular claim a visit as the Emmaus of the Bible: El-Qubeibeh and Amwas: whilst a third place also claims a traditional connection, Abu Ghosh.

El-Qubeibeh lies about 12 miles from Jerusalem; leaving Old Jerusalem by the Damascus Gate we go northwards along the road to Nablūs. The last houses are already in the Judæan hill-country. Our driver, who is a Christian, describes the district through which we are passing, and we now truly begin to appreciate what it is like to be at home in Bible Lands. Geography, history, and religion are inseparably connected here. On the left our driver points out Mount Mizpeh rising from the plain, where Samuel once gathered together the children of Israel to judge them (1 Sam. 7: 5 and 16; 10: 17). The hill is now called Nebi Samwil by the Arabs, and they venerate Samuel's grave here. About 5 miles farther on we come to the slopes of Saul's Gibeah (1 Sam. 10: 26), from which a road goes off to Er-Rām (Rama), the home of the prophet Samuel (1 Sam. 1: 19; 7: 17), and immediately after, to the left, is the road to El-Qubeibeh via Biddu.

We pass stony fields, generally bordered by low dry-stone walls, and we can look across the Judæan hills. Here there are vineyards, with watch-towers of unhewn stone, such as Jesus mentioned in Matt. 21: 33. The villages are surrounded by cultivated fields, and for a few weeks in the year a bright carpet of flowers covers the otherwise dry spaces. The road encircles the high-lying Jib (Gibeon, of Joshua 9), which still has a fortress-like appearance. We pass through Biddu, surrounded by fruit-trees and on rising ground. Leaving Biddu, we turn sharp right to reach El-Qubeibeh. With its trees it resembles an oasis between the bare hills, and from it we have a wide view over the hill-country.

At the entrance to the village, we pass the property of the Sisters of St. Charles Borromeo and then, farther on, we come to the entrance of the Franciscan settlement on the right. The courtyard is paved, and surrounded by conifers, and has an inviting appearance. Entering the church we are shown the foundations of the so-called House of Cleopas, in the left aisle. Later we shall see the still considerable remains of the wide Roman road behind the church .

The church is open all day.

Amwas lies about 18 or 19 miles north-west of Jerusalem, close to the frontier. We reach it to begin with by taking the road to Nablūs as far as El-Bire–Ramallah. El-Bire is the Beeroth of the Bible (Joshua 9: 17) and the first stopping-place of Jerusalem pilgrims returning to Galilee, where, according to tradition, Mary and Joseph first missed the 12-year-old Jesus (Luke 2 : 44). Then the road forks left to Amwas, where we find only ruins, the remains of an ancient church and behind these an empty monastic building, guarded by one monk. Nearby is the Trappist monastery, Latrun, where every visitor is served with a meal, in memory of the supper at Emmaus.

Abu Ghosh, west of New Jerusalem, with a fine Crusader church and a spring in its crypt, is reached by the road to Tel-Aviv, about 12 miles farther on. It is not far from the ancient biblical site of Kirjath-Jearim (1 Sam. 7 : 1).

The Historical Aspect

It is about eight miles as the crow flies from Jerusalem to El-Qubeibeh. That would be the three-score furlongs mentioned by Luke the Evangelist as the distance traversed by the two Emmaus disciples. Excavations have shown that this was an inhabited place in pre-Christian times. But is it really the biblical Emmaus? When the Crusaders attempted to identify Emmaus, El-Qubeibeh was preferred to Amwas because the distance from Jerusalem was more in keeping with St. Luke's report. From the thirteenth century onwards the pilgrim-way from Akko to Jerusalem was via Ramle and El-Qubeibeh.

In the twelfth century the Canons of the Holy Sepulchre built a monastery, with a church and a fort, at El-Qubeibeh. This was said to have been built on earlier foundations, but this has not been verified. During the following centuries this Crusader-church underwent destruction, as did so many others. About 1850 the Franciscans became interested in the ruins, and in 1861 they acquired the land as a gift, and in 1900 erected the present church over the remains of the ancient one.

During the restoration of the church the ruins of a house were discovered in the left aisle. It is now called the House of Cleopas, which Jesus probably entered with His disciples, and it is regarded as the special sanctuary of the Breaking of Bread. North of the church a Roman road, dating from Jesus' day, and considerable ruins of the houses of an ancient settlement were excavated. These remains show that this settlement must have been an important trading-place.

The other place commemorating Emmaus, Amwas, keeps to the biblical name in its Arabic form, and contains tepid springs, in keeping with the meaning of the Hebrew word from which Emmaus comes. But even in a straight line the distance is 23 kilometres (about 15 miles) and thus much more than three-score furlongs from Jerusalem. At the time when St. Luke wrote Amwas was still a village, which later developed into a district-centre, known as Nikopolis.

The historian Eusebius, in 330, and Jerome, in 400, refer to Emmaus-Nikopolis as the home of Cleopas. There was only one place in Judæa bearing the name of Emmaus, namely Nikopolis-Amwas. Therefore tradition, until the time of the Crusades, regarded it as the place where the risen Christ appeared to the two disciples. This memory was never quite lost. The discrepancy of the distance from Jerusalem was explained by copyists' mistakes in later versions.

The ancient tradition of Amwas was verified by excavations in 1875 and 1924–30. These revealed the remains of a large, three-aisled basilica which had been erected on the site of a late-Roman villa. It is not quite clear whether this dates from the third century or only from the sixth, nor whether the villa and later the church indicated the House of Cleopas. During the seventh century the basilica was destroyed, re-built, and transformed into a mosque. The Crusaders built a smaller church on the same spot, and this was also destroyed.

From the Holy Bible

That same day two of the disciples were on their way to a village called Emmaus, which lay about seven miles from Jerusalem, and they were talking together about all these happenings. As they talked and discussed it with one another, Jesus himself came up and walked along with them; but something held their eyes from seeing who it was. He asked them, 'What is it that you are debating as you walk?' 'All about Jesus of Nazareth,' they replied, 'a prophet powerful in speech and action before God and the whole people; how our chief priests and rulers handed him over to be sentenced to death, and crucified him. But we had hoped that he was the man to liberate Israel.'

'How slow you are!' he answered. 'How unready to believe all that the prophets said! Was the Messiah not bound to suffer thus before entering upon his glory?' Then he began with Moses and all the prophets, and explained to them the passages which referred to himself in every part of the scriptures.

And when he had sat down with them at table, he took bread and said the blessing; he broke the bread, and offered it to them. Then their eyes were opened, and they recognized him. They said to one another, 'Did we not feel our hearts on fire as he talked with us on the road and explained the scriptures to us?'

From Luke 24: 13–32.

Emmaus—A Call to Us

Emmaus, the site which speaks of Easter, is not as well-known as the Mount of Olives, Gethsemane or Bethany. But every heart which is enkindled by Jesus, as He once warmed those of His disciples, knows it. Emmaus speaks of sorrow being turned into joy, of men finding again the Lord they had thought to be lost: Him Whom they had buried in their hearts, regarding themselves as deceived by His message. The message of Emmaus is that Joy, not Sorrow, is final, for the disciples found their Lord again as the Living One. It tells of the fulfilling of Jesus' words, 'I will not leave you comfortless: I will come to you' (John 14: 18); and 'a little while and ye shall see me. Your sorrow shall be turned into joy' (John 16: 16 and 20).

Jesus met the discouraged disciples on the road leading from Jerusalem, where He had been crucified, to Emmaus. They had thought of Him as being in the tomb. Now they were allowed to walk the long road in His company and in the end to recognize Him. So Emmaus reminds us that Jesus comes to those who have buried their hopes, who have not been able to comprehend their God in the darkest hour. He seeks out such, He hears their sighs, He shares their grief. He overhears their reasonings as they pass along the road, the thoughts which have been exercising their minds ever since the crucifixion, 'Why did the Son of God have to die? Why was He taken away from them? Who had announced the Kingdom of God more definitely than any before? Who brought it nigh by wondrous deeds and signs, so that the sick were cured, demons were driven out, and the dead raised to life again? Why could He not establish His kingdom and bring the reign of peace and righteousness and joy to this devastated world, full of hatred and war, sickness, death, and sorrow?'

Emmaus tells us, 'He, Who is the answer to all your questionings, is here. He stands beside thee and will bring light into thy darkness, for He is love, and has compassion on thee and cannot endure to see thee in torment with thy thoughts. Jesus, Who once drew near to disciples so heavy-laden with their griefs, will still draw near to us and has an Emmaus ready for us, a time of meeting, a time of replies. This time will come to us, as it came to the disciples in their darkest hour.'

In these Emmaus-times Jesus says to His own, 'O fools and slow of heart to believe! When sorrow and bewilderment come to you, you think all is at an end and that God's ways are beyond your understanding. Why will ye not believe that death will prove a fresh beginning and a new life, that sorrow will be turned into joy, and tears into laughter?' Whilst He still walked this earth, He said this again and again, and His words are everlasting and still true to-day, for Jesus Himself is the witness that death will bring forth life, and suffering and dying become a mighty victory. By the way of sorrow He became the Risen Conqueror, beneath Whose feet all things shall finally lie, when His work shall be accomplished on His Return.

At Emmaus the hearts of both disciples began to burn and when Jesus began to teach, when He revealed Himself, and does this still to-day, what hearts will not burn! We too may experience what they did.

He, the Everlasting, lies concealed under all events. He 'thinks towards us thoughts of peace and not of evil, to give us an expected end' (Jer. 29: 11). As once with His disciples, so to-day He has fellowship with us in the breaking of bread, in which He gives Himself as the precious, blessed sacrifice. He gives us the deepest communion with Himself and makes plain that He has the power to forgive sins because He bore the Cross. He has the power to give us the Bread of Life, which will make of us 'a new creation,' because He Himself enters into us. He makes a new Covenant with us, so that no ill can separate us from Him and His Love—neither trouble nor fear nor danger, not even death. For we are to be united with Him for ever. And so, if we truly encounter Jesus here on earth—each in his own way—as those disciples met Him on the Emmaus road, and if our hearts should burn as did theirs, then truly we shall see Him once and for all as He really is and our hearts will be set on fire in a way that no human word can describe.

The supper of Communion, as the Lord celebrated it with His disciples in the Holy Land, and still celebrates it throughout the world with His own, will at length end in the Eternal Emmaus, when we shall celebrate the marriage-supper of the Lamb in the heavenly halls with joy and singing. Then shall we truly know that all the ways of God lead to glory, a glory far exceeding the sum of the sorrow through which these present ways lead us (Rom. 8 : 18).

Prayer in Emmaus

Dear Lord Jesus,
we give thanks to Thee that Thou hast shown forth in this place that Thou in Thy Love dost come especially to those whose hearts are filled with doubts and questionings. I too come to Thee with unanswered questions and temptations, when I cannot understand Thee, Thy dealings and Thy ways. Deepen my trust in Thee as I ponder the love with which Thou didst join Thyself to the disciples on the road to Emmaus and didst explain to them all their difficulties. I give thanks to Thee that I may know

beforehand that Thou wilt explain my difficulties too. I cast myself down at Thy feet, acknowledging the loving purpose with which Thou didst reproach the foolishness of Thy disciples at Emmaus, and must so often do with me.

Let me take to myself Thy words to the disciples as an answer for my questionings, so that the way of sorrows, if I accept it, may lead to glory, not only for Thee but also for me. Thanks be to Thee that this acceptance of the way of sorrow will resolve all my doubts and bring Thy loving presence nigh. AMEN.

EMMAUS-QUESTIONS, EMMAUS-ANSWERS

I cannot see the way, so dark is the night.
 Only believe, and the night will be light.
My hopes are all shattered, and all is in vain.
 Wait but a short while, the answer is plain.
In vain have I trusted, I am but betrayed.
 God never forsakes Thee, be thou not dismayed.
I may hope neither purpose nor promise to see;
 But believe, O believe, that the glory will be.
My heart it is drowned in sorrow and grief.
 Your tears will be laughter and sorrow relief.
I can never, ah never, comprehend all God's ways.
 But trust in Thy Father, Whose help never fails.

Emmaus—morning has come,
Emmaus—care has gone home,
Emmaus—the Lord He is with us,
Emmaus—our hearts do burn,
Emmaus—our grief has gone,
Jesus, Jesus, is with us
to celebrate the feast of love.

EMMAUS

✝

From whence art Thou coming, O Lord Jesús Christ,
O Thou that art risen from death?
Where is Thy dwelling, O dearest Lord,
Who is there now for Thee careth?

'I need not a roof-tree, have no need of gold,
Nor any to housekeep for Me.
Judas no longer is keeping the purse.
Only angels are now serving Me.'

O where art Thou going, dear Lord Jesus Christ?
Thou that art risen from death?
Is not the Father awaiting Thee now?
Till Thou wilt go to His hearth?

'Love, O disciples, to thy side doth Me draw
Because ye did grieve Me so sore,
But when I have turned all your grief into joy
Then will I go home once more;

'Home to My Father, My dearest and best,
And then all my pain will be o'er,
Then at length I shall sit at His side,
There where I ever was longing to be
During thirty-three years on earth's floor.'

✝

HYMN

Our hearts did they not burn
  As we saw Him?
As He Himself drew near
  Our grief grew dim.

The darkness turned to light
  In this bless'd place
As we then heard from Him
  His word of Grace.

No questions any more,
  And no more pain,
When He His Heart revealed
  And we saw plain.

The way, He proves, must be
  By Sorrow's path;
To rise again will be
  Death's aftermath.

What glory we shall see,
  As through the night
Of death or pain we pass
  And then see light.

Our hearts indeed did burn
  To see Him there;
To share with Him our board
  And know His care.

CHAPTER XIX

JACOB'S WELL

THE road to Nablūs, leading northwards from the Damascus Gate in Old Jerusalem, is already known to us in part from our journey to Amwas. But we follow it still farther northwards, to Samaria, if we are visiting Jacob's well at Sichem. We shall not want to miss the place where Jesus taught the Samaritan woman the truth and thus set her free—even though it lies more than 40 miles from Jerusalem. The journey is well worth while, for it takes us through a district rich in historical memories. Along the road, or only a short way from it, lie Anata (Anathoth, Jer. 1), Gabaath (Gibea, 1 Sam. 10: 26; 15: 34), and a little farther on, Nebi Samwil (Mizpeh, 1 Sam. 7: 6; 10: 17; 1 Macc. 3: 46), Er-Rām (Ramah, 1 Sam. 1: 19; 7: 17; 15: 34), El-Bire (Beeroth, Joshua 9: 17 and, according to tradition, Luke 2: 44), Betin (Bethel, Gen. 12: 8; 13: 3; 28: 19; Judges 1: 22; 20: 26; 2 Kings 2: 2 and 23), and Seilun (Shiloh, 1 Sam. 1: 3; 1: 24; 4: 4).

All these places remind us of events in the history of God's dealing with His people, events inseparably connected with them. And we realize that we can follow the footsteps not only of Abraham, who passed here from north to south (Gen. 12: 6–9) but also those of our Lord as He passed to and fro between Galilee and Jerusalem.

It is a strange landscape which surrounds this journey: many ranges of hills, some of them rocky and bare, some clothed with olive-trees; and in the valleys between, especially in the neighbourhood of the villages, dark brown fields, which are deep green in spring, and whose size increases as we approach smiling Samaria. The fields and the road are bordered by the typical low dry-stone walls.

Now we approach the present-day village of Balata, not far

from the ruins of Sichem, on whose eastern border lies Jacob's well, south of Askar, formerly Sichar. A fruitful plain is here spread out, wreathed by the hills of Samaria. To the west rise two characteristic mountains: Gerizim, thickly clothed with trees, and Ebal, which is arid and stony. In the hollow between them lies Nablūs. Along the road to it we pass by an encampment of refugees, and there, to the right, down in the valley, the parcel of ground of Jacob's well, with its unfinished church surrounded by cypress trees. Just past the camp, the road to Amman forks sharply away from the Nablūs road which curves towards Balata. About 80 yards along the Amman road we come to the entrance to Jacob's well. A Greek Orthodox monk leads us from the choir of the unfinished church down to the crypt, where we can stand by the rim of that same well at which Jesus once rested (see Plate 13).

The Historical Aspect

The genuineness of this well of Jacob by the ruins of the ancient Sichem has never been in doubt. It is the only draw-well in this historically important district, and the situation, at an important road-junction, is in keeping with the description in St. John's Gospel. For, during His itinerant progress from Judæa to Galilee through Samaria, Jesus would have passed here. St. John adds that the well lay near 'the parcel of ground that Jacob gave to his son Joseph.' This 'parcel of ground' is still to-day marked out by the tomb of Joseph. The stone well-head is described by experts as Canaanite work of the eighteenth century B.C., i.e. from the time of Jacob, as the Samaritan woman told Jesus (John 4: 12). She said that the well was deep, and that too is still true: it is more than 110 feet deep. What cannot be ascertained is whether or not it is fed by a spring.

From very early times already Christians commemorated Jesus' conversation with the woman of Samaria here. The Bordeaux pilgrim found a place of baptism here in about 333, to which the water of the well was conducted. And *circa* 380 there was already a church built over the well: Jerome mentions it about 400. This church was destroyed by the Samaritans during the insurrection of 529, but re-built later, though the Crusaders found everything in ruins again. In the twelfth century they built a church of three aisles over the well, and that perished after the Crusaders' departure. Only the crypt, containing the well, remained. During the latter half of the eighteenth century the Greek Orthodox church acquired the piece of land from the Balata commune, and it was decided to re-build the church after the plan of the Crusader one. But the First World War stopped the building operations, when only the crypt and the surrounding walls had been restored, and these have not yet been resumed.

FROM THE HOLY BIBLE

To mount Gerizim and mount Ebal between which the Jacob's well is situated : Behold, I set before you this day a blessing and a curse; A blessing, if ye obey the commandments of the Lord your God, which I command you this day: And a curse, if ye will not obey the commandments of the Lord your God, but turn aside out of the way which I command you this day, to go after other gods, which ye have not known. And it shall come to pass, when the Lord thy God hath brought thee in unto the land whither thou goest to possess it, that thou shalt put the blessing upon mount Gerizim, and the curse upon mount Ebal.

Deut. 11 : 26–9.

Jesus had to pass through Samaria, and on his way came to a Samaritan town called Sychar, near the plot of ground which Jacob gave to his son Joseph and the spring called Jacob's well. Jesus, tired after his journey, sat down by the well. Meanwhile a Samaritan woman came to draw water. Jesus said to her, 'Give me a drink.' The Samaritan woman said, 'What! You, a Jew, ask a drink of me, a Samaritan woman?' Jesus answered her, 'If only you knew what God gives, and who it is that is asking you for a drink, you would have asked him and he would have given you living water.' 'Sir,' said the woman, 'give me that water.' And Jesus said to her, 'Go home, call your husband and come back.' She answered, 'I have no husband.' 'You are right,' said Jesus, 'in saying that you have no husband, for, although you have had five husbands, the man with whom you are now living is not your husband; you told me the truth there.'

The woman put down her water-jar and went away to the town, where she said to the people, 'Come and see a man who has told me everything I ever did. Could this be the Messiah?'

From John 4.

Jacob's Well—A Call to Us

When Jesus was obliged to leave Judæa because of the plottings of the Pharisees, and returned to Galilee, He 'must needs go through Samaria,' as St. John tells us. There may have been obvious reasons why Jesus went through Samaria, though there were other ways by which the Jews could avoid it. But He must also have had inner reasons for taking this route. It would hardly be by chance that He sat down to rest at Jacob's well, between the mountains Ebal and Gerizim, where such great and solemn events in the history of His people had taken place.

The patriarch Abraham had already rested in Sichem (Gen. 12: 6ff.). Here God appeared to him and promised to give this land unto his seed, and Abraham built an altar to the Lord there. And now there sat here, perhaps on the self-same spot, He, of the seed of Abraham, in Whom was fulfilled the promise made to Abraham in the dimness of faith alone. Jesus, resting by the well, was the witness and the proof that God is true, that His promises are 'Yea' and 'Amen' (2 Cor. 1: 20).

Here Jacob had built an altar to the Lord, had 'bought a parcel of a field' (Gen. 33: 18ff.) and had given it to Joseph. Under Joshua's rule the bones of Joseph were brought back to Canaan from Egypt, and buried in this place (Exod. 13: 19; Joshua 24: 32). After the promises which God had given to Abraham, Isaac, and Jacob, the children of Israel had gone over Jordan back to this country, for God had given it unto them for their possession. And here, between the mountains Gerizim and Ebal, as they entered the Promised Land, the Law had been read to them again, with the covenant that blessing or curse would follow, according as to whether they were obedient or not. Then also God had shown Himself to be a God of Truth. Because of their constant disobedience right through the centuries, Israel and Judah had been led into captivity in Babylon.

Perhaps, as Jesus sat here by the well, He beheld in spirit the history of His people, the history of salvation, which He, in union with the Father and the Holy Ghost, had thought out and had brought to pass. Gerizim and Ebal proclaimed that God is the Holy One of Israel, a God that hateth sin. He is the God of Truth Who stands by His condemnation and His blessing. And Jesus had come to reveal and to glorify this God amongst His people.

As Jesus sat by the well, wearied by His journey in the heat, there came to Him the woman of Samaria. Could their conversation be of anything else than of the Truth? The woman was a sinner and, like all sinners, blind to sin and living in untruth, without thinking of the God of Truth, Who had sent judgment upon sinners. She probably no longer gave any thought to her sins but said to herself: God has given us our instincts so that we may follow them. And so she lived in self-deception, as we do. She may have blamed the circumstances which led her into this kind of life and found excuses for herself, as we do. And so a layer of blindness covered her deeds.

But now she stood before Him Who is Truth, to Whom all sin is known; for the light pierces the darkness and shows up all that is sick and ugly and dark and evil. Thus the well cannot but be the well of truth. At first it seemed to be only a matter of water to drink, by which He humbly sought to open her heart. And then it is she who begs for water, and He gives to her the water of life, namely, the truth about herself, that makes her free, this word of truth which, if we will receive it, raises the dead to life again. For falsehood covers up our sins and turns us into living corpses, leading us into the jaws of Hell, where Satan then causes us to taste the pains of a second death. Only the Truth of our Lord Jesus frees us and strengthens us enough by His pardon so that we may not perish but have new life.

As Jesus reveals to this woman, in the light of truth, all her life, with its sin, it is made plain that in spite of her blindness she is 'of the truth' for she is willing to hear the truth. Yea, she is willing not only to hear, but she has the courage to return to the 'city' to tell the men who know 'all things that she ever did,' and to bring them to Jesus who told her the truth about her life. She thus confessed her sin, and her faith in Him. Thus she received drink from the Fountain of Truth and the Water of

Life. Her eyes were opened and she knew what many of her people who met Jesus daily never learnt.

Here is the Messiah, the Son of God, Who reveals sins in order to forgive them and to make of sinners new creations. Whosoever has eyes washed in truth, and has the courage to confess sins, can see the Messiah as the Lord and Saviour with a new clarity. He can come home to the Saviour, released from sin, to become the true worshipper, because the truth which God speaks in love maketh free and leads us into the light.

Talk with Jesus at Jacob's Well To-day

Jesus, my Lord, I am blind—I cannot see myself as Thou dost. Wash mine eyes that they may see in Thy light, and that I may know the truth about myself.

> I am come as the Light of the world, that the blind may receive their sight. If thou wilt know that thou art blind and wilt come to Me, how should I do other than give thee sight?

Jesus, I fear that I may not be able to bear it, if I have to gaze into the abyss of my sin.

> Be of good cheer. If I make thee to see, thou wilt see not only thy sin but also God. Thou wilt see into His heart and thy soul will recover and thou wilt know that God's heart is Love, and Mercy, and Forgiveness.

Then, do Thou give me this insight, whatever it cost, that my soul may be healed, and that I may know Thee, my Lord and my God, as Thou art, and may learn to love Thee as never before.

> Whoso asketh, receiveth. Be it unto thee according to thy faith.

†

To hear the truth about our sins does cause us pain—for it makes us humble and keeps us small.

But it is on such truth alone that God's image in us may be established.

†

Mirror of Truth

The mirror of truth is Jesus.

Gaze into this mirror, and thou wilt see thyself as thou art.

Jesus, though He was God, did nothing of Himself, but only in obedience to and dependence on the Father did He do that which the Father willed.—And thou?

Jesus came, not to be lord, but a servant.—And thou?

Jesus did good unto all men.—And thou?

Jesus had compassion on His people, on all in need.—And thou?

Jesus loves His own, who disappointed Him to the very end. —And thou?

Jesus went into the house of His enemies, the Pharisees, and blessed them.—And thou?

Jesus endured all the wrongs of His Passion in silence.—And thou?

Jesus when He was reviled, reviled not again.—And thou?

Jesus endured without complaint.—And thou?

Jesus bore His Cross, humbly bending under the load.—And thou?

Jesus lived only in order to glorify the Father.—And thou?

Make me shed tears over all my sins
Which seem to thrive as each day begins
In all I think and do and say;
Open my eyes, by Thy grace, to see
What the Almighty wants me to be
Learning the truth with each new day.

Give me the grace, that this I may say
During this journey along life's way,
I alone am guilty of sin.
Give me the grace to bend myself low
Both before God or men here below
Even as Thou didst, O Lord Jesus Christ.

Grant that if I o'er my sin complain,
And in the midst of suffering pain
I cannot but ever lowly speak,
Lord let me have from Thy holy hands
All I deserve after Thy commands
Since my sin makes me frail and weak.

Hymn

O well of Truth, O fount of Life,
Jesus calls us to-day.
He tells us the truth
But, Oh, who will hearken
And take Grace eternal?
Life everlasting will be his reward.

Jesus is living, to-day as before,
By Jacob's well,
In spirit He's near,
He would give us to drink
From a full of life stream
To show us clearly the Truth of His word.

O let us hear then
Words that are true words
Which will enlighten us
Whatever we do.
Water of Life, is this
Which can bring healing
To those whose opened eyes can now Truth see.

O Truth, Thou mirror,
In which reflected
We know and see ourselves
As men full of shame.
Do Thou, O Jesus, Lord,
Provide that clear mirror
Which can reveal for us just what we be.

JACOB'S WELL

We come to Thee, Lord,
As blind from our birth,
O make us to see, for Truth maketh free!
That thus we may know
How Thine eye doth watch o'er us
To see us bend low at Thy judgment throne.

O fountain of Truth,
O life without end,
The searching for Thee is better than gold,
We offer thanksgiving
That Thou Lord dost give to us
Already on earth Thy Truth to enjoy.

O well of Truth, O fount of Life
Jesus calls us to-day.
He tells us the truth.
But, Oh, who will hearken
And take Grace eternal?
Life everlasting will be his reward.

CHAPTER XX

NAZARETH

LEAVING Jerusalem and Judaea behind us, we take the way into Galilee, that other stage of the life and work of Jesus. We go towards the southern hills of Galilee, to Nazareth, the scene of His childhood, where He spent the largest part of His earthly life. When we approach it from the south via Afula and the plain of Jezreel, we see the first hills, and soon we catch sight of the town spread out in front of us. It lies in a wide valley, climbing its slopes .

Nazareth (Hebrew: Nazrat: Arabic: el-Nasirah) to-day is a town of about 30,000 inhabitants, of whom two-thirds are Arabic Christians or members of the different Religious Orders, plus a few thousand Muslims. The continual increase of the population settles in the new Jewish quarter on the slopes towards Kfar Kana. The old town is typically oriental, with narrow winding streets and innumerable steps, tiny courtyards, flat roofs, open-fronted shops, and the chattering of the market In the centre are the grounds of the Franciscan convent which is easily visible because it lies somewhat higher: here are the cave of the Annunciation and the church of St. Joseph.

The rising Casa-Nova-Street leads off to the left from the main road coming from Haifa or Afula. A little more than 100 yards along it we find the entrance to the Franciscan grounds, on the right. We pass through the garden to the convent buildings. To the right of the main entrance steps lead down to the cave of the Annunciation. Passing through the Chapel of the Angel we reach that of the Annunciation, with its original cave-dwelling roof. A large cathedral is in course of erection above this cave, planned to become the largest church in the Middle East. All is given over to the turmoil of building, yet we can perceive a little of the secret of that incomparable hour. A marble tablet in front of the altar bears words: 'Verbum caro hic factum est'—here the Word was made flesh. Next we go to the church of St. Joseph, which lies on the opposite side, to the left of the convent. It is built over a wide cave said to be the Holy Family's dwelling. The lower church is revered by many as the workshop of Joseph.

Recently other cave-dwellings of that time have been found in this neighbourhood. We are directed to the school of the 'Dames de Nazareth,' lying on the other side of Casa-Nova-Street, and reached by a side-road. The sisters will kindly lead us down to the extensive excavations beneath their building where, beside ancient tombs and cave-dwellings dating back to Jesus' day, we find the remains of a Byzantine church. The final results of the work on the excavations are not yet known, but they already reveal, as do those above the Annunciation cave, the character of Nazareth at the time of Jesus.

From Casa-Nova-Street we can look up the rising Bazaar Street—called 'schuk'—to the near-by towers of the Greek Catholic parish church. A modest room beside this commemorates the synagogue in which Jesus taught. To visit this sight we go a short way along the Bazaar street, take the first turning on the left and then the one to the right. Through an iron door we reach the fore-court of the church of the synagogue.

We should also visit Mary's well, lying at a busy cross-road and on the edge of the turn, towards Tiberias. Already from afar we can make it out, by the group of trees and by the mortared vault above it. This well is at the end of a pipe-line from the actual spring, which was probably used in Jesus' day, about forty yards away, in the crypt of the Greek Orthodox church of St. Gabriel. This we reach by a road to the left of the well.

It is not only the dedicated sites of Nazareth which remind us of Jesus. Everything speaks of Him, especially the surrounding hills where He must have spent many hours of prayer. In spring-time the surroundings of Nazareth are indescribably lovely, with flower filled meadows in between the rocks and the shepherds' caves. The silence of these hills is only occasionally broken by the sound of a distant shepherd's pipe or the bleating of a passing flock. Here we can feel very close to 'Jesus of Nazareth.'

All the sites are open during the hours of daylight.

The Historical Aspect

Nazareth, the place chosen by God for the annunciation of the birth of His Son, and where He grew to manhood, is not mentioned in the Bible before the time of Jesus. It only comes into the picture through the Gospels. Jesus was called 'the Nazarene' by His contemporaries, and since then the name of Nazareth follows Him all over the world. Although we do not know definitely when Nazareth began to be, we can tell from tomb finds that it was an inhabited place at least 200 years before Christ. The spring which still feeds the well on the Tiberias road will have attracted the earliest inhabitants; it has given water from time immemorial, and Mary must often have come here to draw water. Nazareth was destined by its very situation to remain unimportant. It lay off the main road, in a side valley. The stony fields meant poverty, even destitution. In Jesus' day Nazareth was apparently so poor and insignificant a town that the Jewish historian Josephus does not mention it at all, while Sepphoris, about four miles away, was for a long time the seat of Herod, and is regarded by Josephus as being of great importance. It can even be said that Nazareth was not a town at all, for though the Gospels (following the Greek Septuagint version of the Old Testament) use the Greek word for 'town,' the Hebrew words denote only a settlement, whether large or small. We cannot but wonder exactly where the message of the angel came to Mary. Was it really the cave over which a huge church is in course of building? Was this truly the Nazareth of old, where the Virgin had her home when the angel Gabriel came to her? The excavations, which began in 1955 when the old church of the Annunciation was demolished, give strong evidence for it. A number of tombs came to light, but these were not Jewish, for Jewish graves were obliged to be outside an inhabited place, but were the tombs of Crusaders, who had a fondness for being buried near the Holy Places. But there were also found the foundations of many houses dating from Jesus' day, showing that this neighbourhood must have been an inhabited one. These are the remains of dwellings such as are frequently found in the East, built in front of natural caves in the rock. The rear portion of the house would have been the cool, dry rock cave, whilst a front of man-made walls was added to it. It was in such a dwelling probably that Mary had her home when Gabriel appeared to her and gave her the heavenly message. The cave of the Annunciation, as we find it to-day, lies amongst the excavated houses of ancient Nazareth. So the tradition is most probably true.

Though the cave has of late years been accredited by the excavators, its previous history is very varied. When the Romans occupied Nazareth in 67, the Nazareth of the Gospels was destroyed. Only oral tradition continued to indicate the site of the Annunciation. It is known that up till about the year 200, later generations of the female relatives of Mary lived at Nazareth. When Nazareth revived many refugees from Jerusalem settled there, particularly after Hadrian drove the Jews out of the whole of Judaea. By the third century Nazareth was again wholly Jewish and its Christian tradition was interrupted. But the Jews must have handed down the memory of these sights, for even denial has a good memory. Somehow a dark mystery lay over Nazareth, for the Christians avoided it and did not seek for biblical sites there. Was this because this city of Jesus had sought to stone her greatest son and remained obstinately deaf to His message? About 359 it is recorded that the Emperor Constantine ordered Joseph the governor of Tiberias to build Christian churches in the Jewish places in Galilee wherever none had yet been built. Nazareth is specially mentioned because 'no Greek nor Samaritan nor Christian dwelt there, for foreigners were strictly forbidden to settle there.' But we do not know whether the governor did use his authority to build a church here.

So it was only in the fourth century that Jewish Nazareth was gradually opened to the Christians. In 368 comes the first mention of pilgrimage, by St. Paula, the friend of St. Jerome. In 400 there is mention of a church here, and the anonymous pilgrim of Piacenza, who is the first to describe the church of the Annunciation, describes in 570: 'The house of Holy Mary is a basilica.' During the following centuries many a wave of war broke over Nazareth, particularly the Persian invasion of 614. When the Persians were driven out by the Emperor Heraclius in 630, it was especially the Jewish settlements which, like Nazareth, had made common cause with the Persians, which were destroyed. It is not known when the Byzantine basilica was destroyed; its beginnings probably went back to the fifth century and the foundations have now been discovered. The Crusaders built a three-aisled church over it, which was destroyed in 1263, though the cave itself was unharmed. In 1730 the Franciscans, who had settled in Nazareth as far back as 1620, built a small church here. They began preparations for the large new building in 1955.★

The cave's exterior has been altered in many ways during the course of centuries, and its significance has had differing interpretations. At times it was regarded as the house of Joseph and the home of the Holy Family. Later it was held to contain the grave of Joseph and Mary. Still later these ideas were dropped. At the turn of the century the gospel accounts and the early traditions began to be more carefully studied, and this led to the abandonment of the tradition that this had also been the house of Joseph. Now only the mystery of the Annunciation is commemorated here.

★ Which is now completed.

FROM THE HOLY BIBLE

In the sixth month the angel Gabriel was sent from God to a town in Galilee called Nazareth with a message for a girl betrothed to a man named Joseph, a descendant of David; the girl's name was Mary.

The angel went in and said to her, 'Greetings, most favoured one! The Lord is with you.' But she was deeply troubled by what he said and wondered what this greeting might mean.

Then the angel said to her, 'Do not be afraid, Mary, for God has been gracious to you; you shall conceive and bear a son, and you shall give him the name Jesus. He will be great; he will bear the title "Son of the Most High"; the Lord God will give him the throne of his ancestor David, and he will be king over Israel for ever; his reign shall never end.' 'How can this be,' said Mary, 'when I have no husband?' The angel answered, 'The Holy Spirit will come upon you, and the power of the Most High will overshadow you; and for that reason the holy child to be born will be called "Son of God." '

'Here am I,' said Mary. 'I am the Lord's servant; as you have spoken, so be it.' From Luke 1: 26–38.

A CALL TO US

Nazareth—the place which heard the marvellous tidings that an angel had come down from Heaven to deliver a message to a virgin whose name was Mary. Sacred city, in which the Holy Spirit of God Himself overshadowed the virgin so that that which was born of her was the Son of God. Here we are led to ponder on the great things that God hath done and to adore in humility the Divine revelation.

Here, in one of the cave-dwellings, the angel appeared to Mary and said to her, the pure virgin: 'Hail thou that art highly favoured . . . full of grace.' Humbly and in astonishment she replied: 'What manner of salutation is this?'; and full of reverence and awe she bowed herself before this heavenly vision. In humble wonder she heard the incredible message of her election: 'Thou hast found favour with God. The Holy Ghost shall overshadow thee; therefore also that holy thing which shall be born of thee shall be called the Son of God.' Mary, chosen by God! That is the highest possible grace; it means being drawn into the closest connection with God, to be used by Him as His instrument. But she who is chosen must also be made worthy of the choice in the furnace of affliction, and bear the full weight of Him Who is man's pardon. For now a person has to travel with the living God by way of faith, not of sight. Election means going the same ways as the Son of God, whether we run before or follow after—ways of deepest humbling, of shame, of countless griefs, producing fruit meet for God, for the coming of His Kingdom.

Thus every election is an offer which we are free either to accept or to refuse. God puts a question to His child and awaits a reply. The reply He desires is our self-surrender, like that of Abraham, who in obedience took the way marked out for him.

What was Mary's reply? She spoke the simple yet mighty words: 'Be it unto me according to Thy word.' This determined the way she had to go. This way, freely chosen by her that day, was a way of poverty, for she would call her child Him Who was the poorest that ever trod this earth. It was a way of innumerable sufferings: persecution, rejection, flight, homelessness—she had to share all with the Son of Man. It is indeed a hallowed room in which God called a virgin so to surrender herself to Him that He might enter into her and His Holy Ghost overshadow her. Hallowed cave which beheld in Mary full of grace a hallowed person—hallowed because God could possess her wholly, because she made no objection and asked no questions concerning the way she would have to tread, but surrendered and at His command had only the one thought: 'Be it unto me according to Thy word.' May there be here in this cave, in silent prayer, spiritual sons and daughters of Mary who will follow her way and unconditionally reply to God when He calls them: 'Be it unto me according to Thy word and Thy will.'

PRAYER

We give thanks to Thee here, O Father, for the wonderful happening to Mary: that Gabriel announced to her the birth of God's only-begotten Son, to be born of her by the overshadowing of the Holy Ghost. We give Thee thanks for the mysterious election of Mary. In her Thou didst find a soul whose reply to Thy call was an unconditional Yea, because her will was wholly surrendered to Thine, whatever shame and difficulty it might bring. May we with her adore the fact that Thou didst behold the lowliness of Thine handmaiden and wast able to do great things through her.

Receive Thou me that I may be humble as she was, willing to follow the way in unquestioning faith and love. May the surrender of my will make it possible for great things to be done for me and through me, so that even my unimportant life may bring Jesus to the world. AMEN.

If we say 'Yes' to God's will, trusting His love in spite of apparent impossibilities, we shall be instruments of God, following Mary's way.

Mary, chosen from all others
Made most honoured of all mothers,
Given the word by angel high
In the hour that God selected
Thou didst hear, thou wast elected
To bear for us God's only Son.

Mary bowed in adoration
Took as true the words then spoken,
That's God's Counsel should prevail
Because she loved God over all things
She received His will over all things
And allowed it to prevail.

Mary acknowledged God more than her understanding. She consented to follow a way she could not understand. God waits for such followers, who will silence the objections of their reason by the words: 'With God nothing is impossible.'

Hymn

It was a sacred hour
  The angel to Mary came
He brought a word of power
  To bring her glorious fame.

He came from highest heaven
  Down to her lonely room.
The light of God shone round him
  More clear than day of doom.

He greets the blest of women
  With words of angelic cheer.
He brings the words from Heaven
  That make the Virgin fear.

'How shall this be?' she asks him.
  She cannot grasp the grace.
She hears the solemn message
  In light before her face.

Mary the ever-blessed,
  God's mother for to be,
Mother of Son most highest.
  O how can such things be?

She bows her down all lowly
  Before this highest grace.
She gives her will up wholly
  To be nought before God's Face.

And from her lips are sounding
  The words for ever dear:
'Be unto me, the handmaid,
  As God has said so clear.'

The angel leaves her praying,
  Returns to Heaven's throne
With 'Yea' from maiden Mary.
  Now can come down God's Son.

†

Let us here bow low with Mary and give consent to God's way with us.

Thy will I e'er would cherish,
Thy longing ever still.
Naught else my soul desireth.
Thy heart shall have its longing
From souls who ask for nothing
But to do Thy holy will.

Take now within Thy caring
My daily life henceforth
Just as Thy will desireth.
I give myself anew
Unto Thy will. O choose Thou
  What Thou with me wouldst do.

THE CHURCH OF ST. JOSEPH

Nazareth having been the home of Jesus, we naturally ask where the home of the Holy Family may be found, where they lived after the return from Egypt, and where Jesus grew to manhood. But there is no definite tradition. Sometimes it was held to be identical with the cave of the Annunciation, or the site of Mary's well, where the church of St. Gabriel now stands; according to the report of the pilgrim Arnulph in 670 a church stood here 'on the site of the house in which our Saviour grew up.'

To-day the home of the Holy Family is venerated in a cave-dwelling of the time of Jesus beneath the church of St. Joseph, which was erected by the Franciscans in 1914; they had built a chapel in 1754 over the ruins of the Crusaders' church. The tradition concerning this sanctuary does not, however, appear till 1600, and then it is called the house and workshop of Joseph. The earliest tradition refers only to Joseph's workshop and does not yet include the dwelling of the Holy Family. Since 1900 both sites have been venerated here.

Though there are no certain traditions about the Holy Family's home, we may be thankful for a worthy site to commemorate the spot where Jesus lived for thirty years, for most of His life. The fact that we can only guess the place is surely in accordance with the whole life of Jesus in Nazareth, the hidden years.

The other important site in Nazareth is the synagogue in which Jesus taught. According to tradition, a new synagogue was built immediately after the destruction of the original, and this was turned into a church in 1137. To-day opinion varies as to where it actually stood. Some think it is in a portion of the Muslim cemetery, but this is not open to visitors, nor is anything at all reminiscent of a synagogue to be found here. The usual tradition has settled on the Greek Catholic parish church, at least on the building adjoining it.

There are varying traditions also as to which is the 'steep

place' to which Jesus was hustled after His sermon in the synagogue. Sometimes it is said to be Nebi Scha'in, the hill against which the ancient Nazareth lay (Luke 4: 29).

But the rounded summit of that has no abrupt slope, though there are steep places lower down, to which the houses cling. To-day the hill-top is built over, with the church and convent of the Salesians. Since the ninth century the Dschebel el-Kafze has been pointed out as the 'steep place,' although this tradition is not a very probable one; it lies beyond Nazareth, and its slope falls abruptly down to the plain of Jezreel.

FROM THE HOLY BIBLE

And being warned by a dream, Joseph withdrew to the region of Galilee; there he settled in a town called Nazareth. This was to fulfil the words spoken through the prophets: 'He shall be called a Nazarene.' Matt. 2: 22 and 23.

Then Jesus went back with his parents to Nazareth, and continued to be under their authority. As Jesus grew up he advanced in wisdom and in favour with God and men.
Luke 2: 51 and 52.

When Jesus began his work he was about thirty years old, the son, as people thought, of Joseph. Luke 3: 23.

Philip went to find Nathanael, and told him, 'We have met the man spoken of by Moses in the Law, and by the prophets: it is Jesus son of Joseph, from Nazareth.' 'Nazareth!' Nathanael exclaimed; 'can anything good come from Nazareth?' Philip said, 'Come and see.' John 1: 45 and 46.

So Jesus came to Nazareth, where he had been brought up, and went to synagogue on the sabbath day as he regularly did. He stood up to read the lesson and was handed the scroll of the prophet Isaiah. He opened the scroll and found the passage which says, 'The spirit of the Lord is upon me because he has anointed me; he has sent me to announce good news to the poor; to proclaim release for prisoners and recovery of sight for the blind; to let the broken victims go free; to proclaim the year of the Lord's favour.'

He began to speak: 'Today,' he said, 'in your very hearing this text has come true.' The large congregation who heard him were amazed and said, 'Is not this the carpenter, the son of Mary, the brother of James and Joseph and Judas and Simon? And are not his sisters here with us?' So they fell foul of him and this led him to say, 'A prophet will always be held in honour except in his home town, and among his kinsmen and in his own family.' At these words the whole congregation were infuriated. They leapt up, threw him out of the town, and took him to the brow of the hill on which it was built, meaning to hurl him over the edge. But he walked straight through them all, and went away.

From Luke 4: 16–30; Mark 6: 1–6; Matt. 13: 53–8.

A CALL TO US

The cave beneath the church of St. Joseph, as the dwelling of the Holy Family, invites us to recall, in the prayerful stillness of the place, the boy Jesus growing up here in Nazareth in lowliness and hiddenness, the Son of God working for years as a carpenter. The cave will make real to us the poverty in which Jesus lived as a child. Nazareth was so poor and unimportant a place that no distinguished priestly families lived there, as they did in the neighbouring Sepphories, called 'the pearl of Galilee.' The whole population was poor and apparently somewhat despised, as we can tell from Nathanael's words: 'Can any good thing come out of Nazareth?'

Perhaps Nazareth had a bad reputation because the inhabitants had few moral qualities. That their spirit was no good one, that the people were prone to anger and hatred, to the point of murder, is shown by their later attitude to Jesus. Although He was their countryman and had grown to manhood amongst them and was related to many of them and friendly with them, yet they were eager, after He had preached to them with 'gracious words,' to cast Him down from a steep place and to kill Him.

Why, we wonder, did God decree that His only-begotten Son, the pure and holy one, should grow up in such a place? The words of Jesus, that He was come to call not the righteous but sinners, apply here. His love, which was at one with His Father's choice, drew Him to the kind of place which we would naturally keep away from. We avoid people who are difficult and handicapped and evil. We prefer other surroundings. But the love of Jesus drove Him to that place where, being most vulnerable to attack, He would have most opportunities for showing His merciful and forgiving love to His enemies. How much may not the child Jesus, so gracious in His ways and expressing His Father's love—for He was indeed a child of Heaven—have suffered here in the streets of Nazareth amongst the other children! The spitefulness of His playmates would have grieved His sensitive and loving heart.

Probably He, the wholly other, may so have been mocked and persecuted by them. Eternal love chose to suffer for love of us, to be born in the Bethlehem stable, and lie in a roughly-made manger, to bear the flight into Egypt through the desert, the childhood in Nazareth, and the years passed in poverty amongst those who treated Him shamefully.

Here the love of Jesus, which drove Him to serve us and suffer for us, found a rich field of action, for the humble carpenter's son was daily obliged to seek out His fellow-men and do lowly service for them. For years He fashioned ploughshares and other tools for them. Here He suffered daily humiliation and took the lowest place. During the years at Nazareth He lived out in His daily life all that He later demanded of others.

Here in Nazareth He revealed more and more His lamb-like ways, which later would be those of the Lamb of God, Whose special characteristic is that of patience. Here Jesus learned what patience meant: to wait, and again to wait, till the Father told Him: Now go forth and preach to the people and work signs and wonders amongst them; reveal Thyself as Messiah and Son of God. When the hour had come He had to experience, here in His home, just this: He came unto His own, and His own received Him not. Here in Nazareth He was the unrecognized, so that His fellow-townsmen could not see the Son of God, or even a prophet, in Him when He told them in the synagogue that the day of salvation was at hand. Here He learned obedience by that which He suffered from His fellow-men (Heb. 5: 8), and towards His heavenly Father and His earthly parents (Luke 2: 51). Here did His Father prepare Him for His Passion.

So to-day we walk the streets of Nazareth in loving adoration, that He chose such a place for His dwelling, such a wretched little town, and among such evil people. Yea, He chose Nazareth as that which 'was not' (1 Cor. 1: 28).

Here in Nazareth He calls us: 'Come, follow me.' Not to dwell amongst people congenial to you, where you will be loved and honoured, but to seek out those who are difficult and who will cause you humiliation. Invite such, and do good to them from whom you can expect nothing in return except that they will despitefully use you (Matt. 5: 44; Luke 14: 12). Give yourselves to that, for that is the way of love, love that humbles itself to serve and help and redeem others, the love of the Son of God. This love which chooses the hidden way of humility desires to live in His own, as the members of His Body, to go to and fro upon the earth, so that Jesus may be amongst them.

✝

Jesus Christ made himself of no reputation, and took upon him the form of a servant, and was made in the likeness of men (Phil. 2: 7).

✝

Considering His person and His gifts, no one on earth has followed such a way of humiliation, of hiddenness and misunderstanding as Jesus, the Son of God, did as a boy and carpenter in Nazareth. Whoever loves Jesus will choose such a way.

HYMN

Nazareth, thou truly bearest
Precious secret in thy streets:
Jesus, Son of God, most highest,
Lord of lords and King of kings.
Dost thou know the grace this brings?

Nazareth, within thee dwelling
None did know who walked therein,
For His greatness kept Him hidden,
Hidden quite from people's gazing,
Humble as the humblest man.

Nazareth, within thee walketh
He that made the world of men,
Walketh humbly as a workman,
Carpenter for thirty years.
Who can grasp His condescension?

Nazareth, much fruit thou bearest
Ripen'd in sorrow and in toil.
As a hero He proceedeth
To the Cross's cruel death,
Without measure, ev'ry breath.

Nazareth calleth without ceasing
To the folk who throng its street
That in humbleness they remember
And in lowliness recall
That here walked Jesus' feet.

†

The way of Jesus in Nazareth tells us that every duty to which we are called must have its preparation in hiddenness and humbleness.

PRAYER

Heavenly Father, we bow before Thee in confusion of face, because Thy beloved Son, Who played here as a child in the streets of Nazareth, was not recognized by us, Thy children. We recall His many childish griefs when, like a stranger amongst the children of Nazareth, He was homesick for His Father's House.

Belovèd, gracious Child, we would love Thee for all who did not love Thee here in Nazareth. We would show forth our love for Thee by following the ways Thou didst walk as a child and as the carpenter's son: the hidden ways of humble serving. Freely will we choose the lowest place, and will love them that are unkind to us.

Grant us Thy Holy Spirit to inspire us to this. AMEN.

CHAPTER XXI

CANA

THE first miracle was wrought by Jesus in Galilee, at the wedding-feast which has made the name of Cana known throughout the world. Now that we are in Galilee we must surely seek out Cana. Two places are claimed as the site of this miracle. The site most visited is Kfar Kana (Arabic: Kafr. Kenna), which lies on the road from Haifa to Tiberias. If we come from Nazareth this village is about six miles beyond; the picturesquely dilapidated Arab houses lie on an eastward slope. The village lies in a smiling landscape, surrounded by olive-yards and pomegranate plantations. At the entrance to the village, on the right, there is a Greek Catholic church, only open occasionally. A little farther, again on the right, a lane leads off to the Roman Catholic church, served by the Franciscans, which commemorates the miracle. Its two towers and its red dome can be seen from a long way off .

Beside it, to the left, is a Greek Orthodox church. Both properties are enclosed by high walls. A narrow paved path between them gives access to the courtyard of the 'Marriage-feast' church. Inside the church, and especially in the crypt, we can well ponder 'the beginning of miracles which Jesus did' at Cana, of which St. John says: 'We beheld his glory.'

Chirbet Kana, the other site, is about six miles from Kfar Kana, and about nine miles north-east of Nazareth. The roads leading to it are very bad.

The Historical Aspect

According to St. John's Gospel, 'Cana of Galilee,' the scene of Christ's first miracle, lay in the hill-country to the west of the lake, for Jesus 'went down to Capernaum' (John 2: 12).

And when He was later again in the same place, 'a certain nobleman,' whose son Jesus healed from afar, bade Him 'come down ere my child die' (John 4: 47 and 49). The third time that Cana is mentioned in the Gospels it is as the home of Nathanael, whom we now call Bartholomew the Apostle (John 21: 2).

The 'Marriage-feast' church of the Franciscans in Kfar Kana (Kafr. Kenna) was built in 1880, and stands on the ruins of former buildings of various dates between the fourth and sixth centuries. An inscription with the name Joseph may indicate that the ruins are those of a sanctuary erected by Joseph of Tiberias, favourite of the Emperor Constantine, who built sanctuaries on many of the sacred sites. But it is also held that the ruins may be those of a synagogue of the same date.

Later a mosque stood here, and in the sixteenth century this was regarded as the spot where the miracle took place, so that in 1566 the Orthodox Greeks built a church opposite. The Franciscans from near-by Nazareth acquired a neighbouring house in 1641; for 200 years they struggled to get possession of the mosque, till at last in 1879 they were able to buy the long-ruined remains and to build their church. Ancient pilgrim reports speak of the crypt as being either the room in which the feast took place or else the place where the water-pots stood; a copy of a Jewish water-pot of Jesus' day now stands in the crypt.

The other site, Chirbet Kana, now consists only of ruins on the hill-top and an ancient cistern. Finds from here show that it was an inhabited settlement from 1200 B.C. onwards, and that it must have been of considerable importance in Jesus' day. But decisive excavations have yet to be undertaken. An ancient tradition asserts that Chirbet Kana is 'Cana of Galilee,' and the name, which has persisted in the Arabic form, seems an indication.

Later the commemoration of the marriage-feast and the miracle was moved from Chirbet Kana to a cave at the foot of the hill, and it was thought that the water miraculously changed into wine was drawn from the cistern still visible upon the hill-top.

Through the centuries traditions have wavered, and many pilgrim-reports do not make clear which of the sites they venerate as Cana. Till after the Crusades Chirbet Kana was much in evidence, but then it became a complete ruin. After the close of the sixteenth century Kafr. Kenna, the Kfar Kana of to-day, was increasingly regarded as being the former Cana, especially after the Greek Orthodox church was built, with the Franciscan one later.

†

'Jesus of Nazareth, a man approved of God among you by miracles and wonders and signs which God did by him in the midst of you.' Acts 2: 22.

Cana proclaims that Jesus is the Lord Almighty Who turns water into wine and Who can still to-day, by one word, transform anything: sorrow into joy, and mountains of difficulty into straight paths. Do we bring our needs to Him?

FROM THE HOLY BIBLE

On the third day there was a wedding at Cana-in-Galilee. The mother of Jesus was there, and Jesus and his disciples were guests also. The wine gave out, so Jesus's mother said to him, 'They have no wine left.' He answered, 'Your concern, mother, is not mine. My hour has not yet come.' His mother said to the servants, 'Do whatever he tells you.'

Jesus said to the servants, 'Fill the jars with water. Now draw some off,' He ordered, 'and take it to the steward of the feast'; and they did so. The steward tasted the water now turned into wine, not knowing its source; he hailed the bridegroom and said, 'Everyone serves the best wine first, and waits until the guests have drunk freely before serving the poorer sort; but you have kept the best wine till now.'

This deed at Cana-in-Galilee is the first of the signs by which Jesus revealed his glory and led his disciples to believe in Him. From John 2: 1–11.

†

Miracles as of Cana still occur to-day, there where God finds those who in faith await His power, as His mother did.

A CALL TO US

Cana reminds us of the great miracle wrought by Jesus at the marriage-feast when He revealed His glory. It stands out from all the other miracles by which He proclaimed His almighty power, for it was His first miracle, the first revelation of His glory as the Son of God, as Scripture tells us.

For thirty years the Son of God went His way unnoticed in unimportant Nazareth. All through those years He Who holds all power in Heaven and on earth chose to undergo humiliation daily as He made tools for His fellow-townsmen and put Himself at their disposal. Year after year—a long time of waiting till He could reveal His mission to His own—learning what sorrow would later make so clear, 'We accounted him as a thing of nought.'

He learned obedience by the things which He suffered and the utter humility which shone forth from beneath the crown of thorns on the way of the cross and in which almighty power lies hidden.

Divine power ripened in Jesus during the long years of waiting, and when He was about thirty years of age, at the wedding in Cana, the time came when He could reveal the power and glory which grows from lowliness and obedience. Here He revealed to the world for the first time what divine powers dwelt in Him, powers such as men until now had never even dreamt of.

At the wedding feast the miracle of Jesus takes place because of this meekness and obedience.

When His mother made known to Him 'they have no wine,' He replied: 'Mine hour is not yet come.' Jesus waited in humble dependence on His Father till permission was given for a deed to reveal His creative power and His mission. He can only do what His Father tells Him. His mother guessed the secret of His being and doing, His dependence on His Father, which is in itself His almighty power, which will be revealed in His hour. Therefore she warns the servants:

'Whatsoever he saith unto you, do it.' For she knew that when He did act He would perform a miracle. He spake the word, and they obeyed, and the miracle took place.

The Cana wedding feast thus shows us a humble but omnipotent Jesus, Who can alter or remove the dilemmas of man. Water which cannot be offered to the guests is changed into wine and the lack is supplied. In place of the water for cleansing is provided the wine for the feast, to mark His eternal mission—that He through the hour of His death on the Cross will lead us to a heavenly feast.

The astonished disciples realized that the simple carpenter's son was truly the Son of God, into Whose Hand was delivered power and might, to Whom nothing was impossible—the fullness of the mighty power of God come down to earth.

We to-day are still apt to regard Jesus as His fellow-townsmen did, as if His powers were limited as ours are. But Cana proclaims to us that Jesus is more than man, that He is God's Son to Whom has been given all power and might, in Heaven as on earth—just because He was the most humble. Cana tells us that we have a Master Who can do all things, to Whom all things are possible, Who will help us in mysterious ways when men can no longer help.

So there need be no more impossibilities for us, for we can bring them to our almighty Lord. As the water was subject to Jesus and was turned into wine, so still to-day all things lie at His feet and do His will, for He, the Son of God, Who was found obedient, now sits at the right hand of God and waits to reveal Himself in our lives in royal majesty. But He desires not only to change our impossibilities but to make us bearers of His glory, that as members of His Body we may show forth His power here on earth. There is no way for us to take except the way that Jesus went before us. The humble will be exalted, and those who have been lowliest will be given the greatest power. Those who wait patiently through long years of hidden service to others, when their hour is come God will make them to serve in the Kingdom of Heaven, and they will bring forth fruit as hundredfold and will reveal His glory.

HYMN

Great is the Lord! Great is the Lord!
To Him be glory evermore.
For His Counsel e'er is sure
And His power shall e'er endure
Jesus, none is like to Thee.

Great is the Lord! Great is the Lord!
Joyously we Him adore.
None can equal all His power
All His Love on us is showered.
E'en to-day it is the same.

PRAYER

Dearest Lord Jesus,
we thank Thee that Thou art a mighty Lord Who turnedst water into wine, yea: sorrow into joy, and mountains of difficulty into plain paths, by speaking but the word.

Here let me praise Thy power and sing to Thee and honour Thee by faith unfailing. We will believe, in all our difficulties, that Thou art to-day the same Living Lord. Thou seest our need and wilt perform miracles for us; Thou wilt help us when we cry to Thee and put our trust in Thee. We render Thee thanks. AMEN.

†

The sphere of action for the power of Jesus, which turns water into wine, and multiplies loaves and fishes, and performs many other miracles, is our powerlessness and our need. These move Him to help us to show forth His power upon us.

CHAPTER XXII

NAIN

THE name Nain comes from the Hebrew word 'na'im,' meaning 'pleasing,' and it calls up a pleasing picture, for here Jesus once raised a young man from the dead and gave back to a widow her only son. But to-day Nain is a small and poverty-stricken Arab village, which reflects but little of the lovely light of the Gospel.

It lies south of Mount Tabor, on an elevated plateau on the slopes of 'Givat Hamoreh,' also called 'Dschebel dahi' or 'Little Hermon.' Coming from Afula, we can see it, well over a mile to the north from the motor road to Tiberias. A bad road leads to it from the main one. A horde of children surround us as we approach the church, and an Arab girl opens it for us on request.

The Historical Aspect

According to Eusebius, who wrote *circa* A.D. 300, and Jerome, who wrote in about 400, the old city of Nain was situated where the present village now is. Ancient rock-tombs have been found to the south-east. The funeral procession probably passed this way (Luke 7: 12). In the neighbourhood of the spot which tradition assigned to the miracle, a church was built in commemoration, but its date is not known, though it is first mentioned by pilgrims about 900.

After the departure of the Crusaders we have reports of a ruined church, as also of a second church near the mosques, which also perished later. In 1880 the Franciscans purchased the ruins of the first church after long-drawn-out negotiations with the local authorities, and they built a chapel over the foundations. Thus the site has been preserved.

FROM THE HOLY BIBLE

Afterwards Jesus went to a town called Nain, accompanied by his disciples and a large crowd. As he approached the gate of the town he met a funeral. The dead man was the only son of his widowed mother; and many of the townspeople were there with her. When the Lord saw her his heart went out to her, and he said, 'Weep no more.' With that he stepped forward and laid his hand on the bier. Then he spoke: 'Young man, rise up!' The dead man sat up and began to talk; and Jesus gave him back to his mother.

From Luke 7: 11–15.

A CALL TO US

The Gospels tell us how Jesus journeyed all over the country and preached in every place the message of the Kingdom. He must have decided one day to visit Nain, which lay away from the caravan road to Jerusalem, to give the inhabitants the gospel of the coming Kingdom of God. Followed by a large number of His disciples, He journeyed across the smiling plain of Jezreel, in sight of Mount Tabor. As He was about to enter the city, He encountered a crowd of mourners surrounding a bier on which lay the body of the only son of his mother, and she was a widow. This was no unusual occurrence—a dead man being carried to his last resting-place. But for Jesus it is not unalterable. He does not, as we do, accept the ordinariness of a funeral cortège. It is written that 'he had compassion on her.' The heart of Jesus shares every sorrow of the human heart. We know how He wept when He heard of the death of Lazarus (John 11: 35).

Nain is for us the place where Jesus revealed His love and compassion, and showed Himself to be One Who could not pass by 'on the other side.' As He met the crowd of mourners, He stood still, and gave His help, raising the young man to life.

God had not sent Him to raise from the dead the thousands who died at that time. The hour for that had not yet come. Death, the last enemy, will only be overcome at the end of time, when all power is put under Jesus' feet. But Jesus gives a sign that He will break the power of death, and that those who believe on Him need not fear a second death. Once and for all as Master over death and in compassion for the widow He speaks the word to her son: 'Arise.' He commands death to recede, and the youth comes back to life. Here death encountered the One Who is greater, Jesus, the Lord of death. Here death was obliged to show that he is the slave of Christ and must obey His commands. What Jesus did at Nain is a sign and a promise that death will be overcome when the battle is joined. They shall not taste death who know through the Resurrection the truth of the words, 'Christ the first-fruits: afterwards they that are Christ's at his coming' (1 Cor. 15: 23).

So Nain encourages us to hope for the hour of the return of Jesus, when for them that are His, death will be swallowed up in victory. But Nain can give us comfort too for the present time when we are still under the power of death. For when, within the church of Nain, we recall how Jesus gave back her son to the widow, we shall realize His compassion, the power of the love that is equal to every sorrow. And though the time has not yet come when He will raise our dead, yet He shows the same compassion as He showed to this widow, when we trustfully bring our sorrows to Him: a miracle will come to pass—the power of sorrow will be broken and it will be turned into joy. For the Son of God still performs miracles. Is it not a miracle when He fills despairing hearts with peace and heavenly love in the very face of death? Divine life conquers.

Nain proclaims: What a Lord is here!
  Let us trust Him and revere.
Jesus, of heroes is the strongest,
  Who indeed the world o'ercomest.
Death itself lies at His feet,
  For God as well has conquered it.

PRAYER

Dear Lord Jesus, I praise the love which could not see the sorrow of the widowed mother and not help her. I thank Thee that her need so touched Thy heart that Thou gavest her back her only son. I thank Thee that Thou dost come to us full of compassion and that Thou wilt transform our griefs.

Let me here take Thy merciful and powerful love deep into my heart, so that in all my sorrows I may wholeheartedly believe in Thy power and Thy love, which now and always find a way to help. Thou canst call back those who are sick unto death; or if Thou dost not give us back our loved ones Thou wilt comfort us 'as one whom his mother comforteth.' Thou wilt come to me, for Thou art almighty and lovest me with an everlasting love. Here in Nain I would praise the victorious power of Thy love. I will await the hour of Thy return when Thou wilt destroy death as the last enemy.

HYMN

Jesus, Thou art our Deliverer,
Thou dost help in all our need
Jesus, risen from the dead,
From death Thou hast me freed.
Halleluja, Halleluja!

Jesus, Thou art our Redeemer,
I can but hail Thy power
Jesus, Thou art victorious,
I bless Thee every hour.
Halleluja, Halleluja!

Jesus, Thou art our Saviour,
Who healest every need.
Jesus, Thou art a Sovereign
Whose power all creatures must heed.
Halleluja, Halleluja!

NAIN

Jesus, Who loosest all bondage,
  Thou Lion of Judah's tribe
Thy fame goes out through all nations
  Thou Lamb of God indeed!
    Halleluja, Halleluja!

Jesus, Sovereign without peer,
  Whom as true Lord we revere,
In whose Presence all power yields,
  To Thee alone must all men kneel.
    Halleluja, Halleluja!

CHAPTER XXIII

MOUNT TABOR

MOUNT TABOR, close on 1700 feet in height, rises in the north-east of the Plain of Jezreel or Esdraelon (Hebrew = Emek Jesreel or just Emek). It is the most conspicuous mountain in the south of Galilee, and it rises in isolation, without foothills or neighbouring heights; it is bell-shaped, and visible from all sides. But it is not only the majestic external shape which makes it remarkable: it is a special mountain for us because it keeps the memory of our Lord's Transfiguration. We think of the three disciples who were chosen to accompany Him to the summit, as we now make our way to the top.

The motor-road from Afula to Tiberias passed close by the foot of Mount Tabor. At the place where this road reaches the foot of the mountain just before Kfar Tevor, the road to Daburie branches off to the left, and it is this one we must take. The Arab village lies on the western side of the mountain covered with boulders and scrub. The road rises in serpentine curves on the north-west slope.

Each curve reveals a wider view. First we see the fruitful plain with its rectangular, well-cultivated fields. It is the biblical 'valley of Megiddo,' called after the 'tell' lying on the south-west, a hill from which the remains of a very ancient city fortress, mostly of the time of Solomon (1 Kings 9: 15), have been excavated. We are reminded of the many ancient battles which this valley of Megiddo (Armageddon) has seen (Judges 5: 19; 2 Kings 9: 27; 23: 29; 2 Chronicles 35: 22) and also of what the name will mean to us in the future (Rev. 16: 16). Beyond, to the west, we see the heights of Nazareth, and even as far as Mount Carmel; eastwards we look across the Sea of Galilee and the Golan highlands. On a clear day we can even see the snow-capped Mount Hermon, to the north-east.

The summit of Mount Tabor is wide and level, with two churches, one Franciscan and one Orthodox. A little-used road leads to the latter, whilst the chief road continues to the right. It passes through the re-built 'Gate of the Winds' in the ancient curtain wall to the Franciscan basilica, which lies at the eastern end of the southern half of the level. The last part of the road is an avenue which goes past the ruins of the ancient Benedictine Abbey. The wide view from the terraces beside the church shows us Galilee, the chief scene of our Lord's earthly activity; both this and the interior of the church help us to recall that mighty hour which prepared Jesus for His way of pain.

The Historical Aspect

Mount Tabor is connected with many biblical and historical events. The village of Daburie on the slope is named in honour of Deborah the Prophetess, who here encouraged Israel to victory (Judges 4).

It was probably by this village that Jesus drove the dumb spirit out of a boy after His disciples had attempted this in vain (Mark 9: 14ff.). The level summit has always been a place of refuge, both in pre-Christian times and when the Jews fought against the Romans in A.D. 70. Traces of the defending wall, dating from that time and later from the Crusades, can still be seen.

But the chief interest lies in the tradition of this being the place where Jesus was transfigured. A modern view regards Hermon as the mount of Transfiguration because, according to Matt. 16: 13ff., Jesus spoke to the disciples about His Divine Sonship at Caesarea Philippi, which is close to Hermon. But an entire week lay between that momentous conversation and the Transfiguration, so we can well assume an expedition to Mount Tabor. And as Jesus found His disciples engaged in discussion with Scribes when He came down from the mount, that would indicate somewhere in a Jewish district and not in a diaspora such as Caesarea Philippi.

As the Gospels give no exact indications we have to fall back on tradition. The apocryphal Gospel to the Hebrews, dated *circa* A.D. 150, refers to Christians commemorating the Transfiguration on Mount Tabor. For a short time it was erroneously supposed that the Transfiguration took place on the Mount of Olives, but in 348 Cyril, Bishop of Jerusalem, certified that Mount Tabor was the scene of Transfiguration, as did also Epiphanius, born 315 in Judaea and later becoming Bishop of Salamis. In the following centuries many pilgrims speak of Mount Tabor as a place abounding in convents and churches. In 518 a synod in Jerusalem speaks of a 'Bishop of the holy mount of Tabor.' The anonymous pilgrim of Piacenza, *circa* 570, reports that three basilicas stood on the summit, in accordance with the words of St. Peter: 'Let us make three tabernacles.' Even after the conquest of Palestine by the Arabs in the seventh century there is mention of a bishop and of monks on Mount Tabor and that there were churches in honour of Jesus, Moses, and Elias.

During the Crusades the Benedictines founded a monastery here, *circa* 1100. They built it adjoining a new church of the Transfiguration, which probably embraced the three earlier buildings. The whole was contained within a defensive wall. In the twelfth century, a church of Elias, belonging to the Greek Orthodox, is mentioned, together with a monastery.

After the defeat of the Crusaders in 1187 the mountain was seized and held by the Saracens and turned into a fortress. In 1631 Sultan Bibars wholly destroyed all the Christian buildings here. Not till 1631 did the Franciscans obtain permission from a Turkish Emir to settle on Mount Tabor. At the end of the nineteenth century the Greek Orthodox began to rebuild their church of Elias, and the Franciscans undertook extensive excavations. The Franciscans erected their new basilica between 1921 and 1924, on the model of a fifth century Syrian church. The two towers at the entrance stand where the two sanctuaries dedicated to Moses and Elias once stood, and contain commemorative chapels.

The Franciscan property encloses the territory which, since the sixth century, has been regarded as a place of commemoration. On the western side, beside the path leading down the mount, stands a little chapel—now closed—called 'Descendentibus.' It commemorates the words of Jesus after the Transfiguration when He commanded the disciples to keep silent till after He had suffered.

FROM THE HOLY BIBLE

Tabor and Hermon shall rejoice in thy name. Ps. 89: 12.

About eight days later he took Peter, John, and James with him and went up into the hills to pray. And in their presence he was transfigured; his clothes became dazzling white, with a whiteness no bleacher on earth could equal. Suddenly there were two men talking with him; these were Moses and Elijah, who appeared in glory and spoke of his departure, the destiny he was to fulfil in Jerusalem.

Peter said to Jesus, 'Master, how good it is that we are here! Shall we make three shelters, one for you, one for Moses, and one for Elijah?' While he was still speaking, a bright cloud suddenly overshadowed them, and a voice called from the cloud: 'This is my Son, my Beloved, on whom my favour rests, listen to him.' And when they raised their eyes they saw no one, but only Jesus.

On their way down the mountain Jesus enjoined them not to tell anyone of the vision until the Son of Man had been raised from the dead.

From Luke 9: 28–36; Mark 9: 2–9; Matt. 17: 1–9.

A CALL TO US

In Psalm 89 David sings that Tabor and Hermon shall rejoice in the name of the Lord. And in ancient times Mount Tabor was a holy mount for Israel, a symbol of witness to the glory of God, a commemoration of Deborah's song of victory. The mount was most probably a sacred place for Jesus, and as it was near Nazareth He would often have looked up to it, and may even have climbed it, during His early years. It therefore had a particular attraction for Him, and we can thus understand why He should choose this spot as the place for His Transfiguration. We do not know whether Jesus knew beforehand the grace that would be vouchsafed to Him on Mount Tabor. But we can guess that for God the Father, Who must have but unwillingly hidden the glory of His Son in His earthly life, this must have been a day of great joy, when He could transfigure the Son. For this was the Son born of His love; and what more could the Father have desired in His heart than to display before mankind His divine glory and heavenly beauty. Only because hiddenness was essential for the redemption of sinful mankind was God obliged to hide His glory.

When Jesus ascended Mount Tabor with His disciples, the time had come near when He would be not only misunderstood and persecuted by the scribes and Pharisees, but be shamefully put to death as a criminal. Because of our sin, His Father had to permit His Son to drink the cup of shame, contempt, and humiliation to the dregs. But here on the summit, in the presence of the three disciples closest to Him, the Father could strengthen the Son in preparation for His rejection. He would show forth what Jesus was in reality: the Son of God, Whose Face shines as the sun and Who would illuminate the city of God and the whole world by the brightness of His love; the Son of God clothed in shining glory, Whose garments are whiter than the snow He created in its splendour.

This hour displayed the glory which God creates out of suffering. For the Transfiguration on Mount Tabor occurs in preparation for the Passion. So Moses and Elias spoke with Jesus of His decease on Golgotha.

Mount Tabor, the mount of transfiguration, tells us that the Father not only transfigured His only-begotten Son, but will transfigure all those who are redeemed by Him. For we have been created to this end and redeemed by Jesus, that we may shine forth as the sun in the kingdom of the Father (Matt. 13: 43). The Transfiguration tells us there is only one way—the way of suffering. For even the Bible tells us that Jesus, Who was without sin, is made perfect through suffering (Heb. 2: 10). Along the road of suffering God will purify us and lead us out of darkness, till our souls are more and more penetrated by the light of Jesus, till in complete transfiguration His qualities can be seen in us: love, humility, meekness, mercy, forgiveness. Yea, love will be manifested so clearly that even our bodies, like that of Jesus, will reflect it. This will be when we are 'raised in glory' (1 Cor. 15: 43).

So only in adoration can we ascend Mount Tabor. We must adore, because not only Jesus, Who so fittingly shines as the sun, wears the garments of transfiguration; but also we, sinful children of men, who are by nature under the dominion of Satan and are full of darkness, are made worthy to show forth the qualities of God.

Mount Tabor asks us whether we are prepared to pay the price, whether we are ready, as was Jesus, to descend from the mount into the 'vale of misery' to tread the way of the Cross, to bow humbly beneath the weight of the Cross. No other way leads to Transfiguration, and only those who are transfigured inherit the glory of God for ever and ever. How relevant that message of Tabor is for us to-day!

†

The Transfiguration of the Son of Man is evidence of the promise that He is come to make us, by redemption, like unto Himself.

PRAYER

Lord Jesus, we thank Thee that we may here behold Thee as the One Who was so wonderfully transfigured, into the beauteous light in which we shall behold Thee above. We adore Thee in the glory of Thy Transfiguration, O Jesus. And we thank Thee that Thy transfiguration tells us that we too may be changed from glory to glory, because Thou hast obtained for us to be made like unto Thee. So we give praise to Thee Who shinest as the sun, Who hast redeemed Thy sinful children for so great a glory that we too shall shine as the sun in Thy kingdom.

Jesus, I am ready to give all that I am and have, that I may be changed into the image of the brightness of Thy love. Purify me—as the refiner does the gold—in the furnace of affliction, that the image of God may shine forth in me and that I may come to glory. Here and now I surrender to the testing of Thy ways. AMEN.

†

The hour of transfiguration came to Jesus at the moment when He was ready to go out into the night of death. As members of His body, we can only receive the grace of transfiguration which He has earned for us, by the same way, the way of humiliation and purging.

HYMN

Jesus transfigured on Tabor's height
Bursts on disciples' adoring sight;
On this mount there is made clear
The deepest truth of their Lord so dear.

Noble and beautiful, glorious too
Seems His clothing as sun shining through
Love is the secret, mysterious mine
Which enables His nature so clearly to shine.

Mount of Transfiguring—listen, the bells
Promise His grace to transfigure ourselves;
Jesus transfigured is for us guarantee
That He will confer grace on you and me.

As after night then only comes day
So transfiguration comes only one way
For those who by judgment their sin clearly see
And have Jesus' forgiveness radiantly.

God wants to transfigure us splendid and clean
That we in His splendour of light may gleam
Through various sorrows He would us make pure
For through purification to rule we are sure.

That we may shine as the sun so bright
As Jesus did once on Tabor's height
For we adoring beheld Him there
Gleaming and shining with Love's image so fair.

†

And because for us there is no veil over the face, we all reflect as in a mirror the splendour of the Lord; thus we are transfigured into His likeness, from splendour to splendour; such is the influence of the Lord Who is Spirit. 2 Cor. 3: 18.

HYMN

Jesus, loveliest of mankind,
  Full of Light and glory now,
Majesty and untold honour
  Like the sun are on Thy brow.
We who see Thee in Thy beauty
  Joys unspeakable may know.

MOUNT TABOR

Jesus, Heaven bows before Thee,
  Powers, thrones before Thee bend,
For Thy glory, none can tell it,
  Power, and love their radiance spend.
Thy disciples, those Thou lovest,
  Thy great glory apprehend.

Jesus, none can e'er Thee equal,
  Even angels come not nigh.
Image of the Father's Person,
  Brightness of His glory high.
In Thy glory Thou dost deign
  For us martyrdom to gain.

Grant us grace, O glorious Saviour,
  To come after to the end,
That Thy Love be shown upon us
  And Thy glory we may spend,
And at length within Thy Kingdom
  Joy with Thee without all end.

CHAPTER XXIV

BY THE LAKE OF GALILEE

WE now approach the king of lakes, the Lake of Galilee, for it has borne our King, Jesus, upon its waves, and its shores beheld His mighty works. It is also called Jam Chinneroth, after the Hebrew word for a musical instrument whose shape it resembles. It is about twelve miles long and two and a half miles wide, and about ninety feet deep at the centre, about 650 yards below sea-level. It is still as lovely as it was in Jesus' day. The warm climate produces a rich vegetation, now that the surrounding land is again in cultivation.

The sites connected with Jesus are to the north and west. We can reach it from either the new city of Jerusalem, from Tel Aviv, or from Haifa, via Afula or Nazareth. The motor road from Nazareth leads to Tiberias, the largest of the lake-side towns, which lies half-way along the western shore. The road which goes north from here, passing through the sites of Jesus' activities, leads to Sfad (Safed). Its curves follow the shore-line. On the left rise hills with rocky summits, on the right is the lake with its constantly changing colour. To the east, beyond the opposite shore, lie the Golan hills, and behind the northern slopes are the mountains of Upper Galilee with Sfad, the 'city set upon a hill.' About two miles along we come to a spot known to us from the New Testament—the warm springs of Dalmanutha (Mark 8: 10). To-day there is only a small Russian Orthodox monastery here and the overnight hostel of the CVJM (YMCA) with its small chapel. One and a half miles farther, on the right, we see the over-grown ruins of Magdala. The remains of the houses are of recent date, but the New Testament Magdala must have lain here. Though these ruins seem so forgotten, yet we cannot forget that here was the home of Mary Magdalene.

The steep hills on the left are farther from the shore, and we come to the fruitful plain of Genesar (Ginossa), extending for about four and a half miles. We see the village of Migdal, which has superseded Magdala, on the height to the left. In front of the village, and soon after we pass the ruins of Magdala, the road divides, the western one also leading to Sfad; about three quarters of a mile along it we reach Wadi Hammam, the Valley of Doves. It was through this rocky defile that in Jesus' day the only road led from the lake-side to Nazareth. We continue along the shore-road, which goes northwards to Sfad, crossing the Genesar plain with its banana plantations, vineyards, and market gardens. The plain ends to the north in a hill, Tell Oreme, which slopes down to the lake. The road goes inland through a pass from which we can see the picturesque little plain of Seven Springs—the Greek: Heptapegon. To the right lie the convent and church of Tabgha, and above that, on the slope, the chapel of the Beatitudes, St. Peter's Anchorage, and Capernaum, the latter about two and a half miles away.

First let us visit the Mount of the Beatitudes, recalling the proclamation of the Kingdom of Heaven uttered by Jesus on these lake-side hills. For this we keep to the Sfad road for about two and a half miles, to where a narrow lane leads to the 'Beatitude,' where Italian nuns run a hospice. South of this is the octagonal church with an open, pillared, vestibule, surrounded by palm and other trees and shrubs (see Plate 8). Here we can easily picture the multitude camped on the plateau or on the slope in front to listen to the Sermon. Between the pillars we see the beauty of the country-side. In spring the many-coloured flowery meadows remind us of the words about the 'Lilies of the field' being greater than 'Solomon in all his glory.' We look out across the lake southwards, to the eastern hills, and to the bay on the north-west with the plain of Genesar the Valley of Doves with the Horns of Hattin behind. These recall the crushing defeat suffered by the Crusaders in 1187.

Across fields and market gardens we see Capernaum, which

stands out by reason of the darker green of its large trees. A narrow path leads down to the road between Tabgha and Capernaum. The fruitful green fields are divided by boulders which have been laboriously cleared from them, and they give the place an air of hope, that the promises of God are being fulfilled after 2,000 years of desolation, and that 'the King cometh.'

But we want to look at the lake-side places closer. To reach them by vehicle we must go back to Tabgha, to where the road branches off from the Tiberias–Sfad road. The approach to the property of the Benedictines, who care for the site of the Feeding of the 5,000, is only a few hundred yards east. A barn-like church covers fifth century mosaics. Thirty yards farther, on the left, we come to some fenced-in ruins on a slope; they are the excavation of the 'Beatitude chapel' of the Franciscans. Another thirty yards farther, on the right, lies the entrance to the Franciscan 'Chapel of the Lord's Appearing and the Primacy of Peter.' It lies a short way down, on the lake-shore, on a rocky spur, surrounded by eucalyptus trees and bubbling springs flowing into the lake. Here, at St. Peter's Anchorage, we can feel very near to the earthly life of Jesus and His disciples by the lake.

Finally we will seek out Capernaum, the place where our Lord once 'found faith,' in the centurion whose servant He healed. Along the road from Tabgha, by the shore, we find, a little over a mile farther on, the wall of the Franciscan property of Kfar Nahum. An avenue leads to the convent, behind which lie the ruins The finds of the excavators line the road, and we come to the steps of the partially restored synagogue. How we long, here as elsewhere, that our Living Lord, so vividly recalled here, may find faith and love in many hearts!

(The church of Beatitude and those of Tabgha and St. Peter's Anchorage are open all day except between 12 and 3. The Franciscan property of Capernaum is also open all day, but there are no guides available between 12 and 3.)

MAGDALA

The Historical Aspect

According to the Gospels, Magdala, also called Magadan, lay on the western shore of the Lake of Galilee (Matt. 15: 39), in the 'parts of Dalmanutha' (Mark 8: 10). The name comes from the Hebrew 'Migdal,' meaning tower, or fortress. The biblical Magdala was, according to the Talmud, a fairly important town by the lake, with a fishing fleet and a population of dyers and wool-merchants. On the edge of the fruitful plain of Genesar it was probably, before Tiberias eclipsed it, the most important of the lake-side towns. Jewish tradition says that it was afterwards destroyed by Jews from the neighbourhood on account of its great immorality.

In the Gospels Magdala is mentioned as the place where the Pharisees asked Jesus for a sign and He spoke only of the sign of Jonas (Matt. 15: 39; 16: 1 and 4). But it is still better known as the home of Mary Magdalene, out of whom Jesus cast seven devils, though it is not stated whether or not this healing took place in her home. Mary Magdalene is afterwards mentioned by the Evangelists as the leading woman of those who followed Jesus during His Galilean journeys and ministered to Him. In the narratives of the Passion and of Easter her name is amongst those women who stood beneath the Cross and later found the tomb empty. She is often regarded as being the unknown penitent who anointed the feet of Jesus in the house of Simon the Pharisee, probably in Capernaum (Luke 7).

Several pilgrim reports mention Magdala. Theodosius writes, *circa* 530: 'From Tiberias to Magdala, from whence came Mary Magdalene, it is two miles.' The English pilgrim, Willibald, visited the 'village of Magdala,' north of Tiberias, in 725. The monk Epiphanius of Jerusalem writes, in 800, of a church on the spot where Magdalene was healed. In 940 such a church is mentioned as being in 'Magdala near

Tiberias.' The Russian abbot Daniel, during the Crusade of 1106, only mentions a 'house of the Magdalene.' And in 1300 a pilgrim states that the church there was used as a stable.

According to later reports, Magdala, about whose position there had never been any doubt, was for a long period deserted. In the nineteenth century a settlement sprang up here but was subsequently destroyed, and it is the ruins of this which we see now. The name lives on in the village of Migdal, about a mile north of the old town, above the lake.

FROM THE HOLY BIBLE

Jesus went journeying from town to town and village to village, proclaiming the good news of the kingdom of God. With him were the Twelve, and a number of women who had been set free from evil spirits and infirmities: Mary, known as Mary of Magdala, from whom seven devils had come out.

Luke 8: 1 and 2.

Near the cross where Jesus hung stood his mother, with her sister, Mary wife of Clopas, and Mary of Magdala.

John 19: 25.

When Jesus had risen from the dead early on Sunday morning he appeared first to Mary of Magdala, from whom he had formerly cast out seven devils. She went and carried the news to his mourning and sorrowful followers.

Mark 16: 9 and 10.

Mary Magdalene proclaims to us that the strongest chains of sin are the opportunity for Jesus' greatest redemption. And that repentance is the most precious of gifts, from which will spring a great love of Jesus.

A CALL TO US

What is it that has made Magdala known still to-day throughout Christendom? Not its former prosperity, but Mary Magdalene who came from here. The woman who was a sinner. And why did she make the place so famous? She, a woman of a rich and self-satisfied commercial town, a woman given over to self-indulgence and lust, who had been possessed of seven devils—there must have been others of the same kind in the neighbourhood. The significance is that her sin and her seven devils were confronted by Jesus.

Then there were extraordinary and powerful results, for Jesus changed this woman. The seven devils came out of her, and the sinner became a rare penitent. Still more: she was changed into the woman who loved Jesus and who was a witness of His Resurrection, to whom the Risen One appeared first of all, in the glory of that blessèd Easter morning and made her His messenger to the others. Few have wept over her sins as she did and found such forgiveness; few have loved Jesus so wholeheartedly, and found such peace of soul.

Mary Magdalene shows us that 'Where sin abounded, grace doth much more abound.' If sin and devil-possession are brought to Jesus and put under the power of His redemption, they are shorn of their power. From broken and contrite hearts God can bring forth wonderful things.

Thanks be to Jesus! Mary Magdalene reveals the power of repentance, that it is the root of true love, love that in humble self-surrender loves with sacrificial intensity.

This humble love makes Mary Magdalene disregard the judgment and slanders of men if only she can be close to Him Who has given her so much. So she is one of the very few, such as the Lord's mother and St. John, who follows Jesus to the Cross, and kneels at its foot when He dies on it as a criminal. After His death she waits, still loving passionately, for His coming again. She watches by the tomb after others have left it, for true love refuses to believe that all is lost, and hopes against hope. She waits to see and find Him Whom her soul loveth, and her love 'maketh not ashamed.'

Mary Magdalene, out of whom were cast seven devils, is the sign of Jesus' power and glory, of the greatness of His pardon, of the rich reward of repentance. Be it Mary Magdalene or another sinner, in Luke 7, Jesus makes her an example to the Pharisee, because in grief for her sin she has done what she could: she loved as few have loved. Over this sinner, who bathed His feet with her tears, He spoke the precious words: 'She loved much.'

So Magdala still to-day speaks praise that sinners who repent are blessed indeed, are the great lovers who will be the messengers and witnesses of Jesus Christ. Magdala cries out: Tears of repentance are precious treasures. May Magdala awaken in our heart a prayer for repentance and love, so that at our life's end He may say to us: Thou hast loved much.

✝

Our hearts hear the voice
Of Jesus Christ, God's Son,
Who makes sinners rejoice.

Our hearts hear the voice
Of Jesus Christ, God's Son,
Who loves beyond words.

Our hearts hear the voice
Of Jesus Christ, God's Son,
Who redeems us to love.

Hymn

Let me lament as Magdalene doth
Let me tell out all my sinning
That I have done unto my Lord.

Let me love as Magdalene doth
As much as formerly I grieved Thee.
Let me do Thee good without end.

Let me repent as Magdalene doth
And lie for ever at those feet
Of Him against Whom I have sinned.

Let me hasten as Magdalene doth
To Thee alone, and stay by Thee.
The sinner must needs keep close.

PRAYER

Lord Jesus, hear my prayer now in this place that commemorates the woman who bathed Thy feet with her tears. I confess that I lack a broken and contrite heart, and that Thou hast hitherto waited in vain for my tears of repentance. The sins and weaknesses of others have exasperated me, but my own sins have left me unmoved. Forgive my blindness and self-satisfiedness and self-righteousness; that I have so lightly judged others instead of myself. Grant me the spirit of truth, that I may see myself in Thy light, and may be afraid of my temerity. Grant me the spirit of repentance that I may bewail my sins as did Mary Magdalene. Let me no longer be of the self-righteous Pharisees, but let me be as the publican who beat his breast and prayed for mercy. I bow down before Thee, Thou Lord of love, Whom I have not loved above all else. So I beg of Thee tears of repentance that mine eyes may be cleansed and that I may behold Thee as Thou art and love Thee with devoted and self-giving love, in response to Thy forgiveness. AMEN.

THE MOUNT OF THE BEATITUDES

The Historical Aspect

From early times attempts have been made to determine the spot where the Sermon on the Mount was preached, but there is no exact tradition. Most probably it took place near Tabgha, in the round of Seven Springs. Capernaum was the centre of Jesus' preaching by the Lake of Galilee and according to the Gospels the site of the great sermon was close to 'His city.' It is said that afterwards Jesus 'came down from the mountain' and 'entered Capernaum,' and that 'great multitudes followed him' (Matt. 8: 1–5). Such multitudes can be most easily envisaged on the road from Seven Springs to Capernaum. There are many places suitable for the encampment of a multitude on the gentle slopes to the west of the road. Most probably Jesus addressed them on several occasions, so that it would be unlikely that a definite memory would be attached to one particular spot in this extensive and lonely country-side.

Already in 385 the pilgrim Etheria reported a tradition for one particular spot. She says that the 'place of custom' of Matthew was on the road between the church of the Multiplication of the Loaves and Capernaum, and that 'near-by is the mount on whose slopes the Redeemer uttered the Beatitudes.' During the Crusades, i.e. about 1150, the site of the Sermon is said to be two miles from Capernaum and one mile from the Feeding of the Five Thousand.

From subsequent reports of the twelfth century it appears that tradition assigned to the Sermon a spot on the heights between Capernaum and Seven Springs. A fourteenth century pilgrim says that 'the mount which excites so much devotion' is hereabouts. In the sixteenth and seventeenth centuries, when access to the parts round the lake had become difficult, other suppositions were current. Even if we cannot now determine the exact place, we can remember the Sermon in the Church of the Beatitudes on a hill above Seven Springs, near Tabgha and Simon Peter's Landing-Place. This church only dates from 1938, when it was built by the Italians, together with a hospice of Italian nuns adjoining.

From the Holy Bible

When Jesus saw the crowds he went up the hill. There he took his seat, and when his disciples had gathered round him he began to address them. And this is the teaching he gave:

'How blest are those who know that they are poor;
the kingdom of Heaven is theirs.
How blest are the sorrowful;
they shall find consolation.
How blest are those of a gentle spirit;
they shall have the earth for their possession.
How blest are those who hunger and thirst to see right prevail;
they shall be satisfied.
How blest are those who show mercy;
mercy shall be shown to them.
How blest are those whose hearts are pure;
they shall see God.
How blest are the peacemakers;
God shall call them his sons.
How blest you are when men hate you, when they outlaw you and insult you, and ban your very name as infamous, because of the Son of Man.
On that day be glad and dance for joy; for assuredly you have a rich reward in heaven.'

When Jesus had finished this discourse the people were astounded at his teaching; unlike their own teachers he taught with a note of authority.

From Matt. 5: 1–12; 7: 28 and 29 and Luke 6: 20–3.

A CALL TO US

Mount of the Beatitudes, mount of enchanting loveliness overlooking the sea of Galilee: thou wast permitted to hear the wonderful words spoken by our Lord and Redeemer to His children; thou art a privileged mount. We cannot but rejoice as we make the ascent. Not because of the view over the lake and its surrounding heights; but because of One lovelier than the loveliness of the lake, One in Whom are concentrated all the beauty of Heaven and earth: Jesus, our Saviour the source of all blessing. Here we remember the Beatitudes, once uttered by Jesus because He desired the happiness of His children. In the Sermon on the Mount He revealed the way to obtain true happiness. In our mind's eye we can see the different sorts of people Jesus called blessed: the merciful, the meek, the peacemakers, those that hunger and thirst for righteousness, the poor in spirit, the pure in heart, the mourners, and those that are persecuted for righteousness' sake. It is a strange collection, and we might well wonder why they should be called blessed. Jesus declared it on this mount, and experience of life will reveal its truth.

The merciful, who are ready to forgive and excuse the faults of others, who look on their brethren with kindly, not with condemning, eyes, whose heart is moved by the miseries of body, soul, and spirit around them—these are truly blessed, for their hearts are filled with love. Nothing brings such happiness as loving, and nothing such unhappiness as hard, bitter, unforgiving hearts. Here on the Mount of Beatitudes we are shown by Jesus which men are truly blessed. We see the peacemakers and the meek, those who are not given to quarrels or resentment, who do not cause strife wherever they go nor let themselves be drawn into quarrels. These are happy, whilst the unhappy are those who live in hate, envy, and jealousy till they are worn down and impoverished. To make peace in humble love is to bring Heaven into our earthly lives.

Then there are those who hunger and thirst after righteousness, those upon whom the Sun of grace has arisen. Richly are they endowed with grace by eternal love. As little children, in want of all good, they cling to God. He will indeed give them all things, all they need, for soul and for body. The Father is merciful to the poor and needy and to those who thirst for Him, to be obedient to His will and His commands, and He gives them life divine. Already in the Old Testament we can read it: 'O that there were such an heart in them, that they would fear me, and keep all my commandments always, that it might be well with them' (Deut. 5: 29).

To the pure in heart He reveals His very Self in Love, because their hearts are fixed on Him alone.

The mourners and the persecuted are rich in the consolations of the Living God and the grace of being fulfilled in love such as only those who suffer can know. The persecuted rejoice, for the spirit of glory and of God resteth upon them (1 Peter 4: 14). Great is their reward in Heaven.

In the fullness of time these people whom Jesus called blessed will attain to the eternal glory of the Kingdom. They will receive the fullness of that which they have tasted here below in struggle and suffering, and that fullness will be theirs for ever.

BEATITUDE PRAYERS

Lord Jesus,

make me willing to be poor—
poor in the gifts of spirit and soul and of earthly things, for Thy sake. Make me rich with the gifts Thou dost shower upon the poor in spirit. I thank Thee that already in this life I may taste Heaven.

Lord Jesus,

give me willingness to bear my cross.
Let me bear it in the certain knowledge that Thou comest in love to those that mourn and dost so comfort them that the hell of suffering becomes Heaven.

Lord Jesus,

give me courage to choose Thy way of lowliness and meekness.
When I am wrongly accused, let me be silent, trusting in Thee. Help me to bear it when I am rebuked, and let me not answer back in anger but remain in love.

Lord Jesus,
release me from self-satisfaction in my spiritual life, which would be unto me death and upon which Thou hast pronounced judgment.

Let me hunger for Thy righteousness,
that I may show forth the image of the truly redeemed. Give me the strength of Thy spirit in my struggle against sin and weakness, so that I may proclaim Thy victory in the knowledge that they who do hunger and thirst after righteousness shall be filled.

Lord Jesus,
Thou knowest my hard heart, so ready to judge, especially those I do not like or who have injured me. Soften my hard heart and *make it a heart of mercy* that will excuse the faults

of others instead of passing judgment upon them, and will show mercy to mine enemies. Let the goodness and pardon Thou showest forth daily work on me to forgive others. I will be steadfast in the faith that Thou hast redeemed me for merciful love.

Lord Jesus,
give me a pure heart,
of which Thou art the only love, and one that loveth Thee above all things. Inflame my heart with that love which will without stint sacrifice and rejoice, which is for ever thinking of Thee and coming to Thee in prayer, and living wholly for Thee. Help me to attain this great and most precious good: to love Thee here on earth so much that in Heaven I may behold Thy Face.

Lord Jesus,
make me a peace-maker,
so that when wrath arises I may say with Abraham: 'Go thou to the right and I will go to the left,' and thus be ready, for the sake of peace, to renounce my rights. Grant that I may bring much peace, and that I may do so gladly, not counting the cost, Thou Prince of peace Who didst bring us peace by renouncing every right.

Lord Jesus,
bring me so close to Thee, that my life may be a following of Thee, even if, as in Thy life, it bring me hatred and contempt and persecution.
Give me courage for love of Thee
to share Thy shame,
to which Thou hast attached such mighty promises. And help me, when I am slandered and persecuted for Thy Name's sake, to rejoice in Thee for Thy great promises. AMEN.

No one ensures happiness like Jesus. Indeed only he experiences such good fortune who seeks it in Him and who travels the path of the Mount of Beatitudes, which can make us and others truly blessed.

Hymn

Who is great as Thou art, Jesus?
My whole heart goes out to Thee.
Jesus, Thou everlasting Joy!

Jesus, Thou source of eternal Joy
Who causest us bliss to enjoy
Jesus, Thou everlasting Joy!

Jesus, our joy-spring from within
Who can to joy turn every sin,
Jesus, Thou everlasting Joy!

Jesus, Thou makest us blessings to know,
Sinners forgiven are made as the snow.
Jesus, Thou everlasting Joy!

Thou Who hast brought down Heaven to Earth's floor
Know'st Sin is regretted where sinners endure,
Jesus, Thou everlasting Joy!

Jesus in Heaven Thou shin'st as the sun
Jesus Thou givest us joy ev'ry one
Jesus, Thou everlasting Joy!

Jesus, so broad and deep Thy Joy
All bliss is ready to enjoy
For us on earth as it is above.

†

Rules for Happiness

If thou wouldst happy be
Take love thy king to be
Who loves shall happy be.

BY THE LAKE OF GALILEE

Choose holy poverty
And God will bless thee.

Bend low beneath thy cross
And Heaven's joy will cover loss.

Leave care for things of earth
For anger, striving, wrath.

Avoid the appearance of satisfaction
To give the hungry cause for faction.

Let mercy enter thy heart,
Mercy to enemy part.

Love only God alone
Then will He see thee home.

Let all selfishness end
Give others peace without end.

Travel by His way of shame
That we may glory in His Name.

TABGHA

The Historical Aspect

The name Tabgha comes from the Greek word Heptapegon, meaning Seven Springs. The district was well known from ancient times on account of its warm springs. The fertile plain, rich in biblical traditions, by the shore of the Lake of Galilee, and in which Simon Peter's Landing-Place is to be found, also commemorates the Feeding of the Multitudes, the Five Thousand and the Four Thousand.

Both miracles have been commemorated here for a very long time, although the Gospels indicate pretty clearly that they occurred on the north-eastern shore and not here. John 6: 1 says: 'Jesus went over the sea'; and Mark 6: 48 says that after the Feeding of the Five Thousand the disciples, in returning to the western shore, got into navigational difficulties. The second Feeding quite clearly took place on the eastern shore for, just before the account of the miracle, it is said that Jesus 'came unto the sea of Galilee through the midst of the coasts of Decapolis' (Mark 7: 31), and that was east of the lake. We cannot determine where exactly the miracle did take place; Scripture only indicates that it was in a hilly part of the country near the shore and not far from Capernaum, from whence the multitude came. Probably it was a meadow where the company could settle itself, Jesus having noted their approach from a higher level (John 6: 3 and 5). But there is no tradition attached to any such place there.

The memory of the site on the eastern shore probably vanished in early Christian times because the district was remote, and the tradition shifted to the western shores near Seven Springs, close to the main road, which was of easier access for pilgrims, who would in any case have come to this district to visit Magdala, the site of the Sermon on the Mount, Simon Peter's Landing-Place, and Capernaum.

In 385 Etheria speaks of a church there where the Benedictine hall-church now stands. She tells of a sacred stone, on which Jesus was said to have laid the loaves and fishes; this can still be seen beneath the High Altar. Excavations, in 1930, showed that a smaller church must have existed here from about 350, and was replaced in the fifth century by a magnificent basilica. Pavement mosaics of that date, depicting a bread-basket and fishes and other symbols, are still in a good state of preservation. This basilica was destroyed some time during the seventh century, probably in 614 by the Persians, for pilgrim-reports of that time, though they mention the site of the miracle at Seven Springs, say nothing of a church. Later the basilica seems to have been partly rebuilt in connection with a monastery which is mentioned in 808 as the site of the Feeding of the Five Thousand.

That both miracles were commemorated here by the lake is attested by St. Jerome, *circa* 400. In Byzantine times, about the sixth century, a small church near the basilica was dedicated to the second miracle. It had been formerly known as the 'church of the Twelve Thrones,' in memory of Jesus' promise to the disciples (Matt. 19: 28). Through a mistaken interpretation of Etheria's description of the site of the Sermon, this church, the remains of which have been revealed by excavation about thirty yards north-east of the Benedictine sanctuary, is now called the 'Chapel of the Beatitudes.'

†

Jesus, Love incarnate, is constrained to help wherever He sees His children to be in want. But He waits for empty hearts, for hands stretched out, wherein He may lay His gifts.

FROM THE HOLY BIBLE

The Feeding of the Five Thousand

Jesus withdrew to the farther shore of the Sea of Galilee (or Tiberias), and a large crowd of people followed. Then Jesus went up the hill-side and sat down with his disciples.

Raising his eyes and seeing a large crowd coming towards him, Jesus said to Philip, 'Where are we to buy bread to feed these people?' This he said to test him; Jesus himself knew what he meant to do. Philip replied, 'Twenty pounds would not buy enough bread for every one of them to have a little.' Andrew said to him, 'There is a boy here who has five barley loaves and two fishes; but what is that among so many?'

Jesus said, 'Make the people sit down.' There was plenty of grass there, so the men sat down, about five thousand of them. Then Jesus took the loaves, gave thanks, and distributed them to the people as they sat there. He did the same with the fishes, and they had as much as they wanted. When every one had had enough, he said to his disciples, 'Collect the pieces left over, so that nothing may be lost.' This they did, and filled twelve baskets with the pieces left uneaten of the five barley loaves. From John 6: 1–13.

The Feeding of the Four Thousand

Jesus took the road by the Sea of Galilee and went up to the hills. When he was seated there, crowds flocked to him, bringing with them the lame, blind, dumb, and crippled, and many other sufferers; they flung them down at his feet, and he healed them.

Jesus called his disciples and said to them, 'I feel sorry for all these people; they have been with me now for three days and have nothing to eat. I do not want to send them away unfed; they might turn faint on the way.' The disciples replied, 'Where in this lonely place can we find bread enough to feed such a crowd?' 'How many loaves have you?' Jesus asked. 'Seven,' they replied; 'and there are a few small fishes.' So he ordered the people to sit down on the ground; then he took the seven loaves and the fishes, and after giving thanks to God he broke them and gave to the disciples, and the disciples gave to the people. They all ate to their hearts' content; and the scraps left over, which they picked up, were enough to fill seven baskets. Four thousand men shared in this meal, to say nothing of women and children.

From Matt. 15: 29–38.

A CALL TO US

By these feedings of the multitudes Jesus revealed Himself as the Lord Almighty, the Son of God, Who works miracles. He took a few loaves, prayed to the Father, and they were so multiplied that thousands could be satisfied. The same with the fishes: He blessed them and gave thanks to the Father, and behold, they proved to be enough for all.

But our Lord had not called the multitude in order to manifest to them His miraculous power. The story shows that He made use of their presence in order to preach the Gospel to them. He only performed the miracle because His heart was moved with compassion for the hungry crowd. He called His disciples to Him and said: I have compassion on the multitude, because they continue with me now three days, and have nothing to eat: and I will not send them away fasting, 'lest they faint in the way.' Here speaks the loving Good Shepherd, careful for His sheep and succouring them when they are sick or lack pasture.

The miracles show us that those that faint in the way will behold the power of God, because the heart of God is full of compassion. His love constraineth Him to help. The description of this story should be: 'It is the poor who receive most from Him.' Love gives such abundance that there is more than enough: twelve baskets of fragments remain. That would not have been the case if the disciples had gone shopping. Thus God revealed His compassionate heart to the faint and hungry, the multitude of simple folk who knew little about Him.

But from His disciples He expects other things. He called Philip to Him, to prove his faith: 'Whence shall we buy bread that these may eat?' Philip failed the test, like the others. As disciples of Jesus they ought to have known to whom to go in such an emergency. Jesus was not wanting them to question where should they go or to whom should they turn. He wanted them to bring the little that they had to

Him, but they did not and He was obliged to ask for it: the five loaves and the two small fishes. So He commands us to bring our poor little all to Him; the least thing given into His hand will be increased. We shall then receive at His hands all that we need, inwardly and outwardly, for the next few hours, the next day. But apart from Him we shall ever want. Human calculation, human endeavour to relieve want are often in vain. But He helps as His wisdom sees fit.

When Jesus, beholding our earthly wants, says to us: 'Bring hither your need to me, put it trustfully into my hand, and I will relieve it,' He makes a further demand. The Evangelists tell us that the people would have made Him king, but that He had gone away from them to the other side of the sea. Many of them followed Him to Capernaum, and He told them sorrowfully: 'Ye seek me . . . because ye did eat of the loaves and were filled.' 'Labour not for the meat that perisheth, but for the meat which endureth unto everlasting life, which the Son of Man shall give unto you: for him hath God the Father sealed.' So the story of the miraculous feeding ends with the heartfelt plea not to set our hearts on earthly nourishment but to seek for eternal love.

To us who have perhaps experienced a similar miracle for our earthly needs, Jesus says: 'Seek ye me, so that ye shall see a greater miracle. I will give you food that perisheth not: Mine own flesh—the bread broken for you, and my blood shed for you. Receive me, in the Holy Supper, and ye shall lack nothing. Whoso eateth the flesh and drinketh the blood of the Son of Man in faith shall have eternal life.' We shall have the life of God Himself, and that means peace and love and joy, and union with Him.

This is what Jesus will give if we come and open our hearts to Him, when we seek Him in His own Supper. If we come, not only in our outward need, but in the misery of our sins and our temptations, He will surely say to us: 'I have compassion on you. I cannot send you away lest ye faint in the way. He will give us heavenly riches, so that we may go forth and give praise that He Who has given Himself for us has given us thereby all things.'

But how few answer when Jesus calls and offers the bread of life. When He first spoke of it then some of His most ardent disciples went back and walked no more with Him, despite the fact that they had seen miracles and signs such as that of the loaves and fishes (John 6: 66). The love of Jesus waits for those who will not leave Him when He longs to give Himself to them, but who are filled with longing to receive Him.

So Tabgha says to us: Come to Him with all your wants and needs, sure of His wondrous help. But there is a further call: Seek for Jesus Himself, Jesus alone, Who will come to you and open His heart to you. Only He can satisfy all your need. But if ye seek only His gifts and to see His miracles, it may well be that one day you will lose Him, as did many in His day.

PRAYER

Dear Lord Jesus,

I thank Thee that Thy loving heart has compassion on our need; that Thou hast testified that Thou art the Creator of soul and body, and that Thou wilt have care for both in Thy divine power, which will multiply a little so that many are filled.

But most of all I thank Thee that Thou art still the same and dost say to me who lack so much: 'Come to Me,' so that Thou canst say over the little in my hand the mighty creative words that will bring increase.

Increase my faith, that I may be sure of help in every greatest need. Henceforth I would seek help not from human powers but from Thee, Who waitest for me to come to Thee, Who art ever ready and able to·help. Yea, I would seek Thee Thyself in my need, not only Thy gifts; for Communion with Thee is the most precious of gifts and the sweetest consolation. Jesus, Who dost wait for me, I will come to Thee and be made one with Thee in Thy Supper, in thanksgiving that Thou art to me the Bread of Life. AMEN.

HYMN

Faith doth grasp the Kingdom of God
Doth move Jesus' hands
Needs shall melt before His power,
He looseth us from our bands.
Where earthly means are wanting,
Faith doth say with cheer:
With God all things can be.

It is the same unto the Lord
Whether our wants are many or few.
Jesus our Helper is wealthy indeed,
Will choose the best to do.
In His love He all things gives.
All that grieves and harasses
He will take away.

Wondrous gift of grace divine,
To believe on such a Lord!
His power can comfort my sore heart.
What can I want e'er more?
He sees the deepest need we have
He can our deepest longing fill
With His own mighty love.

O wondrous word of God indeed,
O promise of our Lord
Thou art the Rock and fortress sure
On which I take my stand.
For what He says will come to pass.
This world itself shall pass away
E'er He can disappoint.

His Name and Might and Light indeed
His Name Amen and Yea.
He brings to pass whate'er doth come
Whate'er He promised.
His Name is Faithful, Wonderful,
His people can but praise
And give Him glory ever more.

✝

Jesus calls us: Come to Me
What you lack I will supply.
Trust to My creating love
Who brings from little much.

Jesus calls: Put trust in Me
As ye believe so shall it be
Thy loving God and Saviour dear
Will help in ev'ry need so clear.

Jesus calls: Whate'er is Mine
To you I give, it shall be thine.
Yea, I give Myself to thee
To be thy treasure without fee.

Jesus calls: Come all is prepared
The blessed Supper here is spread
Hunger stilled by Mine own Self.
I am the Bread of Life.

†

The smallest thing, brought to Jesus in faith in His almighty power, will grow great in His hands.

†

Whoever suffers lack and hearkens to the call of Jesus, 'Bring it here to me!' will live to see that little that He has made more—to-day as hitherto.

For Jesus is the same as heretofore in both His love and His almighty power.

SIMON PETER'S LANDING-PLACE

The Historical Aspect

In the Gospels the sea of Galilee is also called the sea of Gennesaret and Tiberias. It was on the shores of this lake, then densely populated, that Jesus began to preach the Kingdom of God. We wonder why He did not choose Jerusalem or Nazareth or the banks of the Jordan. Jesus retired to Galilee after John the Baptist had been put in prison (Matt. 4: 12; Mark 1: 14), for after John the Baptist had been silenced the Jordan valley was unpropitious, and might even have been unsafe. Nazareth, His home, was to reject Him. But the lake-side district was comparatively safe from Herod and from the zealot of the Sanhedrin. Thus the north-west end of the lake became the centre of Jesus' activity. Its shores keep the most precious memories of that time. Here He called His disciples and began to prepare them for their great mission (Matt. 4: 18–22; 9: 9). Many of the miracles took place here. The waves of the sea obeyed the command of Jesus to be still (Mark 4: 39), and Jesus walked upon them (John 6: 19), and Peter began to sink beneath them when he became aware of the strong wind (Matt. 14: 30). Even the fishes served Him, for one of them bore the tribute-money in its mouth (Matt. 17: 27). The sea of Galilee and its shores, upon which once flourished Capernaum, Bethsaida, Chorazin, and Magdala, repeatedly proclaim Jesus.

But there is one place on the shore more than others connected with the work of Jesus: Simon Peter's landing-place, the little sheltered inlet near Seven Springs, just below the Mount of the Beatitudes. The numerous springs which find their outlet here have made the neighbourhood of the rocky spur into a pleasant grove of shady trees, and this was probably the case already in Jesus' day. The warm springs not only irrigate the soil; when they reach the lake they attract the shoals of fish, so that this inlet has always been the best fishing-place of the western shore.

Fishermen were attracted to this inlet, and we can assume that Peter, Andrew, James, and John had settled here. They would have beached their boats here, and often encountered Jesus. The trees would have provided welcome shade for preaching. Here the multitudes would have gathered when Jesus asked Simon to row Him out on to the water so that He might better address them. And here Simon Peter spoke the words: 'Depart from me, for I am a sinful man!' Because it was Jesus' favourite place, His disciples will have sought it out again after His death; and here the Risen Lord will have appeared to them, calling out: 'Children, have ye any meat?' And He questioned Simon: 'Lovest thou me?' And this inlet would be the scene of the love-feast He prepared for His disciples. Truly, it is scriptural ground.

The Franciscan chapel here has an ancient tradition. Etheria reported in 385 that there was a flight of steps hewn out of the rock, leading down to the water, as they do now, and on which, according to John 21: 4, the Risen Lord would have appeared. Etheria does not mention any church. But there is evidence of a church in Byzantine times, about the sixth century. During the Crusades it was twice destroyed and rebuilt again. Its final destruction took place in 1236, and the present church was only built in 1933 by the Franciscans who have charge of the site.

FROM THE HOLY BIBLE

One day as Jesus stood by the Lake of Gennesaret, and the people crowded upon him to listen to the word of God, he noticed two boats lying at the water's edge; the fishermen had come ashore and were washing their nets. He got into one of the boats, which belonged to Simon, and asked him to put out a little way from the shore; then he went on teaching the crowds from his seat in the boat.

When he had finished speaking, he said to Simon, 'Put out into deep water and let down your nets for a catch.' Simon answered, 'Master, we were hard at work all night and caught nothing at all; but if you say so, I will let down the nets.' They did so and made a big haul of fish; and their nets began to split. When Simon saw what had happened he fell at Jesus's knees and said, 'Go, Lord, leave me, sinner that I am!'

From Luke 5: 1–8.

Some time later, Jesus showed himself to his disciples once again, by the Sea of Tiberias. Morning came, and there stood Jesus on the beach. He called out to them, 'Friends, have you caught anything? Shoot the net to starboard, and you will make a catch.' They did so, and found they could not haul the net aboard, there were so many fish in it. Then the disciple whom Jesus loved said to Peter, 'It is the Lord!' When Simon Peter heard that, he wrapped his coat about him and plunged into the sea. When they came ashore, they saw a charcoal fire there, with fish laid on it and some bread.

After breakfast, Jesus said to Simon Peter, 'Simon son of John, do you love me more than all else?' 'Yes, Lord,' he answered, 'you know that I love you.' 'Then feed my lambs,' he said.

From John 21: 1–15.

A CALL TO US

We cannot but be attracted to this delightful spot, which has so many memories of Jesus. Unlike most commemorative sites, it is not built over, and is probably much the same as it was when Jesus walked here. The same landscape greets our eyes; the waves of the sea sound as they did to Him. Here we can envisage the earthly life of Jesus and His preaching better than almost anywhere else. When to-day we watch the fishermen at work by the shore, we seem to see Peter, James, and John. These fishermen are rough folk, as they probably were then. Amongst them Jesus lived, not only as Rabbi and teacher, but as Messiah and Son of God. And He did not shrink from giving His companionship to these rough, untutored men. He took them as they were: irascible, as was Simon Peter, and yet so weak that they would deny Him. From these He chose His Apostles to fill the world with His name. Jesus was so lowly that He kept company with fishermen; His great love drew Him to the lowliest, who were of no account in the world. He felt in sympathy with them; it was to them He first preached, and to them He revealed His heart. The waves still speak of the great deeds of this lowly Jesus of Nazareth. At His command the fish came together in such numbers that they broke the net and the waves themselves were obedient to His word. But not only dumb creation felt the power of His holiness: the irascible Simon Peter bowed before the power of His holiness and confessed: 'Depart from me, for I am a sinful man!'

Peter's landing-place speaks of the glory and greatness of Jesus, and tells us that whoso believes and obeys the words of Jesus will see that glory, as Peter did. Obedient to an apparently senseless command of Jesus, he rowed out into the lake in broad daylight to fish where no shoal should have been. The command contradicted his whole experience as a fisherman. But he replied submissively: 'At thy word I will let down the net.' For he expected great things of Jesus, and believed that even the apparently impossible was possible to Him, and that it needed but His word to produce a miracle.

Could Peter find followers to-day, who will risk obeying strange commands from Jesus? If so, they will, like Peter, recognize Jesus for what He truly is: the Lord God Almighty, to Whom winds and waves, and all creation, are subject. May he indeed find imitators who, overwhelmed by the glory and greatness of Jesus, will fall at His feet, saying: 'Depart from me, for I am a sinful man.' To such imitators of Peter, Jesus can, after such humble words, entrust great tasks for His Kingdom. The Risen Christ longs to find many who will answer His, 'Lovest thou me?' Shall we not answer it?

Jesus lives—yesterday, to-day, and for ever. And He waits for those who have complete faith, ready to obey commands hard to understand, humbly owning their sinfulness, and answering Love's question. Peter shows us the way. And Scripture tells us: 'Remember those who have spoken unto you the word of God: whose faith follow, considering the end' (Heb. 13: 7).

PRAYER

Dear Lord Jesus,
we give thanks to Thee that Thou didst come down from Heaven and, though Lord of lords and King of kings, didst choose humble fishermen to be Thy disciples. We thank Thee for the patient love with which Thou didst prepare them before they were sent forth. Thou didst teach them to trust Thy words, to be ready to obey commands not understood, as Peter was ready to let down the net into deep water in broad daylight, and then to be enabled to behold Thy power and glory.

Dear Lord, I long to behold something of Thy power and glory in my life. I will surrender myself to Thee with the same words: At Thy word, I will do as Thou sayest, even though it seem hard and impossible. I trust Thee, and I thank Thee that Thou dost reward such faith with a sight of Thy power and glory, with Thine aid and Thy miracles.

But grant yet another prayer, Thou Who dost rejoice when much is asked of Thee, and let me, like Peter, when beholding Thy power and glory, acknowledge what I am in Thy sight: an abyss of sinfulness. Grant me such sorrow as may produce great love. May I here receive, as the gift of Thy grace, my share of that which Thou didst bestow on Peter: faith, obedience, repentance, and love. AMEN.

HYMN

The waves they are saying, was ever the same?
For Peter is prostrate, giving Jesus the fame.

The shores they are wondering, when along them He meets.
The waters are as dry land beneath His fair feet.

The fish come in shoals at the word of the Lord
The nets they are breaking because of His word.

And thousands are flocking, for whole days it may be,
To hear His blessed words on the shores of that Sea.

O Galilee's lake, thou art holy to me,
For the glory of Jesus in spirit I see.

O Jesus, my Saviour, how can I Thee praise
For all that Thou didst in that place in those days?

And still Thou art near me, Thy wonders I see,
If only in Thy Word my whole trust shall be.

†

The deeds and miracles of Jesus are not actions of the past. Jesus is waiting for those, who are still prepared to take risks at His word because they trust His power utterly.

†

Let us here, with Simon Peter, take the Lord at His word and say:

For Thee so gladly will I do
What Thou dost ask of me.
And what Thou askest I will give
Till all shall be to Thee.

For Thee so gladly will I do
Whate'er Thy glory needs.
What more indeed can I desire
Than to Thee myself to give.

For Thee so gladly will I do
Whatever for Thine honour is
To do what Thou dost ask of me
That I may yet extend Thy fame
For that alone I live.

For Thee so gladly will I do
Whate'er the cost may be.
For Thou art worthy, sure, of all.
My heart, my longing, and my will,
My life, I give to Thee.

CAPERNAUM

The Historical Aspect

Capernaum (Hebrew: Kfar Nahum) was one of the chief scenes of Jesus' activity; it was 'His city.' According to the Gospels, it lay 'upon the sea coast, in the borders of Zebulun and Naphtali' (Matt. 4: 13). The prophecy of Jesus about the city (Matt. 11: 23) has come to pass so completely that for a long time the site was uncertain. But to-day excavation and research into ancient sources have made it fairly clear that the ruins which are to be found rather over a mile to the north-east of Seven Springs, on the seashore, are those of Capernaum. They are called by the Arabs Tel Hûm.

Jewish sources state that the city was still in existence in the second century, and the early Christian sources corroborate it. Eusebius, at the beginning of the first century, writes: 'Capernaum, on the shore of the Lake of Genesar, is still a village in Galilee, in the district of Sebulon and Naphtali.' Etheria's report in 385 is particularly detailed. She describes her visit to the synagogue 'in which the Lord healed the man possessed of devils; it is reached by climbing many steps.' When the synagogue at Kfar Nahum was excavated a long flight of steps was actually brought to light, leading from the terrace in front of the synagogue; and this is not found with other synagogues. Thus it is certain that Etheria found Capernaum on the site of the present Kfar Nahum, at a time when Jewish and Christian tradition was still fresh.

Excavations after 1920 showed that the synagogue remains were of a date between the second and third centuries A.D., but it was probably erected on the ruins of its predecessor, of Jesus' day, which the believing centurion built for the Jews (Luke 7: 5). Later pilgrim reports do not mention the synagogue, and the date of its destruction is unknown.

In the time of Etheria a sanctuary was already in existence at Capernaum, on the site of Simon Peter's house. She says: 'The house of the prince of the Apostles was turned into a church, and the walls are still as they used to be. Here the Lord healed the paralytic.' The early tradition, added to the Gospel indications, allow us to assume that Jesus had taken up His abode in the house of Simon Peter, whose mother-in-law and brother Andrew also dwelt there (Mark 1: 29). This house, the scene of so many miracles, became a church dedicated to the Apostle Peter. Traces of an octagonal floor-mosaic, fenced round just in front of the synagogue ruins, are probably the remains of this church.

Later reports of pilgrims, which further confirm that the present Kfar Nahum is the old Capernaum, show that it became more and more a desolate place. Even the Crusaders, who set up sanctuaries in almost all the holy places, did not do so in Capernaum. In the thirteenth century it was reported that there were only seven old fishermen's cottages still standing and the whole district was one of ill-repute, whilst in the fifteenth century the city was quite destroyed and uninhabited 'because of the wicked people in this area.'

Capernaum to-day is uninhabited; it is only a collection of ruins in the midst of palms and eucalyptus trees beside the lake shore. The only traces of the ancient city are the broken columns and some blocks of the synagogue, whose ruins have been in Franciscan keeping since 1894, and which was partly rebuilt with the excavated stones in 1925.

FROM THE HOLY BIBLE

When Jesus heard that John had been arrested, he withdrew to Galilee; and leaving Nazareth he went and settled at Capernaum on the Sea of Galilee. Matt. 4: 12 and 13a.

They came to Capernaum, and on the Sabbath he went to synagogue and began to teach. The people were astounded at his teaching, for, unlike the doctors of the law, he taught with a note of authority.

On leaving the synagogue they went straight to the house of Simon. Simon's mother-in-law was ill in bed with fever. Jesus came forward, took her by the hand, and helped her to her feet.

That evening after sunset they brought to him all who were ill or possessed by devils; and the whole town was there, gathered at the door. He healed many who suffered from various diseases, and drove out many devils.

From Mark 1: 21, 22, 29–34.

When Jesus had finished addressing the people, he went to Capernaum. A centurion there had a servant whom he valued highly; this servant was ill and near to death. Hearing about Jesus, he sent some Jewish elders with the request that he would come and save his servant's life. They approached Jesus and pressed their petition earnestly: 'He deserves this favour from you,' they said, 'for he is a friend of our nation and it is he who built us our synagogue.'

Jesus went with them; but when he was not far from the house, the centurion sent friends with this message: 'Do not trouble further, sir; it is not for me to have you under my roof, and that is why I did not presume to approach you in person. But say the word and my servant will be cured.' When Jesus heard this, he admired the man, and, turning to the crowd that was following him, he said, 'I tell you, nowhere, even in Israel, have I found faith like this.'

From Luke 7: 1–10.

So Jesus got into the boat and crossed over, and came to his own town (Capernaum). Some men brought him a paralytic lying on a bed. Seeing their faith Jesus said to the man, 'Take heart, my son; your sins are forgiven.' At this some of the lawyers said to themselves, 'This is blasphemous talk.'

Jesus read their thoughts, and said, 'Is it easier to say, "Your sins are forgiven," or to say, "Stand up and walk"? But to convince you that the Son of Man has the right on earth to forgive sins'—he now addressed the paralytic—'stand up, take your bed, and go home.' Thereupon the man got up, and went off home. From Matt. 9: 1–7.

'And as for you, Capernaum, will you be exalted to the skies? No, brought down to the depths! For if the miracles had been performed in Sodom which were performed in you, Sodom would be standing to this day. But it will be more bearable, I tell you, for the land of Sodom on the day of judgement than for you.' Matt. 11: 23 and 24.

A CALL TO US

Capernaum is the town which Jesus described as 'exalted into Heaven'; it was His chosen city, where He began His ministry. He would have chosen Capernaum as the best place for coming into contact with large numbers of people; it was the frontier-town between Galilee and the country beyond Jordan, with a custom-house from which, probably, St. Matthew was called. It was also a place of some importance for trade, on the caravan road from Damascus to the Mediterranean. Its lake-side situation attracted fishermen to the town. The population was a large one, and people of all kinds rubbed shoulders there. In Capernaum Jesus could draw a crowd of hundreds, nay, thousands, when 'He spoke as one having authority and not as the scribes' (Matt. 7: 29), and He healed many that were sick. The crowds were so large that He could hardly come out of the house, and sometimes He 'had not leisure to eat bread'; the sick encamped themselves about Him day and night (Mark 1: 32 and 33). Here He opened the eyes of the blind, and set free those possessed of evil spirits. Here the dramatic healing of the man sick of the palsy took place, and the centurion's servant was healed through his master's faith, and Peter's wife's mother was cured of her fever. Capernaum witnessed all these healings, and the raising from the dead of the daughter of Jairus (Mark 5: 22–43).

Capernaum proclaims the love of God which came down to the children of men; the Son of God became Man and dwelt amongst us—here in Capernaum. It tells us of Jesus having compassion on those among whom He dwelt, healing the sick, setting free the possessed, and preaching salvation to thousands. At Capernaum we can see that Jesus is the Good Shepherd, Who careth for His sheep, and leadeth them forth into green pasture.

But Capernaum also heard different words from the Lord (Matt. 11: 23). So it is a sign that not only can judgment become grace if men repent and turn again, but that equally grace can become judgment when God's words and deeds are ignored. We have only to look upon the present-day ruins of Capernaum. In Jesus' day Capernaum, with its many healings, spoke powerfully of what Jesus was Who had done such great things in her streets. To-day Capernaum proclaims with equal power, though without words, that Jesus is the Amen, the faithful and true witness, Whose word is sure, be it blessing or curse. Especially true is that word which says that to whom much is given much will be expected. High as we may be lifted up—and Capernaum is lifted up to Heaven by the miracles of God—we have to humble ourselves and fall down at Jesus' feet, as Simon Peter did when he witnessed the miraculous draught of fishes; he could only say: 'Depart from me for I am a sinful man.' Capernaum witnessed the mighty actions of God, but she did not bow down in lowliness; she made use of Jesus' power and boasted of that which came to pass in her streets. She was high and mighty and self-satisfied, and her heart was not broken and contrite. So the word of God was fulfilled in her. He that lifteth himself up shall be brought low, and he who is raised as high as Heaven, unless he acknowledges the goodness of God by thanksgiving and self-surrender, shall be cast down into hell. The truth of that word of Jesus is visible here to-day. Capernaum, which Jewish tradition describes as sunk in sin, has vanished from the face of the earth; whether by earthquake or by war, we do not know.

The message of Capernaum's ruins to-day is: *Noblesse oblige*. The revelation and grace of God constrain us to bow low at His feet. His goodness constrains us to turn away from the ways which grieve Him to a life of thanksgiving. Capernaum emphasizes the words of the Magnificat: 'He hath put down the mighty from their seat, and exalted the humble and meek.' The columns of the synagogue, which still remain, proclaim how precious to Jesus was the faith of the centurion. Capernaum speaks to us of the truth of both blessing and curse; she begs those who seek out her ruins to take to heart the words of Jesus, so that the blessing of God may be fruitful for our lives.

Capernaum, thou city high,
On which the choice of Jesus fell.
God dwelt within thy streets.
But thou didst not believe in Him,
Him Whose deeds thou didst behold.
Thou didst not heed His mighty words.
God to-day is waiting still
For faith which will Him glorify,
Give heed unto His word.

PRAYER

Lord Jesus,
we thank Thee that Thou didst perform such miracles here and didst proclaim Thy power. But we humbly confess that we are such as once were the inhabitants of Capernaum. Although Thou hast shown forth Thy power in our lives, we confess that we have not thanked Thee but have continued in pride and haughtiness. Thou hast been constrained to turn Thy grace into judgment, to humble us till we lie in the dust, as Capernaum now does.

Dear Jesus, to-day I would render Thee thanks for all in my life that has shown forth Thy power and Thy goodness. Keep me from pride, and let me bow down in lowliness when Thou bestowest Thy grace, that I may glorify Thee. Give me a lowly heart. May Thy goodness so transform me that my life may become, as Thou wouldst have it; that Thou mayest no longer grieve over me, but mayest rejoice in my life of faith, on which Thy blessings and Thy favour can rest. AMEN.

HYMN

Capernaum once could see
Jesus walking in her ways,
Doing wonders day by day.
Thousands who did throng thy streets,
Who did hearken to His voice,
Saw His miracles indeed.

Solitary now that shore,
Hearing only lonely waves
Breaking as they broke before,
Speaking of how Jesus saves,
How He speaks to our life's flow,
Help and healing to bestow.

It calls us still to test our Faith
To launch out in His might
To trust in one who showed Himself
A trusty Captain in the fight.
On Him rely you surely may
For as He was He is to-day.

†

Capernaum calls us
to boldness of faith,
because the power of God and His readiness to perform miracles are far beyond the boldest desires of our believing.

BIBLIOGRAPHY

The following works have been consulted for historical details:

Dr. Clemens Kopp: *Die heiligen Stätten der Evangelien.* Regensburg, 1959

Stenner-Wilmes: *Pilgerführer durchs Heilige Land.* Jerusalem, 1961

Karl Erich Wilkens: *Biblisches Erleben im Heiligen Land.* Lahr-Dinglingen, 1956

Other works consulted are:

Franz Weiser: *In der Heimat des Herrn*

Franz Kaiser: *Hier ist Heiliges Land*

P. S. Meistermann: *Durchs Heilige Land*

We would here express our gratitude for all the assistance received.

The sources for determining the genuineness of the Holy Places are chiefly the early Christian writers and pilgrims. We append a list of those of historical importance.

EUSEBIUS (265–340) 'The Father of Church History,' born in Palestine. He is the best authority for the country during the reign of Constantine.

EPIPHANIUS, born 315 in Judaea, founded a monastery there. Became Bishop of Salamis in Cyprus.

ETHERIA, a nun from northern Spain or the south of France. She made a pilgrimage to the Christian places of the Orient from 385–8. Her reports are very clear.

JEROME, lived from 385 to his death in 400 by the church of the Nativity in Bethlehem. He led and reported on the pilgrimages of St. Paula.

THEODOSIUS (530), left a short and faithful account of the pilgrimage places of the East.

THE ANONYMOUS PILGRIM OF PIACENZA described the Holy Places in 570 at the zenith of their development in Byzantine times.

ARKULF, a bishop of Gaul, who travelled in the East in 670. His reports are valuable.

WILLIBALD, an Anglo-Saxon, who undertook a lengthy pilgrimage 724–6. A nun of Heidenheim wrote an account of his experiences.

EPIPHANIUS (*circa* 751–800), a Greek monk and presbyter in Jerusalem. He put together a description of Palestine from ancient accounts.

DANIEL, a Russian abbot, who travelled the country 1106–7.

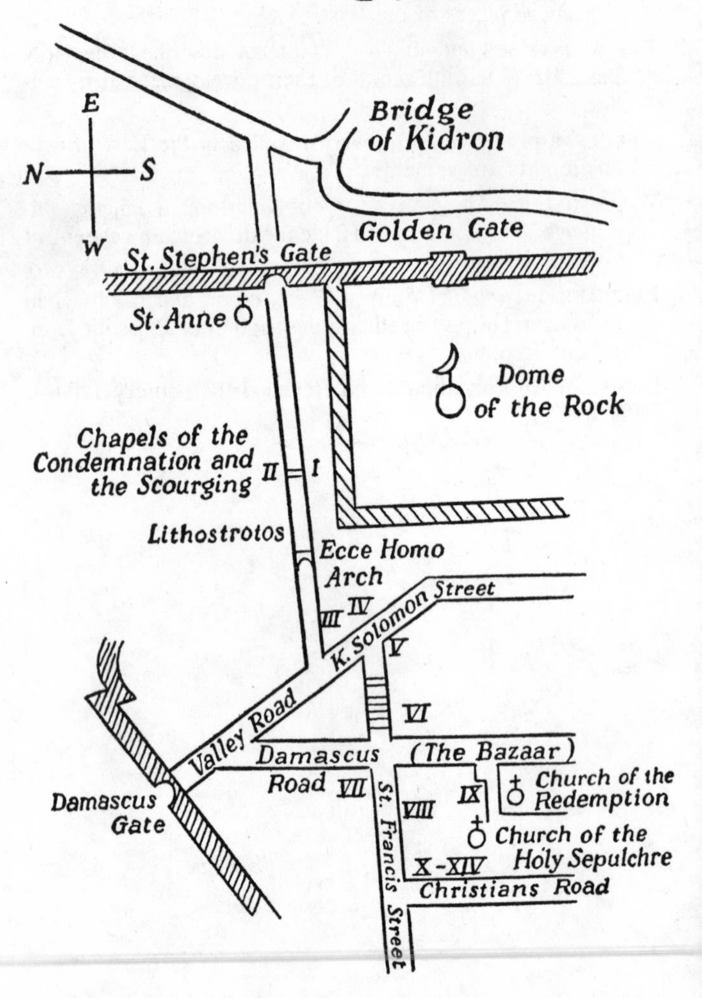
VIA
DOLOROSA
E
N
S
W
Bridge
of Kidron
Golden Gate
St. Stephen's Gate
St. Anne
Dome
of the Rock
Chapels of the
Condemnation and
the Scourging
II
I
Lithostrotos
Ecce Homo
Arch
K. Solomon Street
III
IV
V
VI
Valley Road
Damascus
Road
VII
(The Bazaar)
Church of the
Redemption
IX
VIII
Church of the
Holy Sepulchre
X-XIV
Christians Road
St. Francis Street
Damascus
Gate